PETER B. CLARK

THE STORM PETRELS

THE

The Flight of the First Soviet Defectors

STORM PETRELS

Gordon Brook-Shepherd

Harcourt Brace Jovanovich

New York and London

Printed in the United States of America

Library of Congress Cataloging in Publication Data

Brook-Shepherd, Gordon.
  The storm petrels.

  Includes index.
  1. Refugees, Political—Russia. 2. Russia—
Politics and government—1917-1936. 3. Russia—
Politics and government—1936-1953. I. Title.
DK266.B7   323.1'47   77-84386

ISBN 0–15–185223–5

First American edition 1978

B C D E

To R.R., the Chrysanthemum Man

Contents

CONTENTS x

PREFACE

In the decade before the last war, a handful of senior Soviet officials clambered, one by one, over the walls of Stalin's Russia, to seek asylum and tell their secrets in the West. They were the trailblazers of that long line of Communists who "chose freedom," as one of their later imitators was to put it. They were not only the political heralds of the Cold War. By what they revealed and what they did in exile, this handful of forgotten men helped to shape the course of that great East-West conflict which is still with us.

So far as I am aware, this is the first connected account to be written of these pioneer defectors, in English or, for that matter, in any other language. There is so much high drama, tragedy, mystery, and even romance in the escape stories of the five principal cases described here that they read, at times, more like novels of spy fiction than real-life adventures of the twentieth century. But I have not chosen either those five, or the half-dozen minor cases who also appear in the story, for that reason. The object was to provide a selective balance so that even where similar tales of Stalin's terror at home and subversion abroad are being told, they are given from different standpoints and with different insiders' knowledge.

Thus Bajanov, the pioneer of pioneers, gives a unique political insight into what was going on in the Kremlin itself in the twenties. Agabekov and Orlov, who defected from Stalin's secret police at two different stages of its repellent life, tell the secrets of the OGPU and NKVD respectively. Krivitsky, though briefly an NKVD man before his defection, had served for many years before that in the Soviet military intelligence network, and so gives the viewpoint of the GRU, as that organization is known. Finally, Bessedovsky, the only career diplomat of the batch, provides a glimpse of Stalin's police state as seen by one whose unenviable task it was to represent it, formally and in polite society, in various capitals abroad.

All of these principals involved wrote their own memoirs at some point during their exile in the West. The oldest, Bajanov's (recently rewritten), came out in 1928, in French and German only. All the others have appeared, at one time or another, in English, though it is now almost twenty-five years ago since the last of them was published—Orlov's *Secret History of Stalin's Crimes*.

I want to make it clear that this present volume is in no way a recapitulation or amalgam of these five books of memoirs, which are, indeed, usually summed up in a page or two and then drawn upon only as occasion warrants. There are various good reasons for this. The first is that the books are still available in reference libraries and I have never been partial to paste-and-scissors operations. The second is that, in every single case, these memoirs reveal only a part (and sometimes the lesser part) both of the life story of the defector concerned and of what he had to tell the West. My third reason is that I have been fortunate enough to be able to fill most of the gaps which the authors felt it prudent to leave blank in their time; or, in some cases, gaps which they could never have filled themselves.

The documentary material used here, much of it secret and nearly all of it hitherto unpublished, has been drawn from a wide range of

Western official sources—American, British, British-Indian, French, Belgian, and even Rumanian (which was part of the non-Communist world at the time). Much fresh information has also come out of talks with one or two of these "storm petrels" who are still alive today on both sides of the Atlantic; and who are nearly all still very lucid, despite the fact that the youngest of them is now in his late seventies. In the case of Boris Bajanov, for example, with whom I have had a total of some thirty hours of conversations in France, this new material has covered not only his own life, but also those of his fellow defectors of the period, several of whom he knew personally.

Enlightenment often came from unexpected directions. Thus, in the case of the most romantically tragic of all these defectors—Agabekov—a great deal about his exile in France and Belgium was found in old Rumanian police files, while much material about his secret contacts with Britain originated in New York, where his English-born widow died in 1971.

It all adds up, as I hope the reader will agree, to a fascinating glimpse into some hitherto closed episodes in the history of our times. I have devoted hardly any space to drawing morals from these stories. The defectors themselves are better at that, and are best of all when they do it unconsciously.

Gordon Brook-Shepherd

Hughs,
Hambleden,
Oxon.
February 1977.

THE STORM PETRELS

Chapter One

BORIS BAJANOV:
THE FIRST PETREL

For the tenth anniversary of the Bolshevik revolution, the Russian capital should have been a joyous and confident place. Superficially, of course, it was. The parades were even more elaborate; the fraternal delegations from abroad even bigger; the slogans and banners which swamped the streets even more strident. Yet the reality underneath this veneer of unity and confidence was very different. Moscow in the autumn of 1927 was a city of fading illusions and growing fears. By now, hardly anyone clung any more to the old dream of Soviet Russia becoming a "worker's paradise." Indeed, it was beginning to look instead like the nightmare of a worker's hell.

It was a series of fiascos on the economic front—the regime's failure, quite literally, to deliver the goods—which had disillusioned the nonpolitical masses. In 1921, for example, four years after the

Bolsheviks' seizure of power, the death rate through famine had reached sixty per thousand of the population; industry, smitten by a fuel and transportation crisis, was in a shambles. Lenin, the unchallenged leader of the revolution, had then engineered a temporary recovery, with his bold New Economic Policy (NEP), an attempt to revive industrial output by restoring small enterprises to private hands and, even more important, to give incentives back to the peasantry and so get food flowing again from the villages into the towns.

But by 1927, when the great Lenin was no longer on the scene to think up something else, his theory that "out of the NEP would come Socialism" was already foundering. What had come out of his NEP instead was the dominance of the *kulak,* or wealthy peasant, a grossly counterrevolutionary figure and one, moreover, who seemed no more eager to feed the towns than his collectivized colleagues had been. In this anniversary autumn, the shadows of another great famine were gathering. Grain collections that November had dropped to less than half the level of the previous year. Bread rationing lay ahead, at first in the provincial centers and, later, in the capital itself.

Side by side with these material disappointments—the discovery that the Communist cornucopia looked more like a hollow shell—there had come the spiritual disenchantment of the elite. Lenin himself, brooding over political dilemmas as early as January 1921, had declared: "We must have the courage to look the bitter truth straight in the face. The Party is sick. The Party is shaking with fever."

In the weeks that followed, that fever started shaking the whole country. A wave of unrest culminated, in March, in outright revolt at the naval base of Kronstadt which, by a humiliating coincidence, had been the great stronghold of the 1917 revolution. And what those same sailors and workers were rebelling over only four years later was the regime's ideological betrayal even more than its economic failures. Their cry now was for an end to the growing dictatorship of the Bolshevik party from Moscow and for the restoration, in its place, of "genuine people's government" by local soviets.

The military countermeasures came first—Red Army cavalry clattering across the ice of the Bay of Finland to put the revolt down in blood. Then came the administrative countermeasures: on the economic front, the NEP; and, crucial for the way Soviet Russia was to develop from now on, the establishment on the political front of a closed party dictatorship. The Bolsheviks reacted to the Kronstadt challenge by banning all opposition groups from their ranks. With this ban they gradually stifled not only their rivals, but also their own vitality. The party leadership, like the high priests of old, withdrew into a mystic oligarchy sanctified only by themselves and supported only by brute force and their own twentieth-century brand of mumbo-jumbo. They no longer represented the people. They merely ruled it.

This was the situation which was already crystallizing when, on January 21, 1924, Lenin died. Two strokes had already put him out of action for much of 1922; a third, in March of 1923, had carried him right off the political stage. Yet, despite this abundant evidence that their great leader was mortal, neither the party nor the country at large was prepared for the shock of his actual death. It was, indeed, a shock from which Soviet Russia never recovered.

The next three years, 1924 to 1927, were dominated by the battle in the Kremlin for Lenin's succession, and that battle was, in turn, dominated by two figures, Joseph Stalin and Leon Trotsky. This is not the place to recapitulate the details of that historic struggle, frequent glimpses of which crop up anyway in the stories which follow. All that matters here is to note the method and the timing of Stalin's victory over his rival.

Ideologically, this contrast has always been encapsulated into the conflict between Trotsky's call for Russia to lead a permanent and universal revolution and Stalin's more staid and pragmatic policy of concentrating on "Socialism in one country," that is, the Soviet Union itself. Yet the issue was not crucial to the outcome. Whatever banner Trotsky and his followers had marched behind, the result would surely have been the same. Stalin rose up, and Trotsky was crushed down, by that very autonomous and all-embracing party machine they had both helped to create after the crisis of 1921. The

machine, with its network of committees and commissions, informers and secret policemen, all answerable to a battery of centralized
levers pulled in the Kremlin, was like an unstoppable robot which
bestowed supreme power on whomsoever controlled those levers.

Trotsky, the fiery idealist, never grasped this mundane truth, and
would have had no stomach anyway for all the detailed and weari-
some work involved in mastering the party's administration. Stalin,
on the other hand, as much a bureaucrat at heart as a dictator, thought
of little else, and had been quietly trying to pack every central and
regional organ of the party with his nominees ever since Lenin's first
illness. It was this power base that had enabled him to ride over
that very awkward moment in May of 1924, when Lenin's political
testament, which had unequivocally ruled Stalin out as his heir, was
read to the party's Central Committee (a dramatic event to which
one of the figures in this present book was an eyewitness).

Once he had survived that most formidable of challenges from the
grave, Stalin's final victory over the living seemed inevitable. Yet its
timing was ironically significant. Trotsky's last challenge came during the tenth anniversary celebrations of the revolution itself. On
November 7, 1927, he and Zinoviev, a supporter within the all-
powerful nine-man Politburo, led their followers through the streets
of Moscow and Leningrad in marches which were ostentatiously
separated from the official processions. A week later, they were
expelled from the party. Trotsky's bleak road to banishment, exile,
and assassination had begun.

His fall also marked the beginnings of something else—the great
Stalinist purges, executed, on the budding dictator's behalf, by Yagoda, chief of secret police. All Trotsky's prominent supporters were
packed off to Siberia with their leader. Some fifteen hundred of the
lesser fry were deprived of their party membership that autumn.
Hundreds more only saved their political skins by recanting. It all
added up to an ominous signpost which pointed to more terrible
things ahead.

One who had the eyes to see this, and the boldness to act, had
himself been reared in the Kremlin at Stalin's side and had learned,
as only a handful of men in Russia had done, the secrets of Stalin's
power. Now, sick in spirit as well as fearful, he also left Moscow in

that autumn of 1927. But he was heading south, not east; and the very different trail he was blazing was one which Russians are still treading half a century later, that of the long procession of defectors from Soviet Communism.

Chapter Two

THE FLIGHT
OF STALIN'S SECRETARY

Soon after dawn on New Year's Day, 1928, two young Russians could be seen walking out of Loftabad, a village in the far south of Turkestan, which is itself in the far south of the Soviet Union. They were dressed warmly in hunting clothes and each had a rifle slung across his shoulder. Each also had, in his pocket, a permit, issued at the nearby town of Ashkhabad, to shoot boar in the local forests.

That special pass was needed for security, as well as sporting reasons. The railway they had traveled out on the night before hugs the border with the north Persian province of Khorassan, and the Soviet frontier post itself lay barely a mile ahead through the woods they were now crossing.

The moment it came in sight, the hunting party took on a strange aspect. The smaller and slighter of the two men (who had taken the precaution of keeping all the cartridges they had been issued) unslung his rifle and turned it toward his companion. "Now listen," he said calmly. "I know what your real name is. I know what your real job is and I know what orders you were given about me in Moscow. That's our frontier and there will be little difficulty crossing it today because the guards will still be dead drunk from last night. The other side is Persia and beyond that is British India. That is where I'm heading and I don't advise you to try and stop me. But if you want to come with me, I give you my word I will get you to Europe and tell nobody the truth about you. Here's your chance. I warn you that, if you do cross with me, they will stop at nothing to hound us down, wherever we are. On the other hand, once I'm over that border and you turn back without me, you're a finished man anyway. So make up your mind, and be quick about it."

The other man's expression moved from astonishment to perplexity during this quiet speech. But the last point was decisive and, finally, he nodded agreement. The pair moved cautiously forward to the hut to find that New Year's Eve had, indeed, done its work. No one stood guard outside and, instead of bullets, only snores came from inside. A minute later, they were in no-man's-land and heading for the Persian frontier. One of the most remarkable escape adventures, involving the most important man ever to flee the Soviet Union, had begun.

The one who had hesitated is a mere cipher in this story. He called himself Arkadi Romanovitch Maximov, a former army officer, lately employed by the Ministry of Railways. But, though he did hold the rank of a Red Army captain, his real name was Birger and his real employment was as one of the countless agents of Stalin's OGPU, as the Russian secret police was called at that time. His current assignment was to accompany and report on his companion; not to arouse his suspicions, but to stop him, if need be by any means, from fleeing the Soviet Union.

The companion's name and record explain why these elaborate precautions had been thought necessary back in Moscow. He was Boris Georgeovitch Bajanov, and, though only twenty-seven years old, he had served for eighteen months as personal assistant to none other than Stalin himself and, for nearly two years after that, as secretary to the Politburo, the all-powerful innermost council of the Communist party through which the dictator ruled Russia.

Only this personal link with Stalin had saved Bajanov from arrest and death in the purges that were already beginning to steep Russia in blood. But the then head of the OGPU, the notorious Yagoda, had had his doubts about the "reliability" of this intractable young man for years past; indeed, he had placed him under surveillance even during his Politburo period. This was not merely the compulsive suspiciousness of a secret police chief. Yagoda nursed a personal hatred for Bajanov, who reciprocated with a detestation of the OGPU commander and all he stood for. Once Bajanov, whose outspokenness had got him into difficulties more than once, was relieved, in 1925, of his Kremlin posts, Yagoda's noose steadily tightened. It was unthinkable that such an independent-minded individual, who had held such key positions, should be allowed to flee the country and carry with him into the outside world all the innermost secrets of the Kremlin. However, nothing could be better than for Bajanov to be caught while attempting to escape, for that would be unanswerable proof of his perfidy. In all probability, that was why Yagoda had not tried to obstruct Bajanov's journey to Turkestan, for his OGPU had trapped many a victim along that border. Now, however, on New Year's Day of 1928, the unthinkable had happened. Stalin's secretary was across, taking his police shadow with him.

At the frontier post of Khorassan, Bajanov and the man we will go on calling Maximov were surrounded by an excited crowd of barefooted Persian soldiers—none of whom spoke a word of Russian, let alone French (in which Bajanov was quite proficient). Eventually, the two men were taken to the village police station where they spent an agonizing night, much too close for comfort to that still silent Soviet frontier point. There was nothing the local police inspector could do about it. This was all, he told them, quite above his head, and he had telegraphed for instructions.

The next day, they were taken a little further from the border to the town of Mohammadabad. Here, in the person of the district police chief, they met one of the two saviors who were to come to their rescue in the odyssey ahead. This Persian official, one Basban, to whom they applied formally for political asylum, took it upon himself to help them reach Meshed, the administrative center of Khorassan.

Meshed had ominous associations for Bajanov. He knew that Yagoda had a large and efficient band of agents working there— so efficient that two OGPU officials who had deserted to the Persians from Ashkhabad the year before had been kidnapped by their own colleagues in broad daylight in Meshed and spirited back across the Soviet frontier to face a firing squad. Bajanov was also aware that as Stalin's former secretary, he was a more important quarry than all the OGPU officials of Turkestan put together, and that, by now, all the alarm bells in the Kremlin would be sounding for him, rung by Stalin in person.

Basban, the Persian official, only confirmed these fears. His district was cut off from the interior by a range of high mountains, whose passes were now blotted out by the mid-winter snow. Normally, the only way to reach Meshed in January would be to take the long road skirting the mountains. But Soviet agents had already been reported moving up this road and Basban was convinced they were setting an ambush at Kuchan, a junction through which the hunted men would have to pass if they took that route.

So Bajanov and Maximov found themselves with a guide mounted on hill ponies for a climb straight up and over the ten-thousand-foot-high ridge of the Kuh E Nazar. There was not a track to be seen in the snow and Basban's last advice was: "Don't trust the guide, trust the ponies; they will find the way."

Find it they did, and, after four days plodding, on a southeast course, up and down the massif, sleeping in mountain huts over-night, they came out on the valley road at a village only ten miles from Meshed. The OGPU, realizing their quarries had taken the mountain route, had doubled back from Kuchan and were waiting for them almost as they got off their ponies.

The Russians had arranged matters so that only one vehicle would be traveling that day to Meshed. The driver was in their pay, and waiting to board it with the two refugees was a certain Pashaiev, well known in the district as a Soviet secret police official who masqueraded as a trade representative. Bajanov managed to pull

Maximov and the guide with him into the back seats (which at least gave them the strategic advantage over the two agents in front). Though everyone in the party knew what everyone else was up to, not a word was exchanged as the car, a small Dodge, moved off.

Before they had gone halfway, they were stopped by another car traveling toward them. This contained more OGPU men, including Osipov, the top Soviet agent at Meshed. He and Pashaiev (both of whom were armed) held a long roadside conversation, presumably as to whether the fugitives could be disposed of there and then. But convinced, quite wrongly, that their quarries were armed, they feared a shootout, and the presence of a Persian guide as witness was too awkward to get round. Finally, Osipov left his own car and squeezed himself into the Dodge. This extraordinary jumble of six passengers then proceeded to Meshed. Again, nobody broke what must have been an agonizing silence.

All this time, the wires had been humming from Moscow to the Soviet Legation at Teheran, and from there to the Consulate-General at Meshed. The Kremlin's orders were urgent and emphatic: Stalin's former aide must be liquidated at all costs and by any means on the spot. Comrade Platte, the Soviet consul-general, together with Comrade Osipov and the Meshed OGPU team now did their utmost to oblige, if only because they did not care to contemplate the consequences of failure.

Indeed, they tried to strike as soon as the taxi, by arrangement, dropped the two fugitives off at Meshed's only hotel, the Doganov. While accommodation was being arranged, coffee was offered to the newly arrived guests. Bajanov was about to drink it when he hastily put his cup down, motioning to Maximov to do the same. The knowledge of chemistry he possessed was more than enough to warn him off the very uncoffeelike odor of almonds he had caught in the steaming black liquid.

The OGPU had also been active upstairs. When they were shown to their room Bajanov noticed the inner bolt of the door had been removed. All the other rooms along the corridor were equipped with locks or bolts but all, though empty, were pronounced to be "reserved." Protests proved useless.

The two men, exhausted, then slept for a few hours, to be offered supper when they got up. This· they also declined, which was just as well. Working at the hotel was a Russian Armenian servant called Koltukhchev who had been well and truly "got at" by Comrade Platte. In return for the promise of a small fortune, a Soviet passport, and a safe passage into Russia, the servant had mixed a lethal spice in the fugitives' food.

Still, the OGPU did not despair. In case the poison for some reason did not do its work, they had also provided their assassin with a revolver and ordered him to shoot the two men in their beds. Obediently, Koltukhchev tried to burst in on his victims, revolver in hand, in the middle of the night—only to find himself arrested *in flagrante delicto* by Meshed's chief of police, who seemed to have materialized from the floorboards of the corridor. Quite how such a senior Persian official turned up in the Hotel Doganov at this critical moment is not clear. Bajanov, looking back later on the near-miracle, attributed it either to the suspicions of the Persians themselves or to a tipoff from the OGPU's great rivals in Meshed (and throughout Persia), the British Intelligence Service, which enjoyed a reputation for such omniscience. The reputation flattered, at least on this occasion. The British official documents covering the entire Bajanov saga make it clear that, in early January 1928, the British consul-general in Meshed had no idea of the two fugitives' existence in his town, let alone of the immense importance of one of them.

At all events, for the time being Bajanov and Maximov had found other protectors. Their rescuer told them that, as it was impossible for him to guarantee their safety at the hotel, he would have to take them, there and then, to the Nasmia, the prison and police head-quarters combined. Under some protest, the two men went. Bajanov was somewhat mollified when he found himself given a bed in the chief's private office. They stayed in the Nasmia of Meshed for a full six weeks; and a tense battle of wits and wills it became. From the window of his office-bedroom, Bajanov could recognize teams of OGPU agents stationed all round the clock in the square outside, waiting for him to emerge in the vain hope that he would appear without a strong escort. Comrade Platte also applied more orthodox pressures, appealing to the Persian authorities to hand over the two men to him, on the grounds that they were common thieves who had fled Russia with large amounts in jewels and cash. (As the Persian police had cataloged all Bajanov's possessions at the frontier, including the twelve hundred rubles which represented two months of his salary, this lie was easily nailed.)

Bajanov himself was always uncertain of the Persian attitude, and therefore of the final outcome. He commenced bribery with the only currency he still possessed—information. When he was taken before the Persian governor-general, for example, he produced extracts from the text of a secret report on Soviet-Persian relations made to the Politburo in Moscow only six months before (in August 1927) by Chicherin. In this, the Soviet commissar for foreign affairs had proposed the launching of a coup d'état in Teheran, supported by Red Army intervention, with the ultimate object of annexing Persia to the Soviet Union and denying England, the "supreme enemy," its bridge between Indian and Mesopotamia. Chicherin's proposals, he added, had been accepted in principle.[1] For good measure, Bajanov added another tidbit. The network of Soviet agents planted in Teheran reached, he said, even to the court of the shah. He named the most important of them, a minister called Teimourtach.

Bajanov seems to have got little more than a polite reception from the governor-general. However, it was a different story when he got a chance, a few weeks later, to pass this, and other, intelligence on to the general officer commanding the Persian Eastern Army, Shahzda Amanulla Mirza. Whether the Persian commander took a liking to Bajanov, whether he responded out of gratitude for the information, or whether the Persians had simply decided it was about time to rid Meshed of these politically embarrassing visitors was not clear. At all events, the general now agreed to the refugees' plea to be moved much closer to that Indian frontier which was their target. On February 20, Bajanov and Maximov, with a guard of four Persian soldiers, were dispatched on the long trip south by car to Duzdap,

---

[1]   This document was one of several which Bajanov had brought with him with a special eye to the interested "customers" along his intended escape route. Like the rest, it ultimately ended up in the British archives of the day.

which they reached four days later. The OGPU had followed be-hind them on the first leg of the journey to Turbat-i-Haidiri and only gave up the pursuit when it was clear that the escort had orders never to let their charges out of their sight. From now on, the hunt would have to be switched to Duzdap.

Any hopes that Bajanov may have had of sailing straight on into India and the safe arms of the Raj were dashed when he found that the Persian governor had as little idea what to do with the fugitives as his colleague up at Meshed, and no authority to move them further. This time, they were not taken into protective custody but allotted a rest house near the railway to live in. They were allowed to move as they pleased about the town, and went each day to the bazaars to buy their food. There was not even a guard placed on them or their house.

This freedom was a distinctly mixed blessing, for it could only be a matter of time before the OGPU renewed its extermination campaign. There was, however, one difference. By now, the British had learned of their existence and had begun to take an interest in their future. A gradually and almost grudgingly increasing interest it was, considering all that was to happen later on.

The first mention of the refugees in the British archives is a tele-gram dated February 22, 1928 from the British consul-general at Meshed to his minister at Teheran, and repeated to Delhi and to the vice-consul at Duzdap.[2] It is a rather cross message:

> Two Russians who were arrested in Meshed when they arrived from Turkestan have been in jail for about two months. So far we have not been able to establish their real identity. They state they belonged to Trotsky's party and now wish to proceed to Europe. It was previously decided by [Persian] Governor General to despatch them to Teheran, but on the 18th instant he informed our Attaché that he was sending them to Duzdap whence they would proceed to India. Although At-taché informed him that in Duzdap no visas to India could be given without official reference to this Consulate-General, he ignored this and despatched Russians under escort on 20th.

The only addressee to reply directly to this telegram was the for-eign secretary's office in New Delhi. The reply consisted of one

---

2   India Office records, P. and J. (S) 1928, telegram no. 8–C.

sentence, concerned only with money. "Please let us know," the consul-general in Meshed was asked, "whether Russians can pay their way."[3]

This grave problem of who was to foot the travel expenses was to dog Bajanov—even after his identity and his importance were established—throughout his time with the British. In these early days, it was coupled with skepticism as to whether he was worth even the cost of a bus ticket out of official funds. Nor did an encouraging first-hand impression sent by a British official on the spot do anything to alter this skepticism.

The archives show that, five days after arriving in Duzdap, Bajanov and Maximov were able to pay a call on Captain Macann, the local vice-consul. He showed considerable interest in them in his report to New Delhi that day. The refugees, he said, "have in their possession extremely valuable political secrets which they wish to impart to His Majesty's Government but decline to say more while in Persia; though are prepared to reveal all their knowledge in India. Might they not," the captain asked, "be allowed to proceed to Quetta [the military headquarters town in northwestern India] to prove their statement there?"[4]

All he got back for his pains were negative replies. An "undesirable precedent" could be created if the men were given asylum on British soil. If they were allowed to proceed to Quetta, the government of India would only "be saddled with them." As for their claims about secrets, the foreign secretary in New Delhi commented, on March 1, "Story regarding valuable information does not sound convincing."[5] There was even talk of sending the hapless pair back to Meshed.

To be fair to the British, Bajanov was still at this stage only describing himself as former secretary of the Industrial Bureau's Finance Committee in Moscow; while the OGPU man Maximov, seeking his alias for quite different reasons, called himself simply "late Chief of Commercial Section." Even so, seen in a present-day context, the total lack of official interest in interrogating the two men is bizarre.

3 Ibid., telegram P. and J. no. 402–5, February 23, 1928.
4 Ibid., telegram P. and J. no. 2, February 27, 1928.
5 Ibid., telegram no. 499–S, March 1, 1928.

Bajanov was by now getting desperate. Then, on April 3, his second savior arrived on the scene, in the person of C. P. Skrine, Esquire, His Britannic Majesty's Consul for the Sistan and Kain regions. It would be nice to think that Mr. Skrine (who was in fact an Indian Civil Service officer on secondment in Persia) had his official career advanced by what happened next,[6] for it is partly thanks to his energetic action in that April of 1928, with no encouragement whatsoever from his superiors, that there is a Bajanov story to tell today and a Boris Bajanov alive to help tell it. The next stage of the escape is vividly described in a series of telegrams and letters,[7] all marked "Secret," sent by Skrine in the following weeks to the foreign secretary in Delhi.

Skrine had hurried down from Sistan after hearing from his vice-consul in Duzdap on March 28 about his interview with the two men. He found them at liberty, but far from at ease, unguarded as they were in their isolated railway waiting-room-cum-rest-house.

It was in this strange setting that Skrine started his interrogations. He concentrated on Bajanov, not only because they shared French as a common language (Maximov spoke nothing but Russian) but also because Bajanov immediately struck the British official as more of a kindred spirit. As he commented in the first of his dispatches from Camp Duzdap to New Delhi: "Bajanov is a man of considerable education and intelligence and might be a member of the superior civil service of any Western country."

In the course of two long examinations (one of two hours on April 3 followed by another three-hour session the next day), Bajanov revealed that he had, in fact, been something far more important than that. Skrine now learned that this quiet-spoken, slightly built young man had been no mere bureaucrat, but personal assistant to Stalin and secretary to the Soviet Politburo.

With a sympathetic British official in front of him and the knowledge that the border of the British Raj was only a few miles to the

---

[6] In fact, it seems unlikely. Sir Ronald Wingate Bt., a veteran of the ICS, who was actually serving in Quetta at the time of Bajanov's escape, told the author in 1976 that "Skrino," as Skrine was always known in the service, was somewhat suspect in New Delhi because of his independent views.

[7] India Office records, P. and J. (S), no. 808 (1928).

east of him, Bajanov pulled out nearly all the stops at his disposal. Though there were some highly delicate political matters, he told Skrine, that he would reveal only to the British government in London, he had information on other subjects "of especial interest to the Government of India." These included Bolshevik war preparations against the Raj in central Asia; the Soviet military organization in the frontier area, together with the economic situation there; details of the parts played by Russia in the affairs of China over the past few years; Soviet plans to seize power in both Persia and Afghanistan; and the underground network of the OGPU in various Asian countries.

Bajanov had stressed that, though he was destitute, he was after travel facilities and not cash by way of payment. Any money advances made to him, he told Skrine with serene assurance, would be refunded to the British government "out of the proceeds of my books and articles and the sale of my autographs."

These inducements were considerably more than Bajanov had offered his Persian interrogators at Meshed. He also produced an impressive selection of original documents, all of which he had somehow managed to hang on to throughout the three-month escape. He showed Skrine, for example, the original printed extract[8] (dated August 10, 1923) from the minutes of the "Russian Communist Party [Bolsheviks] Central Committee Secretariat" confirming his appointment the previous day, as Stalin's assistant. (The reverse of the sheet, which is itself marked "Strictly Secret," listed guidelines for preserving the utmost secrecy about all the Central Committee decisions.)

The British consul then found himself looking at what Bajanov assured him was the original written proof, in manuscript, of the eruption of the greatest dispute in Russian history. He might have added that it was also one of the most critical debates in the history of world Communism, and therefore in world history. For what Bajanov was talking about was the crucial quarrel in the early twenties between Stalin, the advocate of "Socialism in one country" (i.e., Russia, with himself as its unchallenged ruler), and Leon Trotsky, the apostle of continuous world revolution, with himself as its prophet.

---

[8] Bajanov papers.

It was a battle which Trotsky was, of course, destined finally to lose on January 20, 1929 when, already outmaneuvered in the Kremlin power game by his rival and banished to Alma Ata, he was expelled, on Stalin's orders, "from the entire territory of the USSR." Eleven years of exile, brought to a bloody close with Trotsky's murder in Mexico in 1940 (also on Stalin's orders), was the end of the story.

Its beginning, at least in writing, was on a sheet of paper that Bajanov now pushed across the table to Skrine in the waiting room of Duzdap railway station. On this paper was the running record, made in the handwriting of the participants, of an argument that had broken out during a Politburo meeting of June 1923, when the Soviet leadership were drawing up a reply to a diplomatic note from Lord Curzon, then British foreign secretary. The argument was not about the reply itself but as to whether the two secretaries of the Politburo had or had not discharged their proper functions correctly in drawing it up. As the two officials concerned, Nasaretian and Towstuka, were both personal appointees of Stalin, that was tantamount to an attack upon him, and the budding dictator had reacted accordingly.

The document, which bears the signatures or initials of almost the entire Communist leadership of the day, reads as follows in translation:[9]

ONLY FOR MEMBERS OF THE POLIT. BUREAU

(23/5/28)

Comrade Litvinoff says that the session secretaries have not made their remarks on the question of this note. This is not right. More correct arrangements will be necessary in future. The secretaries must have had the text of the note before them (I sent it) and ought to have entered their opinions. Otherwise misunderstandings may arise.

Seen.

Sd/-Trotsky
[initialed] V.M. [Molotov]

A stenographer is absolutely necessary.

[initialed] G. [Zinoviev]
[initialed] N.V. [Bukharin]

I agree.

Nonsense. The secretaries would have entered their opinions if

---

9   Bajanov papers.

Trotsky and Chicherin had done so themselves. On the contrary it is better that there should not be separate notings by the session secretaries, in order to preserve secrecy.

> [initialed] I.S. [Stalin]
> [initialed] V.M. [Molotov]
> [initialed] R. [Rudzutak]

No stenographer is necessary.

> [signed] M. Tomsky

A stenographer (a proved Communist to assist the session secretaries) is necessary.

> [initialed] L.K. [Kamenev]

Now all this may well have been a little above the head of His Majesty's Consul for Sistan and Kain as he listened to Bajanov explaining just why this jumble of handwriting was such a crucial fragment of history. He may not even have grasped the immediate point at issue, which was that Stalin was striving to convert the Politburo into a mere rubber stamp for his own decisions, whereas Trotsky, sensing the danger in this, wanted that supreme policy body and its secretaries to retain some independence. But on one point Mr. Skrine was now quite clear.

Bajanov was a uniquely important refugee, the most important ever to be seen in Persia, let alone to pass through his hands. And that meant, to a person of Skrine's resolute character, that whatever the indifference or disdain hitherto displayed in the matter both by higher authority in New Delhi and by his own superiors in Teheran, Bajanov simply had to be got to safety in British hands. As the consul wrote on April 4 to both those capitals:

> After examining Bajanov . . . I came to the conclusion that he was speaking the truth and that his and Maximov's escape from Russia and their anxiety to go to Europe afforded a unique opportunity for His Majesty's Government to secure up-to-date information regarding the inner working of the Soviet Government and their military preparation and designs.

Skrine, who was already preparing to take matters into his own hands, faced no easy task. He wired to Major Steveni, the British military attaché at Meshed, to come down and help him. But the opposition, in the shape of a bevy of Soviet officials, were also descending on Duzdap. They were led, in name at least, by Comrade Platte, the Soviet consul-general who had bungled the assassination attempts at Meshed three months before. In another secret report to New Delhi,[10] written when all the excitement was over, Skrine described how Platte arrived unexpectedly in Duzdap on April 7, "and was seen by an informer loitering in the neighbourhood of the small isolated railway rest-house in which the two refugees were living." Comrade Platte had every reason to pursue the hunt for Bajanov in person. According to a British Intelligence Summary sent from Meshed in mid-March, he had received a visitation there from two senior Soviet officials, one of whom had come from Moscow. Platte must have had a severe dressing-down, for after the visitors—who used false names—had departed, the Russian consul was observed to be "very despondent."

Even more ominous than the reappearance of Platte, Bajanov had recognized known OGPU killers, among them an agent called Osipov, (who had tried to ambush them at Kuchan), also prowling around the area. Major Steveni, who had by now had a chance to interrogate the refugees himself, agreed with Skrine both as to their importance and as to the degree of danger they were in. Platte, it was clear, would exert full diplomatic pressure—mixed with threats and bribery—to get the local police authorities to turn the fugitives over; meanwhile, Osipov and his men would be preparing an outright killing or kidnapping as the alternative.

That evening, the three British officials—Skrine, his vice-consul Captain Macann, and Major Steveni—held a council of war with the hunted men. As the refugees could not safely stay another night where they were, and could hardly be hidden in the Duzdap Vice-Consulate, they had to be got out of the town and across the frontier into India. But how? "No train," Skrine observed, "was due to leave Duzdap until April 11, apart from which it would have been unsafe to try and smuggle the refugees out of Duzdap by train in broad daylight; they would probably have been intercepted at Mirjawa, if not earlier."[11]

At this point, a gentleman with the resounding name of Mr. Jamu-

---

10   India Office records, P. and J. (S) 1127, 1928.
11   Mirjawa is a rail junction close to the Indian border and some sixty miles southeast down the line from Duzdap.

laddin Mullick enters the story as the *deus ex machina*. Mr. Mullick was a prominent Mohammedan merchant of the town. He also possessed its only private motor car, an almost new eight-cylinder Hupmobile which was the pride of his life. Finally, he either doted on the British Raj, or detested Soviet Russia, or both. The upshot was that he volunteered, entirely without payment, to drive the two fugitives himself across the very rough country which led to the advance levy post of India which was in the Kacha Oasis, thirty-six miles due east of Duzdap.

It was the sort of motoring terrain of which Bajanov himself once said: "God has lost the road, but the chauffeur will find it." Skrine happened to have explored most of the area not long before, and thus knew that the border at Kacha was unguarded on the Persian side. The very ruggedness and isolation of the route meant that it would be an awkward pursuit for the OGPU to undertake, especially if the fugitive could get a clear start.

Skrine's report continues:

> Although Mr. Mullick had never been to Kacha before and was doubtful whether, even with my driver as a guide, he would be able to get there in the dark, and although he was naturally anxious not to compromise himself with the Persians, he agreed at once, refusing to accept even the cost of the petrol he would consume, and so it was arranged that he should leave with the two refugees at 11.00 P.M. Their last few hours in Duzdap were spent by Bajanov and Maximov writing against time to complete the intelligence reports they had promised Major Steveni, and it was nearly midnight before we were able to put them in Mr. Mullick's car, together with the food, blankets, etc. which had been procured for them.

Mr. Jamuladdin Mullick was to prove as proficient at escapology as he had evidently been at money making. He managed to dodge all Persian police and customs posts while making his way, in bright moonlight, through the railway station precincts and out of the town. At one point, the track eastward (it could not be called a road) ran through a ragged gorge only eight feet wide, and the sides of his precious Hupmobile suffered accordingly.

But, before dawn, he reached Kacha safely and delivered the refugees, together with a letter of instructions from Skrine, to the Indian jemadar at the levy post. They were now in Beluchistan in

British India, though some way yet from real safety. Mr. Mullick drove proudly back to Duzdap to announce victory thus far.

That day, April 8, when the Russians found the rest house deserted, they started buzzing around the town like a swarm of angry bees. Comrade Platte and his henchmen were observed by the British to be scouting everywhere, including the bazaars and the railway sidings, in their hunt for the refugees. The next day, they enlisted the aid of the Persian police, who conducted an even more thorough search, which proved, of course, equally vain.

On April 10 (Skrine reported with some satisfaction), his desperate Soviet colleague was reduced to paying a formal call on the governor of Duzdap with an official demand that he should "surrender Bajanov and Maximov on the pretext that they had committed a murder in Russia." The governor, who must have guessed by now that the birds, with British help, had in fact flown, solemnly wrote a letter to the Duzdap superintendent of police ordering him to produce the two men. The superintendent, just as solemnly, denied all knowledge of the pair. Skrine (who must have had his informers sitting inside the Soviet Vice-Consulate) learned that Platte had dispatched urgent cipher telegrams to the Soviet missions at Meshed, Sistan, and Kerman that same evening, giving them the bad news. After three more days hanging around in Duzdap, hoping for a miracle, a glum Comrade Platte then returned to Sistan himself.

Skrine was left to savor his triumph and, to do so, had to revert from his Scarlet Pimpernel role to that of the deadpan British diplomat. Though there was no formal approach to him by the local Persian authorities about the missing Russians, both the governor of Duzdap and the garrison commander "mentioned them in conversation," Skrine reported.[12] Before returning to Sistan himself, he told his vice-consul what to do in case he should ever be asked officially about the two men. Captain Macann was instructed to reply "that the Beluchistan Administration will be warned of the escape of two potentially dangerous Russians into British territory."[13]

While all this was going on in Duzdap, Bajanov and his companion

---

[12] India Office records, P. and J. (S) 808, 1928 (secret letter no. 123 from Camp Duzdap, April 10, 1928).
[13] Ibid.

were moving steadily deeper into that same British territory and away from the potentially dangerous border zone. Only one exchange of telegrams in the British archives relates to this final leg of their journey. The first is a message dated April 8 from Skrine to New Delhi informing his superiors that "in anticipation of sanction against the Russians," he had had them "conveyed by night in complete secrecy to Kacha in the Chagai District, where they will await your orders."[14] The second message, sent in reply, shows that the government of India, once confronted with a *fait accompli,* had lost no time in accepting it. Instructions were sent the next day to Quetta requesting "that arrangement may be made to send the two Russians with the least possible delay to Simla [summer seat of the Viceroy] for further examination. . . . A suitable political or other officer" was to accompany them.[15]

Nearly fifty years later, Bajanov described to the author how his escape ended. The Kacha oasis lay at the tip of a triangle where three countries met: Persia, Afghanistan, and, jutting up between them, the Baluchistan salient of British India. The Indian railway line ran on a west-east axis to the interior, but its nearest point lay more than fifty miles south of the oasis. This had been considered much too close to the Persian border for either secrecy or safety, however, so the rendezvous had been fixed by Quetta much further inland. There were roads of sorts leading to this rendezvous; but Russian agents operated throughout this wild frontier area and it was feared that, in the extreme case of Bajanov, they would not stop at an ambush and kidnap attempt even on British soil.

So, after a peaceful night spent at the comfortable bungalow of the levy post (such bliss after their travails that Maximov declared he would happily spend the rest of his life there), the two men were handed over to the local Beluch tribal chief for further transportation. This proved to be by camel—a caravan of about half a dozen animals escorted by a party of Beluch warriors handpicked by the chief. "They take you to train" was the only information provided.

The fugitives spent the next four days and nights crossing the

---

[14]   India Office records, P. and J. (S) 721, no. 8–C.
[15]   Ibid., P. and J. (S) 752–5, April 9, 1928.

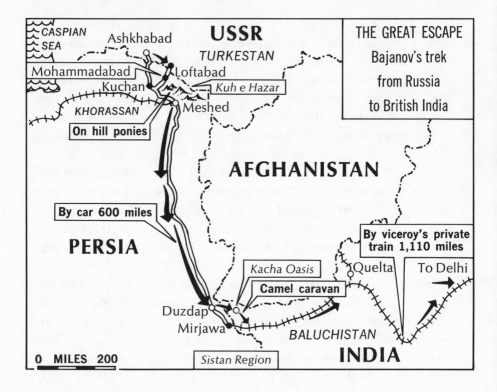

Beluch desert, traveling, both for comfort and safety, only during the hours of darkness. On the fifth evening they reached the railway line at the appointed spot, more than a hundred miles east of the Persian border. It stretched away empty to the horizon and there was one more night of waiting.

But, the next day, nothing less than an Indian Railways special puffed into sight to collect them. From Persian prisons and a station rest house, from the backs of the mountain ponies and desert camels, Bajanov and his companion now stepped straight into unimaginable luxury. He was told that this was the viceroy's own private train, and, though that sounds unlikely, there was little to complain about. The two disheveled fugitives were given an entire sleeping car with bathroom to themselves and, as they flopped gratefully down and the train reversed away, a turbanned servant from the private dining car appeared to ask them what they would like to have served for luncheon. Three and a half months after fleeing from Soviet territory in a hunter's disguise at Loftabad, Stalin's former secretary was being conveyed in style as well as safety to Simla, the summer seat of the Raj.

We should not go on with him there, however, without one last backward glance at Duzdap, and the worthy Mr. Jamuladdin Mullick. Finding that the merchant, on his return from Kacha, was still determined to refuse any material reward, Skrine had asked his government whether he might not at least be allowed to thank the man officially as well as privately.

Many weeks later, His Majesty's Consul for Sistan and Kain was advised by higher authority "that an expression of the appreciation of the Government of India may be conveyed to Mr. J. D. Mullick, for his public-spirited behaviour and for the energetic and effective assistance he gave to you in securing the escape of Messrs. Bajanov and Maximov."

Then official caution suddenly intervened. Simla's message to Skrine ended: "I am however to suggest that the communication should be made orally only; or, if in writing, no reference should be made to the precise incident in question."

That telegram was dispatched on June 27, 1928 from Simla, the very place where Bajanov was busy disgorging the additional secrets he had promised the British government. And one reason for the extreme prudence it displayed may well have been that, by now, everyone in Simla, up to and including the viceroy himself, realized what a sensitive piece of political dynamite they were nursing.

Nearly all the information which Bajanov kept on producing—either out of his head or from the lining of his clothes—was proving of great interest to his interrogators. And one piece of paper, in particular, had made their eyes pop out of their heads. It was another original Kremlin document, in the handwriting of all the Soviet mighty, full of highly damaging comments on none other than a past and future prime minister of Britain.

Chapter Three

A COMMUNIST
IN SIMLA

Boris Bajanov reached Simla in his special train on or about April 16, 1928. For the young man who had served as secretary first to Joseph Stalin and then to the Soviet Politburo in Moscow, this hot-weather capital of the British Raj (it had been used as such ever since 1864) must have seemed a quite extraordinary seat of imperial power.

Instead of the bleak, tightly enclosed gloom of the Kremlin, that fortress whose stone stairways and corridors he knew so well, here was a higgledy-piggledy complex of verandahed bungalows, public gardens, and hotels, sprawling—wide open to the rain or sun—along the hill contours between seven to eight thousand feet up the mountains of Himachal Pradesh. Instead of the Red Square to look out on from barred windows, here was the Mall, Simla's very English main shopping street, with its very English regal name. Instead of the uniformly fur-hatted and gray-coated Red Army sentries, the many-colored turbans and scarlet coats of Indian soldiers and servants. Instead of the bayonet (on the tip of which, as Bajanov recalled, the Soviet sentry would actually spike and carry forward the *laissez-passer* of a Kremlin visitor) the cavalry lance, used in India these days either for ceremony or for pig sticking. Above all, tranquillity instead of tension and the pursuit of pleasure (symbolized by all those tennis courts and croquet lawns) instead of the life-and-death struggles for survival and personal power.

In his anti-Communist outpourings written the following year, after reaching his final asylum in Europe, Bajanov did not as much as mention Simla; nor, of course, did he ever see any of the interrogation reports and official correspondence made on him during the four months he was to be kept there. But talking nearly half a century later about this first summer of his life as a free man, it was, above all, this almost unreal tranquillity of the British Raj which came back to him.

> I met hardly any Indians at Simla and really only mixed with the British officials, and shared the rather artificial life they had there. The great contrast with Russia—where all the functionaries worked like mad— was that, here, everyone wanted to take it easy. They just didn't want to be disturbed, and I got the feeling, soon after I arrived, that, in a way, I was a bit of a nuisance just because I was disturbing their peace that summer. It was such a calm bureaucracy and, though I admired it, I didn't quite like it. Knowing what I did about Soviet aims in the world, it seemed to me all too complacent.

He smiled when told that, running through the many weightier issues concerning Boris Bajanov which were recorded in the British archives, there recurred a nagging concern as to which department of state was to pay for the next stage of the journey. "Well, that's another contrast with the Kremlin I had left behind me," he commented. "There, officials spent what they liked and grabbed what they wanted, and nobody ever bothered to ask where the money was coming from."

After Bajanov and Maximov had been accommodated as distinguished visitors in comfortable quarters at separate hotels in Simla, their military interrogation began. Bajanov scrupulously kept throughout to the promise he had made to Maximov when they had stood together before the Soviet frontier post on New Year's Day: never by a word nor even a hint did he suggest to their British hosts that his companion was an utterly bogus figure. But those hosts easily discovered for themselves that Maximov was both unintelligent and relatively uninformed. Their attention soon concentrated on Stalin's former secretary, and this, therefore, is the only part of their Simla interrogations which need concern us.

Bajanov recalls three principal interrogators. The most senior was a General Isamonger, described by him as the "Head of Intelligence in India." The sessions with him were courteous but formal and always took place in the general's office. The two other officers assigned to examine Bajanov were Colonel Saunders of Military Intelligence and a Colonel Rowlandson, who spoke fluent Russian. His job, clearly, was to gain the refugee's confidence. Their relationship did, indeed, become very relaxed and informal—so much so that the bulk of Rowlandson's "interrogations" took the form of leisurely conversations, conducted without any guards or witnesses or note taking, during strolls around the gardens and bazaars of the hill resort.

One of the first things the British in Simla wanted to establish to their own satisfaction was, of course, Bajanov's genuineness. It was not that his identity and official credentials were suspect: if the personal documents he had produced left any room for doubt on that score, this would have been removed by the OGPU's quite unprecedented campaign to silence him. But everyone (then and ever since) was curious to know just why Bajanov had seemingly abandoned his niche in the innermost citadel of Soviet power and, throwing a brilliant career to the winds, had chosen the perils, and the ultimate oblivion, of flight.

Was he, as had been reported in the first messages out of Persia, a Trotskyite sympathizer, and therefore yet another of those thousands of party officials all over Russia who were now both suspect and vulnerable because they had come out on the wrong side of the great Kremlin power game? Or was it possible that such a privileged Soviet Communist could have fled, not because he was on this losing side, but simply because, out of plain disgust at what he had seen, he no longer wanted to be on the winning side? Men like that were rare in any regime, and any century.

Then there was a bit of a mystery about his relationship, over the past two or three years, with Stalin, formerly his personal chief. Bajanov freely admitted not only that Yagoda, head of the OGPU, had suspected and denounced him long before his escape; he also admitted that, by his own actions and attitudes, he had almost encouraged this lethal hostility. How was it that Stalin had also not turned against him?

All that they had to go on at Simla in the way of a curriculum vitae was a "Statement of Boris Georgeovitch Bajanov," dated April 4, 1928, which had been sent ahead to them by the industrious Mr. Skrine.[1] It answered none of these questions, and raised quite a few more.

In this statement, Bajanov had given his place of birth as Mogilov Podolsk, in the district of Podalian, south of Kiev. He gave the year of birth as 1900, but omitted the exact date. He provided no details about his family background (his father was, in fact, the local doctor).

Despite this bourgeois background, he had joined the Communist party in 1919 while a student at the Saint Vladimir University at Kiev. Thousands of other middle-class students had of course taken the same decision at the same time, though for a variety of reasons. What seems to have drawn the youthful Bajanov to the Communist movement was above all the fact that it had an all-Russian dimension; though a Ukrainian, he had nothing but contempt for the parochial outlook and narrow nationalism of his people.

Of his rapid climb up and down the slippery ladders of Soviet power after moving to Moscow in 1921, he had recorded only this:

> In January 1922, I applied for employment in the office of the Central Committee of the Communist Party, and in the summer of 1923 was appointed Assistant to Stalin, who was then Secretary Politburo. Stalin had two other assistant Secretaries as well as myself. I held the post until January 1924 when I was myself appointed Secretary Politburo. At the end of 1924 I came under suspicion of not being a true Communist and was removed to the Ministry of Finance under Sokolnikov who appointed me Vice-President of the Economic Bureau.

---

[1]   India Office records, P. and J. (S) 1127 (1928), no. 808.

In the autumn of 1926, owing to my press writings on economic subjects, I again became suspect, and when I applied for leave to go abroad it was refused by the OGPU. I was removed from my post and put in charge of the "Financial Gazette" of the Ministry until the stopping of that journal by the Government in November 1926.

After that I continued to act as Adviser in the Ministry on economic subjects and worked a great deal with the professors of the Higher School of Economics, who were at heart, like myself, anti-Bolshevik to a man.

In 1927 I organized a Correspondence College under the auspices of the Finance Ministry called the "Central School of Financial and Political Science." It began to function in the autumn of that year and, by the time I left, had fifty professors and six thousand students from all over the Soviet Union on its books.

Then came the question of his escape. Throughout 1926 and 1927, he said, he had been trying in vain to get out of Russia. (He later elaborated on this by saying that he had first planned to cross by the shortest route to western Europe, that is, over the Finnish or Polish borders. Both were too closely guarded, however, with bloodhounds and air reconnaissance backing up the regular military patrols.) The issue was decided for him in October of 1927, when the OGPU informed him that he was to be banished from Moscow, and must choose a remote province of the Soviet Union in which to reside.

He picked Turkestan with the deliberate aim of escaping across the Khorassan frontier into Persia. As the OGPU authorities at the capital, Tashkent, had his dossier, he had moved on in November to Askhabad in the border zone where, he said, nothing detrimental was known of him and he was even given a job by the local Communist party secretary, Ibrahimov.

One great puzzle arising from Bajanov's bald account of his life was how—under a cloud for the past four years and actively provoking the regime for the past two—he had managed to survive at all, let alone enjoy the favor (or at least the tolerance) of the morbidly suspicious Stalin himself.

Part of the explanation Bajanov provided was the fact that, though the political purges had begun in Russia by the mid-twenties, Communist party members like himself still enjoyed special protection, the Bolshevik equivalent of parliamentary immunity. Accusations against them had to be brought, in the first instance, before the Central Control Commission of the party. Only after this commission had considered and accepted the charges and had expelled the suspect from the party's ranks could the OGPU take direct action against him. Until then, he carried his membership card around with him like a protective shield, a shield that was not to be swept away, along with much else, until the frenzied persecutions of the thirties.

As to Yagoda's hostility, Bajanov seems actually to have made capital out of this with Stalin. He recalled at least one occasion when the dictator confronted his aide with a file showing the OGPU's accusation of "anti-Communism" against him. What had Comrade Bajanov to say?

Comrade Bajanov had replied that he and Comrade Yagoda certainly did not see eye to eye on many things but that this dossier was nothing more than a personal vendetta on the police chief's part. And he described one of their quarrels, which could easily be verified. Both men had served together on the supreme Sports Council for the Soviet Union. Young Bajanov, with typical audacity, had argued that it was no use simply trying to squeeze more and more output from the exhausted factory workers. A range of enjoyable recreations had to be provided for them as well, and this could only be done if the so-called bourgeois sports like tennis and riding were brought out of ideological banishment and revived. Yagoda had violently opposed such counterrevolutionary sacrilege but had been defeated on the council. He had never forgiven his opponent for the humiliation. Apparently, this explanation not only satisfied Stalin, it pleased him. Rivalries between others were what he throve on; and here was another useful one. That his secretary would be playing his bourgeois tennis on the courts of Simla only a year or two later never entered the dictator's worst nightmares.

The second puzzle unresolved by Bajanov's personal statement was his real motive for flight. But his interrogators realized there was no immediate answer to this. His claim that he had rejected and flown from, not Stalinism, but simply Communism as such could only be borne out by studying the character of the man, as well as the startling variety of information which he now started to produce.

Simla's formal interrogation report on Bajanov (supported at some points by information from Maximov) is a document fifty-eight pages long. It is divided into two parts: a sixteen-page "Index of the Questionnaire" and a forty-two-page summary of the answers.[2] It was considered at the time to have been of such importance that a special print was made of it for dispatch to all interested departments in India and England and to British missions throughout the Middle and Far East. The bulky document shows General Isamonger and his staff doing an extremely thorough professional job, and Bajanov responding, for the most part, quite frankly. Only occasionally did he defer his answers "for the competent higher authority," by which, of course, he meant London.

Inevitably, Indian Army intelligence experts spent a great deal of their time on the military and technical aspects of the Soviet threat along their northern borders. What is the capacity in trains per diem of the Trans-Siberian Railway? Is the branch of the Merv-Khuskh line to be extended to Takhta Bazaar? Is the Soviet intention to attack the British Empire through Afghanistan? If so, how soon after a declaration of war would they move troops over the River Oxus? What is the normal means of crossing the Oxus at Termez, and what sort of boats are available? Are Soviet passenger or military aircraft yet fitted with wireless? Are there any amateur wireless "radio clubs" in existence? How long would a land-line telegram take to reach Leningrad from Tashkent? Are there any poison gas factories in existence in the USSR, and what are Soviet plans for "liberating" gas from aircraft? Are there any all-metal aircraft in operation, and can they land in snow? Are there any balloon units in the Soviet Central Asian Military District? How many Red Air Force planes crash in training and what types of bombs and machine guns would the planes carry in action?

These and a host of other specific points were showered over the two men, and it is impressive to note how many they could deal with between them. (Some technical replies formed Maximov's main contribution to the entire paper.) But apart from such a detailed examination, wider issues were also not forgotten at Simla; and here the interrogation report takes on a certain historic value.

At the beginning of his examination, for example, Bajanov was

---

[2]   Bajanov papers.

asked whether it was still Soviet policy to bring about world revolution, and if so, how? Moreover, assuming this led to hostilities, how did the Kremlin view British policy in the event of war, and how did they propose to counter this policy?

Stalin's secretary replied:

> Worldwide revolution is still the Soviet policy. Attention is now being directed more to the East than the West. Methods vary according to the country being exploited. In spite of failure in China, which the Soviet admits, efforts there will be continued.
>
> The Soviet thinks that England will organize Poland, Rumania, Finland, and other small nations bordering on Russia into a "block" against them and that England will supply the money, arms, and munitions, but not necessarily troops. The Soviet thinks England's policy is dictated by Churchill, Amery, and Birkenhead, and that the greatest of these is Churchill.

As for Soviet countermeasures, the Kremlin regarded the British Empire as "its greatest enemy" with whom war was, one day, inevitable. Their plan was to weaken it from within so that the armed struggle, when it came, would be that much easier for the Soviet Union to win. Propaganda and agitation were "the chief weapons" in the campaign. Diplomatic missions and trade agencies were all centers for the dissemination of such Soviet propaganda and, where the Soviet Union had no such outposts, subversion agents were dispatched with false passports manufactured at a special Moscow factory.

The Society for Cultural Relations, Bajanov went on, was nothing less than an organ of this Bolshevik propaganda. Its three objects were "to throw dust in the eyes of educated persons in the West"; to organize societies to help Russia; and to pass agents into foreign countries.

As for India, Communist agents "were at the bottom of every strike there." The Russians were playing chiefly on Indian nationalism. They hoped to secure the approaches to India (i.e., Persia and Afghanistan) and to stage revolutions there when the expected war with the Western powers broke out. Across the Himalayas, the Soviets considered they already had absolute control over Mongolia and intended to absorb it into the USSR at the right time. The so-called national republic there was a sham, as power was in the hands of the Bolsheviks. Through their recently founded front organization, the so-called

People's Party of Mongolia, they ran things at Ulan Bator, as the old capital of Urga was now called. And this, Bajanov stressed, was the takeover pattern they would henceforth try to follow everywhere in the world.

There is not a great deal about that laconic survey which will be new to any observer of the Soviet scene today. Moreover, some predictions, such as an Anglo-Russian war for the approaches to India, were canceled out by a very different war in which Britain and Russia actually fought for four years as allies, and in the aftermath of which British India disappeared altogether.

But much of this was new to Colonel Rowlandson as he listened to it in those strolls round the Simla public gardens. And what is remarkable, looking back, is how many of these basic features of Soviet strategy—the seizure of power through political front organizations; the abuse of cultural societies for espionage and the hoodwinking of Western intellectuals; the fomenting of industrial unrest and so on— remain just as valid today as when Bajanov first expounded them to the British in the spring of 1928. On the other side of the account, the Kremlin's prediction that Churchill was England's coming man commands respect. This was more than most English observers would have said of the statesman who, for more than ten years to come, would still remain in the political shadows.

Yet, though Bajanov had painted a disturbing picture of Soviet ruthlessness and determination, it was not all strength that he portrayed. Indeed, in one of the special papers he wrote at Simla, entitled "The Bolsheviks and the Coming War,"[3] he described how highly secret discussions in the Kremlin had led to the conclusion that, for the time being, a war against England and France in Europe was out of the question for the paradoxically capitalist reason that Stalin's Russia simply could not finance it by the old-fashioned methods still under consideration. Here, Bajanov's service as a senior party official at the Finance Ministry in Moscow stood him in expert stead, as well, of course, as his long spell inside the Kremlin.

The starting point of this paper was a series of Politburo discussions in the early twenties (all of which Bajanov had attended as sec-

---

[3] Bajanov papers.

retary) to decide whether war with the West should be regarded as "probable" or virtually "unavoidable." There was a parallel clash of views as to whether the Soviet Union should try to precipitate the struggle or postpone it (the OGPU being for the first course and the People's Commissariat for Foreign Affairs supporting the second). The Politburo finally decided that war was indeed unavoidable, but hedged its bets as to the timing. The commissar for foreign affairs was told to delay a conflict as long as possible, while the Soviet armed forces were told to prepare for it as soon as possible.

But in the end it was, apparently, neither the Soviet diplomats nor the Soviet generals who held the key to the problem but that archaic figure, the tax collector. A special Finance Committee, sitting at the headquarters of the Red Army General Staff, eventually came to the dismal conclusion that "it would be impossible to wage war for more than three or four months against the expected confederation of neighbouring states headed by Poland even if not one of the Great Powers came in against Russia."

The weakness was not manpower (the necessary army of 1–1.2 million men could "easily be mustered") but the lack of capital resources to feed the enormous industrial output which would be needed to equip and supply such an army. According to Bajanov, the Communist finance experts (who doubtless included a few tsarist bureaucrats) drove home their argument by drawing the following contrasts with Russia's prewar position:

> In 1914 there existed a market for securities amounting to nearly 20 billion rubles. This provided an extremely mobile reservoir on which to draw for the needs of war by war loans and so to arrange for the provision of the necessary means and the proper disposal of the national-economic resources, adapted to the changed conditions of wartime. There is now no market for securities in Russia at all, and this important form of mobilization of war means in Russia is nonexistent.
>
> Bank assets amounting to many billions provided a valuable source by the help of which the Government could arrange war loans on vast capital. The bank assets under the present national-economic system represent the actual means by which industries are carried on, these industries being of necessity entirely dependent on bank credit, and any attempt to draw on this source deals a heavy blow at industry and greatly increases the dearth of commodities in the country, already sufficiently scarce. This problem now has an entirely different

significance from that of former days. In 1914 there were enormous reserves of commodities in the country, sufficient for many months. Now there are not even reserve sufficient for a fortnight, so much so that any check to continuous industrial production means immediate growth of queues in the towns and political tension.

Before the Great War, there were 2 billion rubles' worth of small savings in the savings banks alone. By the summer of 1927, these had shrunk to deposits amounting to not more than 100 million rubles.

As for other alternatives, the report concluded, the sale of gold and foreign currency reserves in the State Bank to purchase supplies would serve no purpose in a military emergency because the West would impose an economic blockade, "while in the East there is nothing of value to be bought." Increased customs duties would have "a negative political effect"; manipulation of the budget would only lead to a collapse of exchange rates; and increased direct taxation would yield little, "in the absence of any bourgeoisie." Paper issues of war loans, which would cause a further concealed reduction in general living standards, offered the best fundraising option; but even so, "the financial catastrophe would begin after the third month of war."

This sobering analysis, Bajanov stated, had been reluctantly accepted by the Politburo in September of 1927, only a few months before his escape began. He himself signed his recapitulation of it at Simla on April 21, 1928. Looking back, it may go a little way toward explaining the lack of military, as opposed to ideological, aggressiveness which Stalin was to display over the next few years.

Though this must all have sounded very important to the officers of the Raj, it was a bit remote for them, and also highly technical. Much more fascinating (and immediately understandable) was another document Bajanov turned out three weeks later, and which has also survived.[4] It is addressed "To H.B.M. Government," marked "Extremely Secret," and signed, rather endearingly, "With sincere respects, Bajanov." This dealt with a more tangible Soviet financial asset: a pool of precious stones from the tsarist era which the Politburo members had, it seemed, stowed away for themselves, just in case the revolution went sour on them.

---

[4]   Bajanov papers.

Bajanov described how, in February of 1924, soon after the shock of Lenin's death, he, as Politburo secretary, had to draw up a distribution authorization relating to the Gosbank's reserve of diamonds and other gems. There had been no open discussion as to their disposal, the decision having evidently been taken by the leading members of the Politburo (Stalin, Kamenev, and Zinoviev) beforehand. This did not arouse any suspicions in Bajanov's mind at the time. Such decisions, at least as regards foreign currency reserves, were often taken in private when it was a case of providing urgently large sums of ready cash to support revolutionary movements abroad.

But he was reminded of it sharply three years later when fulfilling his last party function in Moscow as a senior official of the People's Commissariat of Finance. One morning, he was about to enter the office of Bryukhanov, the commissar, when something made him pause on the threshold.

Bajanov, in his paper, described what happened next:

I had half-opened the door when I heard him rung up on the automatic telephone. (The automatic system in the Kremlin, with a strictly limited number of connections, serves only the principal Bolshevik Government officials, and was put in to ensure greater secrecy in conversations.) I paused without entering, not wishing to disturb him. It was Stalin ringing him up. There was no one else in the anteroom where I stood, the secretary having gone out, and as the door of Bryukhanov's private room was not quite closed, I heard Bryukhanov's replies distinctly.

From them, I learned that there exists a strictly secret pool of precious stones (probably the same as that dealt with in 1924, when I was working in the Politburo). Bryukhanov gave an estimate of its value, putting it at several millions. Stalin apparently asked if it could be more accurately valued. Bryukhanov replied: "I should find it difficult to do so. Its value in general depends to so great an extent on various factors, and the home market (for precious stones) is no index, and all these jewels, moreover, may have to be realized abroad, and under conditions entirely unforeseen. Anyhow, they are worth several millions. I will determine the approximate figure (of course a very rough one) and ring you up."

The eavesdropper then discovered that this secret hoard of gems was earmarked exclusively for the members of the Politburo, and held against the eventuality of the downfall of Soviet power in Russia.

His Simla report continued:

Although Bryukhanov was speaking in a low tone, I clearly heard him, first, when he said laughingly to Stalin: "As you so disagreeably call it, 'in case of the loss of authority.' If Lev Davidovich [Trotsky] heard you, he would accuse us of lack of faith in the possibility of the victory of Socialism in one country."

At that, Stalin evidently stressed the need for complete secrecy, for Bryukhanov hurriedly replied: "Of course, of course, I understand perfectly. This is simply a timely precaution against the eventuality of war. It is not only "anonymous" but, further, we have nothing whatsoever on paper about it." Bajanov went on:

Secondly, I heard part of a question asked by Bryukhanov: "I understand that this is for the members of the Politburo, that is, to prevent a stoppage of the work of the center in case of extremity. But you said that you desired a change in the means adopted to safeguard it. What am I to do in this regard?"

Thereafter followed a long reply from Stalin, then Bryukhanov said that he fully agreed, and that the best place for the pool would indeed be in the private flat of Claudia Mimofeevna.

Elaborate precautions were to be taken to carry out the transfer through a chain of trustworthy persons, none of whom knew of more than his own link in the chain. As for the members of the Politburo itself, they were allowed to be told of the existence and the emergency purpose of the gems hoard, but they would not know where it was. Only Stalin, Bryukhanov, and the lady herself would know everything.

She, Bajanov went on, was well known to him by name and reputation. She was the widow of the late president of the Central Military Executive Committee, Yakoff Sverdlov. She had two prime qualifications to be selected for this signal honor. She was held to be quite incorruptible; and her private apartment was handily situated in the Kremlin itself.

Bajanov then described how, in order to get confirmation of this astounding piece of information, he had deliberately cultivated the friendship of Madame Mimofeevna's teenage son, Andrei, who lived with his mother. In the late summer of 1927, he had managed to draw the boy out on the subject. His report continued:

Andrei stated that he had twice happened to see his mother open a fireproof cupboard in her room (she had acquired the documents of her late husband, which were kept in this cupboard), and that there was a very large number of precious stones there. When he questioned her she replied that these were family jewels and worth nothing, but she was annoyed that he had seen her. He believed his mother: "Of course they are false," he said to me. "Where on earth could my mother get such a lot of precious stones?" Naturally, I agreed with him.

Bajanov ended his paper by appealing to the British government "to acquaint the smallest possible number of people" with this information. The secret, he argued, was only of importance so long as it was kept.

His Simla hosts would clearly have been intrigued by this tale, which smacked more of the *Arabian Nights* than Karl Marx. Moreover, if he told the story then with the same disgusted venom as he repeated it many years later, they might also have begun to believe in his assertion that it was an outraged moral conscience and not a frustrated ambition which had led him to abandon first the Kremlin, and then Communist Russia.

But the real treasure, from the British point of view, of Bajanov's collection of reports and documents was not produced until May 12. And, in true Simla style, it was drawn out of him, not by any formal interrogation, but by a casual conversation at the tennis club.

As well as having been largely instrumental in reintroducing tennis to Bolshevik Russia, Bajanov (who was in fact an excellent all-round sportsman) played a good game himself, and had become a regular visitor to the club. Once, when waiting for a court to become free, he found himself talking to Mr. O'Hara, a senior official of the Viceroy's Department for External Affairs. "What was your party number?" was one of the first questions the Irishman shot at him; and that impressed Bajanov mightily, for nobody else had asked him that detail, which, for any Communist, was such a vital one.

By the time they stopped chatting and went on the court, Bajanov had decided that O'Hara was the man he would like to play his trump card with. (Indeed, looking back on these eventful months he was to conclude that, of all the British officials he met, only Skrine in Duzdap and O'Hara in Simla seemed to have grasped the wider political significance of his flight.)

So the next day he turned up, by appointment, in Mr. O'Hara's office and pushed a short handwritten minute across his desk. It was drawn up in several different hands, but a good deal neater than the similar document he had shown to Skrine in Persia the month before.

However this, too, was all in Russian, and Bajanov had supplied with it, by way of explanation, another of his notes addressed to "H.B.M. Government," and signed "With sincere respect."[5] This key showed that the minute itself, dated May 23, 1924, had been written by Bukharin, while the initials and comments had been added by Comrades Stalin, Zinoviev, and Kamenev, the trio who, at that time, ran Soviet Russia among them. But even more interesting than the signatures on the minute was its subject—Ramsay Macdonald, the then Labour prime minister of Britain.

The minutes was, in fact, a sarcastic joke, though the discussion preceding it had been serious enough. This had all taken place, Bajanov said, at a session of the Politburo in Moscow on May 23, 1924, with he himself being present throughout as secretary. The conversation of the Soviet leadership had turned to England and there had been general agreement that political events there were shaping up very promisingly indeed from the Kremlin's point of view. The left-wing policies of the Labour party under Macdonald were judged, all round the table, to be "profitable to Moscow," as Macdonald was unconsciously preparing the way for a Communist takeover of the country.

Then Bukharin, while admitting that the Communist "already had their prime minister in London," suggested that Macdonald was unfortunately not bright enough for the job, because "he did not understand what he was doing himself." All he was fit for really was a post as a petty Communist official in some remote Russian provine like Kyshtym. He certainly deserved some reward for his great services to Communism, but that was about all for which his intellectual capacity qualified him. Macdonald, in turn, should be replaced by a worthy Soviet figure, someone like Comrade Tomsky.

There was, Bajanov recalled, laughter at this, and then the joke began. Bukharin wrote out the gist of what he had said in the form of a

---

5 Bajanov papers.

spoof Politburo resolution, and this was the sheet of paper he had brought with him to Simla. It read, in translation:

> Act of the Secretariat of the CCRCP dated May 23, 1924. Comrade Macdonald to be appointed secretary of the Ukom in Kyshtym, passage being guaranteed on the same ticket with Comrade Urquhart [British president of the Lena Goldfields concession in Siberia].
> Comrade Tomsky to be appointed Premier in London, at the same time two starched collars being provided for his use.

The first signature to follow was that of Stalin, who wrote "For" in front of his name and added "For the members of the Orgburo." Zinoviev and Kamenev followed, each also indicating assent before his signature. According to Bajanov, joke or not, Soviet protocol was such that this paper was handed to him for recording as though it were a formal resolution.

The spoof had begun seriously and it ended even more seriously; the sequel, in fact, is the most important thing about this oddity. Bajanov's intention in handing it over was, as he told Mr. O'Hara, to have it published in the British press, and thus expose the leftist leanings of the Labour leader. He was puzzled, after he had left India and had moved on to Europe, to see that the months passed, and still nothing had appeared in the London newspapers.

There came a time, as we shall see later, when British Intelligence approached him for help and guidance over a most delicate problem. Bajanov asked his contact to make inquiries in London about the fate of his Kremlin document. The answer brought back was that when the paper had turned up on the desk of the head of British Intelligence, this gentleman had thought of a far better use for it than publication. He had sent it round personally, with a covering note, to Ramsay Macdonald himself at 10 Downing Street. The Labour prime minister was said to have been much chastened by its implications; indeed, Bajanov was assured, Macdonald's awakening to the dangers of extreme left-wing views had been powerfully helped by the sight of it. Be that as it may, Bajanov was satisfied with the outcome. He even felt that perhaps he had helped to correct, if only by a degree or two, the drifting course of British Socialism.

In between his interrogations and the writing of all his various reports (the papers described above being only a small proportion of his output) Bajanov read a great deal in his hotel. He also spent much time pondering over this unfamiliar imperial gentility which now enveloped him in such an atmosphere of security. Clearly, his hosts were doing everything in their power to achieve the impossible, namely to make him feel at home. They had enabled him, for example, to earn some money by asking him to serve on the examining board which sat at Simla to test the proficiency of Russian-language students among the Indian Army officers. (With the money, he kitted both himself and Maximov out with clothes from the Simla shops and tailors.) It was a tactful gesture to make him feel he was not living on charity.

The tact and good manners of the British community in India had, indeed, struck Bajanov particularly. He was to remember all his life, for example, one regimental dinner in the General Staff officers' mess at Simla at which he was the guest of honor. It was a big affair, with some fifty seated at table, Bajanov being placed between the senior officer of the mess and his own interrogator-cum-interpreter, Colonel Rowlandson. It so happened that, on that particular evening, Simla was having its first eagerly awaited showing of the silent film epic *Ben Hur*. The film was due to start after dinner, and everyone present was making straight for the cinema as soon as the port had passed.

Bajanov, who always dressed simply and informally, had no hat to collect when the meal ended: and so simply stood up and made for the door. When he emerged on the street, however, and turned round, he saw that every one of the fifty officers following him was also bareheaded. They had, Colonel Rowlandson explained, all left their uniform caps behind as a gesture of politeness to their guest of honor. Bajanov had never known anything remotely resembling this in the Communist Russia he had abandoned. Nor, as he admitted later, was he ever to experience any such considerate gesture quite like it in the long years of exile in Europe which were to come.

Yet, though touched and ever impressed by such graciousness (which, he realized, was also a mark of confidence and strength) Bajanov's final verdict on the British Raj was much as his first impression had been—a strong doubt about its capacity to survive the political tempests ahead.

This was summed up in one particular conversation he had with

Colonel Rowlandson. The two men had stopped talking about the future of Communist Russia and were discussing, for a change, the future of British India.

"Are you," Bajanov had asked, "here to fulfill an imperial mission or are you here because you feel a moral responsibility toward the Indians?"

"We are here," the colonel replied, "to protect England's interests."

"Then you won't be here much longer," Stalin's secretary said simply.

That must have sounded like a remarkably confident, even somewhat cocky tone for a twenty-eight-year-old Russian, almost straight from Moscow, to strike in the summer capital of an India about which he knew next to nothing.

Yet it was absolutely in character with this outspoken, calm, and totally uncompromising man. He had spoken to Stalin like this in the life he had left behind him. And, though neither he nor Colonel Rowlandson would have dreamed it at the time, he was to strike precisely the same attitude in the life that lay ahead of him, first with British Intelligence itself and then with Stalin's alter ego, Adolf Hitler.

While the Military Intelligence community at Simla were busy questioning Bajanov and absorbing the documents he presented them with, their colleagues in the viceroy's Home Department, working in another office in the same hill station, were almost equally preoccupied with the problem of how to get rid of the fugitives. Bajanov never saw this steady stream of letters and telegrams which passed, throughout the spring and summer of 1928, between Simla and various Whitehall departments in London. This was just as well. They did not exactly flatter anyone's reputation, including his own.

Before judging the authorities—and especially the home ministers involved—too harshly, the effort must be made to get back into the historical perspective of the time. The modern word *defector*, with all the associations it carried later on, was seemingly quite unknown in 1928; at any rate, it never shows up once in all the contemporary official correspondence about Bajanov. And what that implies, of course, is that the concept of a global ideological conflict between

East and West—the battle of nerves, blackmail, subversion, and propaganda which was eventually to merge in the so-called Cold War—was also unknown. So, both in London and Simla, Bajanov and his uninteresting companion were considered basically deserters or, at best, plain fugitives. Moreover, the British took a lot of convincing (especially those outside the Intelligence world) that it was a creed rather than a country from which they were fleeing.

As for the threat posed by Russian colossus, this was felt, as it always had been felt, primarily by India rather than England or Europe as such. Even the Raj itself was perhaps more comfortable with this impoverished and chaotic Communist neighbor north of the Himalayas than it had been in the old days of the menace from tsarist Saint Petersburg. To have sensed in 1928 the enormous implications both of Bajanov's flight and of the information he brought with him, one would have needed a feel for the future in one's bones. As we have seen, Bajanov had encountered only two British officials who shared this dimension with him.

The rest, including the authorities in London, regarded him at the time of his escape not as the absolutely priceless capture he would be seen as today, but with indifference mixed almost with disdain. A gentleman, one can almost hear them murmuring, just does not turn his coat, even if that garment had been a violent Bolshevik red. Moreover, unfortunately for him, Bajanov was the first such important turncoat ever to confront Whitehall. That meant, on top of everything else, repeated genuflections before the bureaucrat's god of precedent. And so the fugitive secretary of the Politburo, a figure for whom, in the modern world, the NATO alliance would move divisions and armadas to secure, was shunted around instead like some awkward house guest.

The first message to London on the files about Bajanov and Maximov was sent from the Home Department in Simla on April 30, 1928, that is, about a fortnight after the couple's arrival there. It referred to the useful information the two had already given to the military, and also to several documents which, at the time, they were still withholding. The General Staff in India were "definitely of the opinion that it would be worthwhile to send the Russians to England for examination by the authorities there." So, would the India Office and other government departments concerned "wire urgently" whether they wanted this—and, if so, whether "they are prepared to meet part of the cost of passages and travel expenses?"[6]

The reply from London, dispatched on May 5 from the secretary of state to the viceroy, was distinctly unenthusiastic. All departments concerned, Simla was told, were "unanimously opposed to the proposal that these men should be granted permission to come to England." Their withholding of "certain alleged items of information" was seen as "a ruse," and one which "should not be permitted to succeed." However, once they had told all they knew in India—and once their material had been proven genuine—then London was prepared to consider "the question of suitable rewards."

A month later, Simla tried again. By now, the two men, and especially Bajanov, had produced seven statements and two documents between them. The viceroy's government, said a further message to London on June 4, thought the information to be both genuine and "of value." Then came the first attempt to pass the bureaucratic buck over the case.

> As His Majesty's Government are aware, their entry into India was not premeditated by the Government of India. They were assisted out of Persia by the Consul at Sistan, acting on his own authority. . . . We recommend therefore that they should be sent to Europe where they should be able to settle down. . . . If His Majesty's Government agree to their being permitted to land in England, but are unwilling to meet part of the expenses, we are prepared to pay their way as far as England, and sufficient for their subsistence until they have had a chance to look for employment. Early decision requested.

Simla had thus placed the responsibility on London because it was an official of a Whitehall department who had been responsible for the fugitives' escape. In London, the India Office now seized on the same thought, namely to try to make the Foreign Office (Mr. Skrine's employers, after all) pick up the baton.

"We might try to persuade the F.O. to do what they can," runs an internal minute written the day the Simla telegram was received, "on the grounds suggested that it was the Consul at Sistan who originally

---

[6]   This, and all the following correspondence from India Office records P. and J. (S) 1127 (1928) and from Bajanov papers.

sponsored these individuals." That word *individuals* expresses, more than volumes, the official attitude.

And so it went on, throughout June and July. With both England and India ruled out, the problem was to find another haven; and the authorities *did* regard this as a problem, for what, today, would be considered comically pompous reasons. "The only alternative," another internal Whitehall minute reads, "appears to be some country on the Continent, but it is open to doubt whether any other country would be prepared to take in persons whom we ourselves refuse to admit." ("Very much so, I should say!" commented the minute writer's superior in the margin of his draft.)

In fact, it was very much not so. In bringing the Foreign Office in on the problem, the India Office was thinking of France as a dumping ground for the two fugitives, though with no great hope of success, as the following memorandum shows:

> France has a large colony of Russian refugees and is probably the only country in Europe who would accept Bajanov and Maximov. If we explain to the Foreign Office that we have been more or less landed with these men . . . they may be induced to approach the French government. . . . There is just a bare possibility that this might succeed, provided the negotiations were carefully handled.

To be fair to the British government, its worst crime at this stage was indifference; it was trying to do the decent thing.

"After all," the same memorandum continues,

> these men are quite likely to be genuine refugees, and it may be considered a new departure for the British Empire summarily to eject harmless persons who seek, and who have already in some measure received, our protection.

Nonetheless, the writer added, he could not feel "particularly optimistic" about the Paris reaction.

In the event, the French government seems to have jumped at the opportunity to pick the brains of Stalin's former secretary in their own capital and at leisure. Fearing a rebuff, the first approach to Paris was made informally; the French promptly indicated that they would be quite happy to receive the two refugees. A gratified British government now realized it could go ahead with an official application but it was determined to get the cash out of the viceroy first.

"Before making *definite* suggestions to the French authorities," read another internal Whitehall letter at the end of June,

> we want to be quite sure that the Government of India will:
> (i) provide the expenses of Bajanov and Maximov's journey to Marseilles and arrange for their departure to that destination, and
> (ii) supply them with a sufficient sum of money to provide them with the wherewithal to live for, say, a fortnight after landing.

These weighty matters took some time to clear up for, ten days later, Simla sent a message to London saying that the two men were "restless and anxious to know the decision arrived at concerning their future movements." Bajanov was said to be in poor health, his condition "aggravated by the altitude of Simla." Indeed, there was the possibility of him becoming "seriously ill if detained here much longer." Could final orders for the men's disposal therefore be issued "at a very early date"?

As Bajanov never recalled afterward feeling anything but fighting fit in Simla's pleasant climate and surroundings, this particular message probably owed more to the "restless and anxious" state of mind of his hosts. At all events, soon afterward, both hosts and guests were put out of their misery. There was a final flurry of activity over the perennial question of paying for the fares, and also over documentation. Any issue of British passports was, of course, ruled out, as this might subsequently be construed "as entitling them to British nationality." There were even dangers lurking in the provision of so-called British Emergency Certificates by the government of India. It ought to be made perfectly clear, London warned Simla, that these certificates were available only for the single journey to France, "otherwise there might be a danger of the men attempting to secure entry into Great Britain where, as you know, they are not wanted."

On July 27, a telegram to the viceroy announced the end of the imbroglio. France would definitely take the two Russians (indeed, the message added, as though with faint surprise, "the French authorities appear to be anxious to question these two men"); and the French consul-general in Calcutta was being instructed to stamp the necessary visas in their one-way travel papers. The only favor that the French authorities seem to have asked for in return was to be shown the full results of their interrogation so far while in British hands. No objection was raised to this.

On August 14 Simla sent its final message about Bajanov. Arrangements had been made for him and his companion to sail for Marseilles on the S.S. *Maloja* leaving Bombay on August 18. The Raj said goodbye at the quayside. No guard or escorting officer was sent with them on the voyage.

One ironic aspect of the whole affair was that the British government's determination to prevent Bajanov from getting British papers and living in England had been quite superfluous. France had been his intended destination from the start and he had never had the slightest wish to go to London except, perhaps, for a transit stop in order to pay for his passage to Paris with further interrogation. The muddle had arisen because, on arrival in India, he had immediately expressed his desire to "settle in Europe." The haughty expatriates of Simla had automatically assumed that he could only mean England.

Bajanov's only vivid memory of that voyage was the heat. He took the temperature of the shower in his cabin when going up the Red Sea. It was 34°C, as high as the hottest of summer days in Moscow. Otherwise, the trip was uneventful, and they docked at Marseilles as scheduled on September 1, eight months to the day after slipping across the Persian frontier at Loftabad.

There was not a soul to meet them. So, like any ordinary travelers, they stepped straight on the train to Paris, where they arrived that same evening. Bajanov seems to have been neither surprised nor offended at the absence of a reception committee, or even of any special message as he cleared the immigration authorities. He was given by them only the routine instruction, issued to all arriving émigrés, to report to the local police as soon as he had found somewhere to live. He assumed—rightly as it turned out—that the French republic would promptly take it up from there.

Chapter Four

THE PARIS DOSSIER

When Bajanov got off his train at Paris on September 1, 1928, all that he had to start his new life on was a modest sum of money and, in the way of personal belongings, little more than a pistol for protection and the clothes he stood up in. He found a cheap room at the Hotel Vivienne, which lay centrally between the Bourse and the Opéra. It was the first of several Paris hotels he was to move in and out of over the coming months and years, the aim being, if possible, to keep one jump ahead of the assassins he knew Stalin would send after him.

When he reported, as required of all émigrés, to the local prefecture of police, he found that his safety was one of the two matters also preoccupying the French authorities. The prefect warned at their first meeting that his life must be considered as being permanently in danger, and that if any alarm were passed down from the Ministry of the Interior, there would be nothing for it but to take him into pro-tective custody. Things could move so fast, the prefect added, that his men might be forced to pick Bajanov up off the streets without any explanation. He would have to be prepared for this in advance.

The fugitive, who had already been forced to accept six weeks of such protective custody in Persia, said he quite understood the posi-tion. But he then set the prefect back with a warning of his own.

"I must tell you straight away," Bajanov said, "that, if I am suddenly tapped on the shoulder in the street by a stranger in civilian clothes and pushed toward a car, I shall simply shoot him down with the pistol I now always carry with me. I shall not stop to ask whether he is one of your people because I dare not take the risk that he is not really an OGPU agent—of whom, as we both know, there are plenty in Paris. You must understand that, and explain it to your men."

The police chief swallowed hard before nodding reluctant agree-ment.

The second communication which the local police prefect had to pass on to Bajanov was the expected summons for interrogation. Would he report as soon as possible to a certain Lt. Colonel Josse at a military address in Paris that he was now given?

The French Intelligence authorities tackled Bajanov with a style and a purpose that were in complete contrast to those employed by their British colleagues at Simla. To begin with, there was nothing leisurely or informal about their approach. He was interrogated intensively al-most every day over the next two weeks (the interpreter being a Russian-speaking Pole), and it was all hard office work, with no strolls along the boulevards. The thrust of the French questioning was also entirely different. Not a single military point seems to have been raised, although a military officer was in charge of the examination. Instead, Colonel Josse concentrated on the political side: he wanted to know in particular, for example, exactly how Moscow financed Communist party funds in France and other Western countries. And when it came to conditions inside the Soviet Union, Bajanov was in-vited to explain, not the social or economic problems, but the Krem-lin power game: how were the various rivals in that game playing it, and who was likely to come out permanently on top?

The result was a document, over two-hundred typewritten pages long, which provided the first authentic picture, painted by a Russian from the inside, of the Soviet leadership and the struggles that divided it. It is the portrait of Bajanov's former master which dominates this dark canvas.

Stalin at home: morose, unsociable, uncommunicative. "Do you know," his eldest son Yashka once said to Bajanov, "my father spoke to me on Tuesday." "What brought that about?" "Well, I was reading, and my father came up to me and asked, 'What are you reading?' " "And that was all?" "Yes, that was all." It appeared that the boy, whom Bajanov got to know quite well, would often go for days on end without a single word from his father, although, at the time, they lived at the Kremlin together.

Stalin at work: "extremely cunning, with an unbelievable power of dissimulation and, above all, very spiteful." The ruler of a country who scarcely read at all (in the eighteen months Bajanov served him as secretary, he estimated that his master acquainted himself properly with less than a dozen official documents). A similar display of indifference at Politburo meetings, where Stalin would never take the chair himself, and would only pronounce on any point after he had heard the views of all his colleagues.

Yet this disdain, both of paper work and formal procedure, only masked the driving passion of the man for supreme power and his ruthlessness in using the apparatus of the party to achieve that power. Bajanov gave this, among many examples:

> Stalin goes every day to the Central Committee and spends several hours there. Plunged in thought, he paces up and down the office and the corridor. At first, this habit puzzled me, and I asked myself what he could be thinking about all this time. I found the key to the enigma by watching him closely. One day, at the end of an hour of this pacing and meditation, he ended, abruptly, by going to the telephone and asking for Molotov.
>
> "Viacheslav Mikhailovitch," he said, "it seems to me that the President of the Central Executive Committee of the White Russian Republic is not sound and ought to be replaced."
>
> This is Stalin's sole occupation. For hours, he will ask himself who is sound and who is not, whom he should remove and whom appoint. He tries to guard himself on every side so that he may continue to wield uninhibited power. Everything else interests him but little.

And Bajanov went on to describe how, through this tireless manipulation of party posts, Stalin had succeeded in building up, brick by
brick, an impenetrable wall behind which he could shelter and which
eventually closed out his greatest rival, Leon Trotsky. Bajanov called
Trotsky "the most gifted of all the Bolsheviks," a romantic tribune of
the people who could organize anything, except that dull party
machine whose growing strength he never understood. By now,
the struggle had been lost for him. Only the outbreak of war might,
in Bajanov's view, revive Trotsky's chances, for the Red Army
admired him as much as it disliked Stalin.

The political rout of Trotsky did not mean, however, that Stalin's
hold was, as yet, unchallenged. Bajanov described how a group hostile
to Stalin had emerged when, in 1927, the question arose of replacing
Trotsky as a member of the Politburo. There were, at that time, nine
full members of this supreme Soviet body, and, in the vote to fill the
vacant ninth place, the eight other members had split exactly into
two groups.

Stalin had proposed Valerian Kuibyshev, whom Bajanov described
elsewhere in his report as "notoriously incapable, very idle, and also
an inveterate drunkard." He was, however, the servile creature of
Stalin, on whose behalf, as head of the Control Commission, he had
purged the Communist ranks. His master had already secured his
election to the party's Central Committee and now sought to promote
him further. According to Bajanov's account, Stalin was backed by
Molotov, Rudzutak, and Voroshilov. Bukharin, on the other hand, had
proposed Choubar, president of the Ukrainian Soviet of Commissars,
for the vacant place, and had on his side the votes of Rykov, Tomsky,
and Kalinin.[1] The deadlock was such that, for a time, the Politburo
continued with eight members only. But, in the end, the Plenum of
the Central Committee duly endorsed Kuibyshev, and Stalin's favorite
took his seat to give the dictator a built-in majority of Politburo
cronies.

Bajanov's assessment, by the time he left Moscow himself at the end
of 1927, was that if anyone could be said to have taken over Trotsky's

---

[1]   Out of this particular quartet, only Kalinin escaped with his life in Stalin's great
"show trials" of his supposed rivals in 1936–38. Bukharin and Rykov were sentenced
to death and executed; Tomsky committed suicide before trial.

mantle as Stalin's challenger in the Kremlin, that man was Bukharin ("the only one of real value in the Politburo"). But he warned against the illusion that the overthrow of Stalin by a so-called moderate Communist leader would transform the picture for the West. Moderates and extremists alike realized that a return to anything approaching normal conditions would mean that Russia would be opened up toward the great powers of western Europe. This would, in turn, invite dependence and, even more painfully, comparisons. Bajanov commented:

> As a result of the weakness of her industry and the imperfections of her economic system, Russia would then find herself condemned to play the part of a tenth violin in the European concert.

Any successor of Stalin's drawn from the existing hierarchy would thus follow the dictator's example in seeking, not only domination within Russia, but isolation from the rest of the world. Their Bolshevik road was paved, like his, with inferiority complexes.

Bajanov made it clear to his Paris interrogators that such speculations were, in any case, largely academic. The potential threat from Bukharin, and whatever loose tactical grouping he might attract around him, was hardly a serious one. By now, the dictator was too firmly entrenched in all the concentric circles of Soviet power—in the innermost ring of the Politburo; in the larger Central Committee and its five-man Secretariat which Stalin also dominated; in the All-Union Congress of the Communist Party (theoretically the supreme organ but convened in practice only when when Stalin wanted it to meet and rubber-stamp decisions he had already taken); and, outside Moscow, in the regional, district, and cantonal committees through which the country's million or so party members ruled the lives of the ordinary people the length and breadth of the land. By the end of 1927, Stalin had his local Kuibyshevs packed into most of these as well.

Then there was the OGPU, of which Bajanov provided, as part of his Paris interrogation, a detailed thirty-page organizational description, the first such complete breakdown to be seen in the West.[2] Stalin's hand was on the hilt of this blood-stained secret police instrument too. Both the president of its so-called *Collegium*, a nonentity

---

[2]   He had produced a much briefer paper on the OGPU at Simla.

called Menjinsky, and his two "assistants" who really ran it (Yagoda for domestic affairs and Trilliser for the Foreign Section) held their posts by Stalin's favor and could lose them at his whim—as, indeed happened with Yagoda in 1936.

The OGPU did not merely hold the country down for Bolshevism; it also helped to hold the party down for Stalin. Blackmail—political or personal—was its principle weapon in the latter task, and Bajanov's Paris report gave this revealing example.

Michail Ivanovitch Kalinin, one of the four Politburo members who had voted against Stalin in the matter of a successor to Trotsky, was a lightweight in politics but a considerable bon vivant in his private life. One of his amorous adventures concerned a well-known singer at the Moscow Opera called Tatiana Bach, whom he proceeded to shower with favors at the state's expense. His most lavish present to her was, in fact, at the expense of the murdered tsarina. This was a sable cloak, reputed to be the finest in all Russia, which was valued at 37,000 rubles and had been deposited, with other Romanov family possessions, in the Kremlin.

In 1927, soon after she had been given this imperial gift, Mlle. Bach applied for permission to go on tour abroad with the opera company, and listed the cloak among the items of value she wished to take with her. The OGPU, not knowing it was a present from a Politburo member, sent agents to her house to discover how she had obtained the magnificent fur. At first, the opera singer maintained a sulky and haughty silence. But when she was threatened with arrest, there was nothing for it but to ring up her illustrious lover and explain her plight. Kalinin gave orders over the telephone that his mistress should be left in peace, and should also be allowed to take "her" sables abroad should she so wish.

The OGPU men apologetically withdrew, but reported the matter to their chief, Yagoda. As it concerned one of the nine most prestigious men in the country, Yagoda promptly rang up Stalin and described the whole affair to him. The dictator's reaction was characteristic. He ordered that the OGPU inquiry should be closed, with no further action taken, but that a detailed report on the incident should be forwarded to him in person. This report, Bajanov was told, had been placed by Stalin in his special secret files, where incriminating material of every description about his colleagues and potential rivals was preserved for future use.

When it came to foreign affairs, the French authorities were interested above all to learn from Bajanov what plans, and what weapons, the Kremlin possessed to subvert the Western democracies by strikes and terrorism. There is nothing in his Paris interrogation report about such schemes for France, but in a separate paper he gave them a vivid account of the most ambitious Soviet subversion campaign launched to date in Europe. This was the Kremlin's attempt in 1923 to bring about a Communist coup d'état in Germany. It was an insider speaking. As secretary of the Politburo at the time, Bajanov had attended, and taken the minutes of, all the secret sessions at which the Soviet leadership of the day had thrashed out the issue.

The first such meeting had been held in the Kremlin on August 23 of that year. Karl Radek had been called in for the occasion, as the representative of the Comintern, to brief the Politburo on the prospects. He painted a glowing picture of the rapidly swelling wave of unrest and Communist fervor among the German people, which, he claimed, would reach its climax in the coming weeks; Radek then asked his masters for instructions.

As might have been expected, Leon Trotsky, at that time still the revered and powerful preacher of worldwide revolution, was in favor of striking while the German iron was hot. If the Communists could seize power in Berlin, he argued, it would mean the beginning of the end for that detested bourgeois order which still began at Russia's frontiers. But he warned his colleagues that they would be playing their trump cards. The future of Communism in Russia itself, as well as in Germany, would be at stake. Yet, for him, it was worth even this risk.

Bajanov noted how the others, and notably Stalin seized on the peril rather than the prize, and argued at first for postponing action. The outcome was a compromise typical of the Politburo of the day. Without sharing entirely in Comrade Trotsky's optimism, a series of very energetic measures were passed, all designed to bring Germany to a rapid crisis point.

A Quadrumvirate was nominated to provoke and then direct the

German revolution. It consisted of the *rapporteur* from the Comintern, Karl Radek (who was also on the Central Committee of the Russian Communist party); Yuri Piatikov, a vice-president of the Supreme Economic Council; the vice-president of the OGPU, Unschlicht; and the People's commissar for labor, Vassily Schmidt. This high-powered quartet were duly dispatched to Germany with false passports, each with his appointed task in the great conspiracy.

Piatikov was made responsible for agitation and propaganda, and also for liaison with Moscow. Radek was the emissary of the Comintern to the German Communist party, who were to act as the political façade of the uprising. Unschlicht, as befitted his murky calling, was to do the dirty work—first to organize the so-called armed *sotnias* or "Red Companies," who were to execute the coup d'état, and then, immediately after this had been completed, to set up a German branch of his own OGPU to exterminate the bourgeoisie and other enemies of the Bolshevik cause. Schmidt, the labor expert, was to raise revolutionary cells in the factories and to prepare the Trade Unions Committee for its appointed task of becoming a temporary "nucleus of state authority," in which capacity it would draw up Germany's new Communist constitution.

Soon afterward, Bajanov's account continued, a fifth member was added: Krestinsky, the Soviet ambassador in Berlin. He was needed for administrative purposes—to transfer from Moscow and distribute the vast sums of money which would be needed, and to parcel out the scores of special agitators dispatched by the Kremlin. The German Communist leaders (notably Brandler) were only used in an advisory capacity in all this planning, and their own domestic network was similarly bypassed. Instead, the entire Bolshevik diplomatic, consular, and commercial system inside Germany was mobilized, at the Politburo's express orders, for the operation. The embassy in Berlin supervised the creation of the *sotnias* and the workers cells; the trade delegations imported the Russian agitators (German or German-speaking Communists); the weapons and inflammatory pamphlets came in under the protection of the diplomatic mail. All these gigantic preparations were financed in part by the gold reserves held for ordinary commercial transactions by the Russian State Bank in Berlin.

At the end of September, Piatikov reported to Moscow that all would soon be ready; and, at a particularly secret meeting of the Politburo, and with no outside attendance, even from the Central Committee, the date was fixed. Bajanov, as secretary, actually signed this report and locked it away. November 7, 1923 was the day named on which Germany would be stormed. It was the anniversary of the Bolshevik revolution, which would provide the ideal pretext for mass gatherings in the streets. In the course of these, the "Red Companies" would provoke clashes with the German police. These, in turn, would strike back and be accused of brutality against the masses. The "spontaneous uprising," leading to a seizure of all state offices and institutions, would follow.

What happened next is a matter of history. The great revolution misfired, partly because a last-minute order from Moscow postponing it reached most, but not all, of the party centers in Germany in time. The courier for Hamburg, for example, arrived too late, and the "Red Companies" started a bloody battle there which lasted three days. There was total confusion at the other party centers who did not know whether to lie low or come out in sympathy with the Hamburg comrades. A series of half-cocked uprisings spluttered into life, which were fairly easily extinguished by the German Army and police.

Moscow blamed the entire fiasco on Brandler and his German Communists—the very network excluded by the Kremlin from real responsibility. Bajanov, in his report, conceded that there were plenty of blockheads among their ranks. But the Bolsheviks were themselves partly to blame for that. It was largely at Stalin's behest that peasants and workers had been placed in key Communist posts, both inside and outside Russia, without regard to intelligence or ability. Wherever the blame lay, however, the select circle of people reading Bajanov's disclosures in 1928 would have been just as alarmed by the prodigious scale of this Soviet subversion attempt in the heart of the European continent as consoled by its failure.

Among that select circle of readers were British Intelligence officers, who now belatedly realized what a plum they had allowed to slip through their fingers. It was clear from this massive Paris dossier that Boris Bajanov was a unique and irreplaceable expert to help them sort out any conundrums emerging from the Soviet Union. And it so happened that the British had one especially intriguing conundrum on their hands at the time. The upshot was that, early in 1929, a Mr. Dunderdale called on Bajanov in Paris, announced himself quite openly as a senior member of British Intelligence, and asked for his advice on the following problem.

It concerned the enterprising activities of Comrade Gaidouk, resident chief of the OGPU in Riga, the capital of Latvia, which was then, of course, still an independent Baltic state.[3] Through the British Mission in Riga, he had made contact with London, offering to sell His Majesty's Government nothing less than copies of the minutes of the Soviet Politburo itself. The price was astronomical, but so was the level of intelligence, and Mr. Gaidouk's samples looked, to British eyes, completely convincing. So a deal had been done and London settled down to savor one of the espionage coups of the century. Their confidence had only been strengthened by seeing secret Politburo decisions, as reported by Comrade Gaidouk, filtering out officially through Soviet announcements made weeks later. Nonetheless, in Boris Bajanov, they had the former secretary of the Politburo itself, and the only man in the Western world, therefore, who could put the matter beyond any doubt for them. There was, after all, the possibility that this was an elaborate deception game on the Kremlin's part. Would he be so good as to look at the specimens Mr. Dunderdale was producing, and just confirm their authenticity?

Bajanov, on the contrary, immediately pronounced the documents to be crude forgeries, and Comrade Gaidouk to be an unscrupulous fraud. There were several reasons why he could be so emphatic. To begin with, he knew that the OGPU "resident" in Riga, important as he was in his own trade, would never have official access to such material. Moreover, there seemed to be no way by which Politburo minutes could have reached him unofficially. The most elaborate precautions had always been taken to insure that what went on inside the Politburo was only communicated—and then in condensed form—to a handful of senior party men outside it.

---

[3] Latvia was forcibly incorporated into the Soviet Union in 1940.

Bajanov had been a key figure in this security process for eighteen months. Though, as he had told the French, Stalin never sat as chairman of the Politburo, the dictator, he emphasized, was always careful to edit the minutes of each meeting himself. Only when he had approved the final text were copies made for the privileged recipients—notably all the members and deputy members of the Central Committee. Those in Moscow received them that same evening by hand—delivered in pink envelopes, by the rather comic means of Kremlin cyclists.

Those away from the capital had their copies delivered to them, whenever they were in the Soviet Union, by special messengers belonging to the Courier Corps of the Kremlin. These darkly clad, heavily armed giants were sworn to their duty on pain of death, and were considered utterly loyal to their masters. (To hear Bajanov describe them puts one in mind of the Dark Riders in Tolkien's *Lord of the Rings*.) Every copy sent out bore Stalin's own stamp and was marked for its recipient, who had to return it after perusal, to be burnt by the Politburo's Secretariat. Admittedly, there might be a traitor in the top echelons of the party; the strongest messenger could be overpowered, or one of those Moscow cyclists waylaid. Stalin would soon have heard about the second or third eventuality, however; while the first, in this pre–Cold War age, was almost inconceivable.

Bajanov was also able to point out what were, to him, obvious blunders in the so-called minutes, whether these were errors of facts or simply mistakes in the styling and layout. But the real reason why he knew that they were forgeries was one which he may or may not have communicated to Mr. Dunderdale. Comrade Gaidouk had actually had the nerve to come to Paris and look up the former secretary of the Politburo with a business proposal. Cheerfully admitting that he was doing a lucrative trade in "Politburo minutes" with the British, but that he was now running rather short of inspiration, he had proposed that Bajanov should contribute his unrivaled inside knowledge to the swindle in return for a share of the profits. Bajanov had thrown the man out. He had refused money from the French secret service, he was not going to take it from the very OGPU who were out to kill him.

Perhaps understandably, both Mr. Dunderdale and his superiors in London (to say nothing of his colleagues in Simla) were reluctant to accept Bajanov's verdict. It was not pleasant, when you thought you had struck a hidden vein of pure gold, to be told that this was, in fact, fools' gold, and specially manufactured for the prospector at that. But, in the end, Bajanov's judgment had to be accepted. Comrade Gaidouk found that his services were no longer required by London, and, though he would never have known it, the British taxpayer of the day was saved a considerable sum as a result.

For Bajanov, this was the beginning of a long-term relationship with the British Intelligence Service, which consulted him at intervals over the next ten years on a variety of Soviet problems. The relationship seems to have been a pleasant one and it was only a turning point in European diplomacy which was eventually to bring it to an abrupt and less pleasant end.

By now, the turn of the year 1928–29, Bajanov was settling into the life—at once tense and monotonous—of the anti-Soviet émigré in Paris. He earned his living in this prewar phase mainly by his pen; yet whatever the difficulties of making ends meet, he never sold that pen. There were, for example, two Russian-language daily papers published in Paris at that time. Stalin's former secretary was a valuable contributor for either to win. One paper, which had leftist tendencies, offered him two francs a line. The other, which was right-wing, could only pay one franc. He chose the right-wing journal.

He had not been contributing to it for long when a compliment, no less handsome for being unspoken, was paid to the importance of his work. He noticed that some of his articles on conditions within the Soviet Union, though fully paid for, were not appearing. As it was the journalistic platform which interested Bajanov even more than the money, he demanded to know what was going on. His paper finally admitted that the Quai d'Orsay (the French Foreign Office) were buying some of his contributions as authoritative reference material for their archives and were, accordingly, insisting that they should not be published.

Bajanov seems to have managed fairly well on his journalist's income, if only because he needed so little. Even as a young man he was a person of plain, almost Spartan tastes. He was a nonsmoker and a complete teetotaler (even abstaining from the occasional glass of wine); for him, food was essentially something with which you nourished your body rather than indulged the tastebuds. Nor did he ever acquire either valuable possessions or a fashionable wardrobe. Economical though all these habits may have been, they were scarcely conducive to social success in a capital devoted to the good things of life and within a Russian émigré community which, by instinct and tradition, had always spent lavishly more money than it possessed.

That community, ten years after the Bolshevik revolution, was still almost entirely White Russian. The arrival, in their midst, of Stalin's one-time secretary must have been an extraordinary event, for, quite apart from his former position, he was the first apostate Communist most of them had ever seen. The introduction was arranged for him en bloc by M. Gourkassov, wealthy owner of La Renaissance, the paper for which he had opted to work. It was, Bajanov recalled many years later, an impressive gathering of the banished tsarist world, complete with grand dukes, former generals, and industrialists. He chatted easily with them all, giving them the latest news of Moscow.

When the last of them had left, he asked his patron what impression he had made.

"A bad one," replied M. Gourkassov.

"But why?"

"Because you are only twenty-seven," the newspaper proprietor replied. "Several of them remarked to me that if the Kremlin has many more like you, then we monarchists really have no hope."

Where Bajanov did fit in with the Paris scene was in his admiration for a pretty woman. Yet though he eventually wound up his existence in hotel rooms and risked moving into a small furnished apartment which he could call a home, he never married.

Asked, when looking back on his émigré life, why he had remained a bachelor (despite one or two close attachments), he replied simply:

I did not have the moral right to take a wife. She would automatically have become a likely hostage in Stalin's eyes. Quite apart from that, she could so easily have ended up as a widow.

He was not being unduly morose. Even after eliminating all accidents which might have been truly accidental, Bajanov was left with at least half a dozen separate and unmistakable attempts by the OGPU to murder him during the first ten years of his stay in Paris. Some were crude, like the attempt to stage a car crash for him in Nice, or the knife attack made on him in the garage of his apartment house by a Spanish thug hired by Stalin's agents. Other approaches showed a little more finesse, and into this category came the OGPU's innuendos to a notoriously jealous and violent husband that Bajanov had slept with his pretty wife. The husband did indeed go for Bajanov (who was quite innocent of the charge); but after a bout of fisticuffs, hostilities ended with nothing more lethal than a few bruises on either side.

On one occasion Stalin sent the most famous of all his executioners to France in person to silence his renegade secretary. His name was Jacob Blumkin and, ironically, in his very first interrogations at Simla, Bajanov had prepared a special paper on the man, whom he had singled out as one of the most dangerous of all the Kremlin's assassins. Long before Bajanov's flight from Moscow, Blumkin had carved out an unsavory reputation for himself as a ruthless operator on an international scale. Apart from its bearing on Bajanov, the story of Blumkin's rise and fall is an instructive vignette of the violence and treachery of this Bolshevik age.

Blumkin had started his career in 1917 as a member of the extreme Left Social Revolutionary party in the Ukraine, a group which, though allied at the time with the Bolsheviks, was in many ways even more fanatical. The alliance was broken off altogether after the signing on March 3, 1918 of the Treaty of Brest-Litovsk. This was the instrument by which Lenin's still vulnerable regime in Moscow, desperate for a breathing space, had opted out of the Great War and come to terms with the Germans and their allies. The Social Revolutionaries, appalled at this "betrayal," decided to seize power from the Bolsheviks. The signal for their revolt was to be the murder of the German ambassador in Moscow, Count Mirbach, and Blumkin was given the job. He accomplished it on July 6, 1918, though rather messily.

With a sailor named Borisov as his assistant, he managed to get an interview with the count in his office on the pretext of an inquiry concerning the ambassador's brother. As soon as he was inside the room, Blumkin drew a revolver from his attaché case and fired. Despite the short range, however, he missed. Blumkin then pulled out his second weapon, which was a bomb, and hurled that at the envoy— who by now, not surprisingly, had decided to terminate this unorthodox interview and take to his heels. But the bomb also missed, or rather, fell to the ground without exploding. It was, according to Bajanov's account, the assistant executioner who picked it up and hurled it again at the fleeing German. This time it went off, killing the ambassador and wounding several of his staff.

Though it was an obscure Russian sailor who had actually administered the coup de grâce, it was Jacob Blumkin who, from that day on, claimed and occupied his own murky little niche in history as the murderer of Count Mirbach. At first, it did him little good. His party's revolt failed to materialize and Blumkin found himself outlawed and hunted by the Bolsheviks. After several months on the run in Moscow and Saint Petersburg, he returned to his native Ukraine. When this was reoccupied by the Bolsheviks in the spring of 1918, after the German peace treaties, Blumkin realized that the game was up and decided to save his skin by reconciling himself with the victors. This he did, in characteristic fashion, by betraying to them the entire organization of his own Left Social Revolutionary party, which had by now been driven underground. His reward was a nominal sentence for the Mirbach murder, after a somewhat farcical trial staged by the Bolsheviks in Moscow to save appearances, both diplomatic and domestic.

By the autumn of 1919, Blumkin was already at liberty and active again, this time in northern Persia, as adviser to the Communist bandit Kachuk Khan. After a spell on "special duties" with the Red Army, the seal was set on Blumkin's rehabilitation when, in 1923, he was enrolled in the foreign section of the OGPU.

For the next stage in his colorful career, the clean-shaven Blumkin grew a full moustache and beard. His first OGPU assignment was subversion in the Middle East based in Palestine (then under British mandate). His new alias, Moses Huffinckel, was as florid as his new appearance, though the headquarters, a laundry in Jaffa, was rather more mundane. By the following summer, he was back in Moscow, from where he was appointed commandant of the OGPU frontier force in Transcaucasia, to help in the bloody suppression of the revolt which had broken out in Stalin's native Georgia. That accomplished, he was transferred in a similar capacity to Outer Mongolia.

By now, the German government had learned that the man who had murdered one of their ambassadors was held in such high esteem in Moscow and given such responsible posts. Chicherin, the Soviet commissar for foreign affairs, was sharply questioned on the matter when on a visit to Berlin in 1925. The commissar was assured by the German authorities that this was quite a different Jacob Blumkin; he simply happened to have the same unfortunate name as that reprehensible assassin of 1918.

Such was the odious figure detailed to murder Bajanov. Though he never succeeded, Stalin could not admit failure. So, to demoralize the underground opposition (and to dissuade any more of its members from following in Bajanov's footsteps), word was spread around, all the way from the Moscow cafés to the Siberian concentration camps, that Blumkin had again got his man. How successful the rumor was at the time is shown by an echo of it which appears today in Solzhenitsyn's *Gulag Archipelago*. Writing of the talk among political prisoners during Stalin's reign of terror, Solzhenitsyn describes a discussion about Blumkin, and goes on:

> After the 1918 rout of the Left SRs, Blumkin, the assassin of the German Ambassador Mirbach, not only went unpunished . . . but was protected. Superficially, he converted to Bolshevism and was kept on, one gathers, for particularly important assassinations. . . . At one point, close to the thirties, he was secretly sent to Paris to kill Bakhenov [*sic*], a member of the staff of Stalin's Secretariat who had defected, and one night he succeeded in throwing him off a train. . . .[4]

Quite which of the various attempts made on his life were, in fact, directed by Blumkin, Bajanov never discovered. There was indeed one scuffle on a train; but this had ended, like the Nice car accident, with the intended victim safe and sound. Nor did Bajanov

---

[4] Alexander Solzhenitsyn, *The Gulag Archipelago* (Fontana Paperback Edition), 1: 370.

ever come face to face with Blumkin, bomb or revolver in hand. But what he did discover was that Blumkin had succeeded in recruiting, in Paris, one particularly interesting assistant for his murder plot. This was none other than Captain Maximov, the man whom Bajanov had brought with him in safety to the West and whose false name and identity he had protected ever since, true to that promise given at the Soviet border on New Year's Day of 1928. Now, after only a year or two of "going straight" in Paris, Maximov had reverted to his original self and had been reenlisted into OGPU's ranks. To bring about this reverse metamorphosis, Blumkin had used, apart from blackmail and bribery, family pressure. He was, it turned out, Maximov's cousin.

Maximov's perfidy and ingratitude toward him does not seem to have surprised Bajanov unduly. He had always regarded his fellow refugee as *un sale type*, like nearly all of his odious profession. Moreover, possessing neither intelligence, charm, nor journalistic facility, the OGPU man, as Bajanov knew, had found it difficult to get either a social or a financial foothold on the French capital. But outraged or not, Bajanov could have been forgiven for taking a wry satisfaction in the fate, first of Jacob Blumkin, and then of the double-traitor he had recruited. Their end is part of the Bajanov saga.

On January 20, 1929, Stalin's great rival, Leon Trotsky, who had already been living for a year in exile at Alma Ata in central Asia, was banished with his family "from the entire territory of the USSR," and dispatched to Turkey. Here he had been consigned by the nervous authorities to a dilapidated villa on Buyuk Ada, one of the remote Prinkipo Islands in the Sea of Marmora, which could be reached only by a long steamer journey from Constantinople.

But Trotsky's influence could not be isolated like his person. He was to remain, down to his eventual murder and beyond, the magnet of international Communism; and visitors from all over the world traveled to Turkey to take the steamer out to the red-cliffed Buyuk Ada. Among these visitors was Jacob Blumkin, who was then doing a spell of duty as chief of the OGPU station in Constantinople.

Blumkin, it will be remembered, had started his career as a member of the Left Social Revolutionary group in opposition to the "moderate" Bolsheviks. Perhaps there was a spark of political idealism left in him so that now he looked to the banished Trotsky as being in some way the inheritor of his own youthful fanaticism. Perhaps Blumkin was merely being the eternal opportunist, resolved to keep in the fallen hero's good books in case his fortunes should change. At all events, the OGPU agent agreed to deliver to Trotsky a highly secret letter from his supporters in Russia.

The man who had betrayed so many people in his brief career was now betrayed himself. By the summer of 1929, Blumkin was back in Moscow and already under suspicion for his reputed Trotskyite sympathies. But the days of indiscriminate purges had not yet begun in Moscow. A veteran revolutionary who was also a senior OGPU official with many brilliant successes recorded on his file could not be eliminated on rumor alone. Yagoda, his chief, set out to get proof. He offered, as bait, something that Blumkin, who was as debauched as he was unscrupulous, would find hard to resist—a pretty woman. Lisa Gorskaya, one of the most attractive female agents on the staff of the OGPU's Foreign Section, was instructed to make herself amenable and available to the suspect, and to persuade him to spill out his secrets over the pillow.

Blumkin swallowed the bait with alacrity; and it must be presumed that the beautiful Lisa provided not only him, but also their mutual master Yagoda, with everything required of her. It seems that Blumkin not only confided to this seductive stool pigeon the fatal details of his courier missions to the Prinkipo Islands, but even tried to convert her to the Trotskyite cause. Yagoda now had the evidence he required. He struck the night after receiving Gorskaya's report, some time at the end of August or the beginning of September. An OGPU car arrived at Blumkin's Moscow apartment in the early hours of the morning just as he was driving away from it with Lisa. There was a brief car chase through the empty streets, and a volley of shots, before Blumkin surrendered. As he gave himself up, he was said to have denounced his Delilah bitterly for her betrayal; but that part of the story may well have been apochryphal. At all events, he knew what was facing him.

There was no trial, merely a discussion by the OGPU council. Of the supreme trio who debated his case, Yagoda, who had trapped him, was for the death penalty. Trilliser, his immediate chief in the

Foreign Section, was against it. The nominal chairman, Menjinsky was, as usual in such situations, neither for nor against. The matter was accordingly referred up to the Politburo and to Stalin, who pronounced the death sentence. He was reportedly appalled and alarmed that Trotskyism had penetrated the higher echelons of the secret police, the Praetorian Guard of his dictatorship. It was indeed a turning point in the violent history of his rule, and one that was to take its full effect in Stalin's large-scale and almost indiscriminate purges of the OGPU that were to follow in the late thirties.

Jacob Blumkin was only thirty when he faced a firing squad, made up of his former colleagues, in the cellar of some Moscow prison. He had shown a certain panache throughout his eventful life, so it was appropriate that there should have been a touch of colorful irony about the way he was officially declared dead. His code name had been *Vivant*. The message now passed round the service was: "*Le Vivant est mort.*"

Maximov's end did not come until seven years later, and was much closer to home for Stalin's secretary. For reasons that remain obscure, in the summer of 1937 he jumped—or was pushed—from the top observation platform of the Eiffel Tower. As befitted the intrinsically insignificant figure of Bajanov's companion in flight, Maximov's death caused few ripples in Moscow, and attracted little attention anywhere.

The removal of these two assassins from the scene, with that same sudden violence by which they had lived, lightened somewhat the dark pressure which Bajanov always felt around him during this first decade of exile. But Stalin's secretary was not really to breathe easily again until 1953, when Stalin himself died, taking his thirst for personal vengeance with him.

Chapter Five

GRIGORY BESSEDOVSKY: AN ENVOY DEFECTS

Dodging assassination attempts was not the only excitement of Bajanov's first year of exile. On Wednesday, October 3, 1929, a more cheerful surprise awaited him when he learned that he was no longer the only top-level Communist defector in the French capital. The newcomer was none other than the chargé d'affaires at the Soviet Embassy in Paris, Grigory Bessedovsky; and, in contrast to Bajanov's own escape—an odyssey which had stretched across three months and some ten thousand miles—the renegade diplomat was faced with only a short walk, or rather jump, to save his skin. However, whereas Bajanov had kept his secret police guard at the right end of the gun when it came to making a dash for it, Bessedovsky had been staring down the muzzle of an OGPU man's pistol within seconds of reaching freedom.

The first paper to break the news of Bessedovsky's flight was *Le*

Matin of October 3. The following day, not only all the French papers, but the entire world press reverberated with the scandal. No Soviet envoy had ever defected before, not even an OGPU official in disguise, let alone a career diplomat who, at the age of only thirty-two, was an embassy counselor senior enough to be left in charge of his mission, a man, in short, with a brilliant professional career ahead of him. The question on everyone's lips in Paris when they read the first bare reports was: what on earth made him do it?

No proper answer was forthcoming at the time, and no completely satisfactory explanation can be constructed nearly fifty years later, with the benefit both of hindsight and of much fresh information. But we could do worse than begin by examining, before discarding, the one piece of the jigsaw puzzle which quite certainly does not fit, despite the fact that it was designed specially for that purpose. This is the version which, after nearly three days of stunned silence, Bessedovsky's former masters put out at the weekend, in the form of a Tass communiqué distributed via the stricken Paris mission.[1] These are the relevant passages:

> The ex-Counselor of Embassy, Bessedovsky, who for some time past has been leading a life far beyond his means, has embezzled a considerable sum of the monies entrusted to him and is unable to render an account of it. On September 24 of the current year, the Commissariat of Foreign Affairs requested Bessedovsky to resign his post, and to come to Moscow, in order to give explanations in connection with his actions.
>
> Since Bessedovsky did not comply with this order, the member of the *Collegium* of the Commissariat of the Labor-Peasant Inspection, Roisemann, was instructed to audit the accounts of the ex-Counselor of Embassy. For this purpose Roisemann came to Paris on October 2. Wishing to avoid the necessity of rendering account, and chiefly for the purpose of escaping responsibility for his actions, Bessedovsky left the Embassy surreptitiously.
>
> In order to lead public opinion astray, Bessedovsky attempted in a deceitful way to represent the affair, which is of a purely criminal character, as a political one, which it certainly is not. The Embassy declares in the most categorical way that Bessedovsky never expressed any difference of opinion with the Government, either to the Government itself, or to the Embassy. Nonetheless, hoping by means of a

---

1   Published in *Izvestia*, October 8, 1929.

scandal to divert attention from his unseemly actions, he invented a fairy tale according to which his family and he were detained in custody at the Embassy, with their lives in jeopardy. In bringing to public knowledge these facts, the Embassy most emphatically denies all the fantastic assertions that may crop up in this connection.

What appears to be true about that pained and defensive statement is that money did have a lot to do with the affair, though on a larger scale even than the ample cash reserves that would be found in the coffers of a major Soviet mission. It is certainly true that Comrade Roisemann (or Roisenmann as the name appears elsewhere) did arrive in Paris on October 2, the day of the actual escape, and on a special mission from the Kremlin. However, his real job in life was far more sinister than anything implied by that harmless title by which the communiqué described him, while his orders from Stalin went a great deal further than simply "to audit the accounts." Bessedovsky, on the other hand, had not "invented a fairy tale" when claiming that the lives of himself and his family had been in jeopardy. The fairy tale at this point is the Tass denial.

As for any political differences between the chargé d'affaires and his government, what needs to be remembered is that, however loyally he had served Moscow to date in his career, Bessedovsky had never enjoyed the unqualified confidence of the Moscow regime. A Ukrainian Jew (born at Poltava in 1896), he had originally belonged, like Blumkin, to the extremist opposition party of the Social Revolutionaries. After this had been absorbed by the Bolsheviks, the young Bessedovsky, as one of its suspect leaders, was sent abroad in 1922 to do diplomatic work, more or less as a political exile. Abroad he remained; and although, over the next seven years, he rose steadily in rank, with successive postings in Vienna, Warsaw, and Tokyo, his career was always a form of banishment.

However, it was not until the summer of 1929 that, for reasons we shall examine later on, the Kremlin's latent distrust took on sharper form. The OGPU, which operated in the Paris Embassy (as it did in all Soviet missions abroad), started putting Counselor Bessedovsky under special surveillance. His mail was examined and photographed; his private apartment (also in the Embassy building) was searched whenever he took his family out of Paris for the weekend;

and agents even shadowed him when he went to have his boots cleaned at the Gare Saint-Lazare, which was the nearest place he could get this service performed. His nerves began to go to shreds, all in a very Russian way. To ease the tension, he started firing revolver shots up at the ceiling of his office. When he attacked it for the last time it was already riddled with holes.

This bizarre behavior (duly reported, of course, to Moscow) can have done nothing to increase confidence in high places. But the crisis did not come until September, when Bessedovsky ignored an order to spend his annual leave in the Soviet Union, having already evaded an earlier summons to Moscow for "official consultations." The day the second recall order arrived, the Soviet ambassador in Paris, Dovgalevsky, was leaving for London for critical talks with the Socialist foreign minister of the day, Arthur Henderson, over the resumption of diplomatic relations between Britain and the Soviet Union, ruptured two years before. Dovgalevsky was indispensable for this mission, as he had personally conducted all the earlier, abortive negotiations on the subject that summer. So, despite the crisis brewing in his Embassy, the ambassador was obliged to depart, and had no choice but to place his harassed, pistol-happy counselor, as the next senior official, in temporary charge. Thus it was that Bessedovsky, as acting ambassador of a major Soviet Embassy, stood on the highest rung of his career just as the ladder was to be pulled from under him.

The Kremlin had a special henchman for doing this, a man reserved for cases like Bessedovsky's, who was an old party member as well as a senior Soviet official serving abroad. This henchman was the said Comrade Roisemann, and he enjoyed, in addition to the elaborate function described by Tass, the much shorter and more pregnant title of "Honored Chekist," that is, an ex officio member of the Cheka, as the Soviet secret police had earlier been called. Roisemann's main function in life was, in fact, the purging of any Soviet individual or institution abroad which had fallen under suspicion, for whatever reason. The local OGPU network was placed under his total command for any of these operations, and he was usually authorized to stop at nothing to carry them out. His professional colleagues would not, therefore, have been surprised to learn that he had arrived in Paris on October 2 with a very large custom-built trunk, inside which, if need be, the body of the condemned chargé d'affaires could be transported, drugged or dead, back to his homeland. Yet on this occasion there was a proviso. It had been made clear to Roisemann that, whatever methods he adopted, diplomatic relations with France had somehow to be preserved in the process. These were always important in Soviet eyes, and doubly so in view of the current breach with London. Even for this experienced operator, it was to prove too tall an order.[2]

At first, all went well for the Kremlin's executioner. He arrived from Berlin on a false passport with a French visa which had been arranged by the Paris Embassy without Bessedovsky's knowledge. As soon as Roisemann reached the Embassy building in the Rue de Grenelle, he armed both guards in the hall and gave them orders to prevent anyone, by force if need be, from leaving the premises without his permission. "Does that include the Comrade Acting Ambassador?" "That includes in particular the Comrade Acting Ambassador." Roisemann then summoned a conference of the Embassy staff to inform them officially of his mission and finally, at about three in the afternoon, he announced his presence to the chargé d'affaires himself.

The moment Bessedovsky heard that this dreaded "Honored Chekist" was not only in Paris, but in the Rue de Grenelle and requesting a meeting with him in Room 82 (which was the main OGPU office in the building), he knew that the game was up. What was more to the point, he could not relieve this situation by firing aimlessly at the ceiling. He sent a message to Room 82 postponing the meeting for a while and used the delay to slip along to his private apartment, where he warned his wife to pack and to prepare both herself and their ten-year-old son for a sudden departure. Then, at tea time on a gray and rainy afternoon, came the confrontation with Roisemann.

---

[2] The account which follows of the events of October 2 is a balanced blend of Bessedovsky's own published descriptions (which appear distorted or exaggerated at many points); French press reports, based on French police information; a detailed account from a contemporary official source; and material supplied to the author by Boris Bajanov, in whom Bessedovsky confided some private details after his defection.

Bessedovsky's own published version of this[3] needs taking with a barrel-load of salt, like almost everything he wrote. He claims that, when accused by Roisemann of criticizing the Soviet government, "not only in your dealings with non-party sympathisers but also in your dealings with foreigners," he replied with a long passage of oratory attacking "a Stalin régime that depends on a gang of besotted lackeys directed by a megalomaniac Dictator." The Soviet revolution, like the French revolution before it, "needed its Thermidor," and he, Bessedovsky, had decided to stay in France and direct this regeneration from afar: "I shall know how to make the Russian masses understand the cry that is tearing my heart." There was, he claimed, much more, all in the same evangelical strain.

It is a highly improbable harangue, and for at least two reasons. In the first place, never, in his long and successful career to date, had Bessedovsky given the slightest inkling of such ideological scruples; he had throughout his life played the system for all it was worth. Quite apart from that, it would have been sheer lunacy (as well as an obvious waste of breath) to direct such remarks at a man who was known to be one of the most ruthless of those same "besotted lackeys" in the dictator's service. This version of the encounter must be regarded as being produced by an exile, in calculated retrospection, and with his new Western audience primarily in mind.

However, all the various accounts of that February afternoon that are now available do more or less agree on what happened next. When Roisemann threatened to take the disgraced diplomat back with him to Moscow "dead or alive," Bessedovsky stopped arguing and started running. Having alerted his wife once again on the way, he ran down into the front hall, past his downstairs office with the words "Embassy Counselor" inscribed on a porcelain nameplate. He got out without difficulty into the large gravel courtyard, but then found that the outer waiting room and the concierge's lodge, through which he would have to pass to reach the street, were securely in the hands of Roisemann's men. The two guards with revolvers barred his way. Though both of them knew him and, a few hours before, would have obeyed him unhesitatingly as their acting chief of mission, they were

---

[3] *Revelations of a Soviet Diplomat* (London: Williams and Norgate, 1931), pp. 264–70.

now far too scared for their own skins to bother about Bessedovsky's. He was told, in tones of agitated determination, that if he took another step, he would be a dead man.

As he could not go forward and dared not go back, Bessedovsky did something that had evidently not occurred to his redoubtable opponent. Yet it was logical enough: he simply went sideways. Leaving the guards alone in their lodge, he threw his coat over the wall of the Embassy courtyard, which was not very high, and clambered over after it. He landed in a damp garden, the only safe exit from which was another side wall which led onto the premises of a private house. This second wall was, however, at least ten feet high, and Bessedovsky was beginning to despair when his wife's voice, heard shouting through the open window of their Embassy apartment, lent him new wings. The wings took the practical shape of a garden chair, which just enabled him to get his fingers round the top row of bricks and haul himself over.

A certain M. Rambeau, the concierge of the building he now entered, was the first of many Frenchmen to get the shock of their lives that evening; (it was now about 7:00 p.m.). The second was the inspector of the local police station; the third was M. Benoist, the commissaire at the prefecture to which the local inspector promptly proceeded with his charge. Several more high officials followed in rapid succession, both in the Ministry of the Interior and at the Quai d'Orsay, the French Foreign Office.

It was to this last department that Bessedovsky applied all the pressure at his command; and this was hardly to be resisted. He was, after all, the duly accredited acting ambassador of the Soviet Union in Paris and, as such, the French authorities were responsible for insuring his safety. If, therefore, he was literally fleeing for his life, he had to be given protection. Moreover, if he so directed, his wife and child, who enjoyed similar privileges, would have to be brought out of the Embassy to join him.

So, at 8:30 p.m., Bessedovsky, accompanied by an armed French police escort headed by M. Benoist himself, returned to the concierge's lodge of 6, Rue de Grenelle, though approaching it this time from the pavement side. There followed a three-way telephone conversation with an enraged Comrade Roisemann in the main building, who could have seen his escaped prey across the courtyard had it been daytime. But it was a case of "so near, yet so far." Stalin's special envoy remembered his orders to seize Bessedovsky without damaging formal relations with the French government. To attempt a public shootout now, and with the commissaire of police in person, would have created the gravest of diplomatic rows, as well as the worst of all international impressions. After a while, the figures of Madame Bessedovsky and her small son were seen crossing the courtyard with their luggage. At around 9:00 p.m., her husband drove them off in triumph at the end of what, for all three, must have seemed the longest six hours of their lives.

The three political refugees (as they became from this moment) were escorted to quarters in the Hotel Marigny in the Rue des Arcades, a quiet establishment where the Ministry of Interior hoped that Bessedovsky could live undetected until he had found his feet. But within a few days of settling in, the former chargé d'affaires, whose name had now been struck off the Soviet diplomatic lists, received a communication from Moscow, sent to him in person at the correct address. Inside was a summons calling on him to present himself at a Moscow courtroom on such and such a date to answer charges of treason. Bessedovsky later told his fellow fugitive Bajanov that he had immediately fired off a telegram to the judge of the Moscow court telling him, in effect, to go to hell. Not that the Kremlin had ever seriously expected Bessedovsky to turn up. They merely wanted to show the renegade that they already knew exactly where they could lay their hands on him.

For the significance of this Paris scandal, we must look at its origins, which lay across the Channel. The story had really begun in London at 4:30 p.m. on the afternoon of May 12, 1927, when a substantial contingent of uniformed and plainclothes police forced their way into No. 49 Moorgate. This housed both the official Trade Delegation of the Soviet government in Britain and also a Soviet-controlled enterprise known as Arcos, which was registered as a joint stock company in accordance with U.K. legislation. The activities of the police on that spring afternoon suggested that something other than commerce was being conducted from that City building. As soon as they entered, they disconnected all telephones, searched all the employees, seized all the mail, and even took the ciphers which the trade delegate had been authorized to use. There were one or two physical scuffles before the search ended at midnight; but they were nothing to the political rumpus which broke out the following morning. The Soviet Embassy launched a furious protest, and, when the General Council of the British Trades Union Congress promptly backed that protest, followed in Parliament by the Socialist Opposition (the government of the day being the Conservative administration of Stanley Baldwin), it was clear that a domestic crisis had flared up alongside the diplomatic one.

The home secretary, Sir William Joynson-Hicks, was in some difficulties when he had to disclose that a highly secret British document (which the raid had been launched to retrieve from the improper possession of someone in 49 Moorgate) could not, in fact, be found. The prime minister himself had to confirm this in a long-delayed statement to the House of Commons on May 24. Yet, he insisted, plenty of other evidence had been found which proved conclusively that espionage and subversion were being conducted from the premises. Indeed, one of the Soviet employees was found to know so much about British secrets that he was described (rather lamely perhaps) as a "human document in himself."[4]

The Opposition were probably letting their imagination get the better of them when they claimed that the entire incident had been stage-managed by the Conservatives with the deliberate object of bringing about a rupture with the Soviet Union; but this was what now followed. On May 26, Britain announced that "existing relations between the two governments are suspended" and gave the Soviet chargé d'affaires in London, Maisky, and his staff ten days in which to pack and go home. Maisky duly left from Victoria Station on the morning of June 3, waved off by a large crowd of sympathizers, including several prominent Socialist politicians and trade union leaders. They broke into the *Internationale* as the train steamed out.

What has always been intriguing about the "Arcos affair," as it came

---

[4]   The failure to find the incriminating document which the police had sought obscured the value of the material uncovered by the raid. This included evidence, not only of subversive operations in Britain, but of similar activities in America, conducted under cover of the Amtorg Trading in New York.

to be known, was that the fateful raid in Moorgate was launched the day after an agreement had been signed between the Midland Bank and the self-same Trade Delegation for a credit of £10 million (a vast sum in those days) to finance Soviet purchases of British goods.[5] Now it was a bit too drastic to suggest, as the left-wing camp did, that the Tories had been so alarmed by the pro-Soviet implications of the Midland Bank deal that they had immediately engineered the Moorgate raid to sabotage it. (It was also far too neat. Democracies, and especially the sleepy one of Mr. Baldwin, simply do not function with that speed and precision.) But the coincidence does serve to highlight the ambivalence, even among right-wing circles, of attitudes toward the Soviet Union in Britain at the time—and today, for that matter. On the one hand, it was feared, as a police state, for the corrosive power of its propaganda and subversion. On the other, it was prized as a vast, undeveloped market which offered the City (London's Wall Street) and British industry the prospect of even greater profits than those they had enjoyed, until only ten years before, in the earlier Russia of the tsars.

It is this ambivalence, and the impact of the whole Arcos affair, which brings us back to Grigory Bessedovsky. He was reappointed from Tokyo to Paris in the late summer of 1927, soon after the rupture in Anglo-Soviet relations, and, according to him, was specially instructed, while passing through Moscow, to do all he could from his new post to repair the shattered bridges between the Kremlin and the British Conservative party. A revival of the Midland Bank credit scheme, or some equivalent financial project, was suggested as the best way to get things moving; and Moscow (again according to Bessedovsky) even recommended a promising contact man for the task. This was one Vladimir Bogovout-Kolomitzev (whom we shall henceforth call Bogovout for short), a Russian émigré who was then on excellent terms both with the Bolshevik regime in Moscow and with leading capitalists in Paris and London. Whether the original introduction came from Moscow or not, Bessedovsky met Bogovout soon

---

[5] Trade between the two countries had reached a peak in 1925, when Soviet exports to Britain, at £31,412,000, were more than matched by British exports to Russia totaling £35,645,000. The credit was intended to restore that high level of exchanges.

after arriving in Paris in October of 1927, and the two men became close friends.

Bogovout later described Bessedovsky to a Paris friend as a "dedicated individual with high intellectual capabilities, but weak-willed and given far too much to the bottle." Bessedovsky's own admiration for his new friend, was, on the other hand, without such reservations. He found Bogovout to be the *"entrepreneur par excellence,"* a man of strong personality and great persuasive powers, and ruthless in the exploitation of his private contacts.

It seems clear from all this that the first approaches by the Bogovout-Bessedovsky team to London were made with the general blessing of the Kremlin. But then, after Bogovout had paid several visits to London early in 1928 (in a characteristically ambitious attempt to get the chairman of the Midland Bank, Mr. McKenna, not only to renew the old credit line but to extend it to £15 million), Moscow suddenly started to blow cold. Bessedovsky was informed that he had exceeded his authority, and the negotiations slowly fizzled out.

It is from here on that the roles—and the motives—of the Paris duo become, to put it mildly, more obscure. Bessedovsky himself admits in his memoirs[6] that, when he used his official position to resume financial discussions with London in the summer of 1928, he was acting on his own:

> I had to assume the entire responsibility for the conversations, so that the Politburo might suddenly find that the thing was done. My being forced in this way to take the initiative amounted to a kind of plot against my own government; the slightest mistake or check and I should pay dearly for it.

This, it must be noted in passing, is strange-sounding stuff indeed to come from a career diplomat who had behaved conventionally and obediently until that moment and who, according to his closest partner in the enterprise, was anyway notable for his weak will.

But, whatever the new basis on which it was launched, this second initiative of 1928 made steady progress. Bogovout made several trips to London during that summer and seems to have concentrated on

---

[6] See *Revelations of a Soviet Diplomat*, pp. 251–52.

prominent Conservative political figures rather than on his earlier contacts in the City. Among them were Ernest Remnant, editor of the *English Review*, Sir Arthur Balfour, and Major Kindersley. Bessedovsky records that on September 8, at a time when he was acting as chargé d'affaires, he received Mr. Remnant in his Paris office to discuss the prospects with Bogovout. The energetic editor, who appears at this juncture as the prime mover from the London end, wrote a week later to say that he was confident of assembling a delegation of British financiers who were willing to go to Moscow to discuss a major new credit. All that he needed was "a list of the works envisaged by the Soviet Government, accompanied by an approximate estimate of the sums to be invested."

That, of course, would have presented no problem at all had Mr. Remnant and his friends really been dealing with the Soviet government. But it was quite a poser for Messrs. Bessedovsky and Bogovout, two individuals who were handling the entire affair themselves, in a deep secrecy which excluded not only their colleagues at the Embassy but also their masters in Moscow. However, the resourceful chargé d'affaires proved equal to the challenge. He merely asked the Soviet Trade Delegation in Paris to let him have a copy of the main capital projects currently being planned for the Soviet Union by the Council of Economic Planning (Gosplan) and sent this off to London as his general "shopping list." It was enough to open the eyes and excite the appetite of any Western financier.

The "items" ranged from the reequipping of the entire Soviet river and maritime fleets to the construction of a Moscow underground railway; and from the cutting of a Volga-Don canal to the building of a giant power station at Dnieprostroy. It was not surprising that, when Bessedovsky toted up all the cost estimates, they came to the gigantic total of nearly 5 billion gold rubles. What he was suggesting to Mr. Remnant's financial backers—though without saying so—was that they should pay for the entire modernization program of the Soviet Union. Bessedovsky had hinted that what they would get for Britain in return (apart from the profits) was a cessation of all Communist propaganda activities, which, in fact, formed the main bone of contention between the two countries. The two Paris schemers were now swimming in truly deep and dangerous waters. They were pretending to conduct official negotiations on matters absolutely crucial to the political as well as economic future of their country.

Bessedovsky's account of his own doings from this point forward becomes as full of holes as a shrimping net. He concedes that by now (November of 1928) his government had some right to be let into the great secret, and relates in his memoirs that, on a brief visit to Moscow during that same month, he decided to "prepare the ground." But beyond saying that, on that trip, he had "talks with certain Communist leaders, and dangled before their eyes the five milliards roubles of foreign money," he gives no details whatsoever. It seems inconceivable that, if Bessedovsky really did reveal any of his machinations while in Moscow, he would have excluded his own foreign minister, Chicherin, with whom he was on good terms, and to whom he had been professionally responsible for most of his career. He is even vaguer as to how the entire grand design collapsed, blaming some complicated intrigue within the Politburo. But collapse it did over the next few weeks, despite another visit to the Paris Embassy in January 1929 by Mr. Remnant, this time accompanied by Sir Arthur Balfour and the other political sponsors. Bessedovsky describes how he himself "lost interest" in the affair from now on. He claims that his partner Bogovout became so irate and frustrated that, three months later, he not only washed his hands of the British loan muddle but also severed all contacts with the Soviet government, including its Paris Embassy, in protest.

If there is a key to this extraordinary maze of intrigue, it may lie in a completely different version of events which Bessedovsky himself confided to Boris Bajanov soon after his defection, and which Bajanov relayed to the present author nearly fifty years later. According to this version, Bogovout had persuaded Bessedovsky, after the collapse of the official talks, to let him use the Embassy as a "front" for something that was not merely to be launched as a private enterprise but was intended to remain so all the way. In other words, all Bogovout was interested in from first to last was his own profit from the London deal. This he was to lay his hands on by getting the London bankers, after an "agreement in principle" had been reached, to forward a down payment to him at the Paris Embassy, as a token of good faith. With such gigantic sums at stake, even that token would have made Bogovout a rich man for life.

What makes this version on balance more plausible is that it accounts completely for the effrontery of the two conspirators in bypassing Moscow. Indeed, Bajanov was told, that was the whole subtlety of the trick. Formal relations between Britain and the Soviet Union were suspended, and attempts to renew the Midland Bank loan officially had failed. Credits from capitalist financiers were anyway a delicate topic for Bolsheviks. So, in all these circumstances, what could be more plausible than to tell Mr. Remnant and his friends that, to save any embarrassment should those talks collapse, the Kremlin had deliberately chosen to conduct them through its Paris Embassy, the London mission being still closed? As an additional refinement, the British negotiators were to be told that, should they ever make any direct inquiries in Moscow, the Kremlin would have to deny all knowledge of this latest Bogovout operation. However, according to this same Bessedovsky "confession" (and it would seem an odd thing to boast of), those inquiries were discreetly made by the British at some point in 1929.

Chicherin was the first to get wind of the scandal, and he promptly reported it to the Politburo. From then on, it was a short road to the telegrams summoning Bessedovsky home, and to his own leap over the Embassy wall. There is some irony about the coincidence that, on October 2, 1929, as he was making that leap in Paris, his own ambassador Dovgalevsky was putting his signature, across the Channel, to the protocol declaring Anglo-Soviet relations to be restored.[7] Thus Bogovout's swindle, and whatever part Bessedovsky may have played in it, would inevitably have been exposed in any case once the Soviet mission in London resumed its normal operations.

It is important to try to fathom Bessedovsky's real motives for defecting, and compare them with the reasons he gave at the time,

---

[7] The Tory Opposition of the day attacked those negotiations as "Edgar Wallace diplomacy." They were certainly unorthodox. The foreign secretary, Arthur Henderson, was at Brighton that week, attending the annual conference of the Socialist party. Dovgalevsky also repaired to Brighton "for his health." But, for extra secrecy, the two men had met at the White Hart Hotel in Lewes, where the final agreement was hammered out.

not only to tell the full story of his escape, but also to assess his reliability as an informant afterward. This was indeed the question which preoccupied everyone who came into contact with him in October 1929—the Russian émigrés, the French press and police, and the Western intelligence services who soon started pumping him for information. One member of these services stationed in Paris was very quick off the mark in this respect and had a two-hour talk with Bessedovsky on Saturday, October 5, only two days after his flight became known, followed by another hour of conversation with him on October 9. The official's conclusions were not very flattering. He came away with the distinct impression that Bessedovsky was "smart and intelligent, but neither frank nor principled, and quite possibly not honest." In addition, he was "extremely talkative and indiscreet and a poor judge of people."

The White Russian press in Paris had formed much the same opinion; for this, Bessedovsky had only himself to blame. Immediately after his escape, he had contacted their right-wing organ, *Vozrojdenie,* and agreed to do a series of articles for them. But he soon discovered, as Bajanov had done two years before, that the left-wing Russian press paid far better money. In contrast to Bajanov, he dropped his convictions and went for the cash. It was soon noticed that he had adjusted his views on the Soviet Union accordingly. Thus he had begun by affirming (which was probably true) that any Socialist-type movements of the Kerensky mold still left in Russia were so compromised as to enjoy no real following. But the moment Bessedovsky switched to the left-wing émigré papers, he published statements in flat contradiction, presumably because he knew that it was what they and their readers wanted to believe. As a result, many people even began to think again about those Tass allegations, so prominently carried in the French Communist party's organ, *L'Humanité,* that some financial scandal was the real explanation for his defection.

Bessedovsky's initial crop of writings were not all as suspect and unsubstantial as those contributions to *Vozrojdenie* and its rivals. Of more interest were a series of seven pieces which he wrote, between October 22 and November 12, 1929, for the moderate Russian daily of Paris, *Poslednia Novosti* ("Latest News"). The first, which gave details of two alleged meetings with Stalin, concerned the Kremlin's French policy, and contained a key quote that must have startled the Quai d'Orsay: "We can spit on France." A later companion piece on Anglo-Soviet relations made the curious assertion that the famous Zinoviev letter was genuine, despite the fact that Zinoviev himself did not sign it. A fourth article, on October 28, authoritatively nailed down the lie that the Comintern was somehow separate from the Soviet government (a myth assiduously, and effectively, spread in the West by the Kremlin's disinformation services). Other pieces gave catty, but on the whole accurate, pen portraits of various Soviet ambassadors and analyzed Moscow's expansionist aims in the Far East. Yet even this series did not restore, in Western and Russian émigré circles, the damage Bessedovsky had done himself with those first newspaper articles.

However, the fact that Bessedovsky had leapt so swiftly into print, and compromised himself just as swiftly in the process, may have saved his life, whatever the damage done to his reputation. It is known that the Kremlin's immediate reaction to his defection was to organize an assassination squad to go to Paris to complete the work that Comrade Roisemann had left so palpably unfinished. These plans were called off soon afterward. One reason for their cancelation was, clearly, second thoughts about the political repercussions of such a drastic step against a man who was a career diplomat duly accredited to the French government rather than a secret service agent in disguise. But another calculation in Moscow may well have been that, if their former chargé d'affaires was to go on making such an ass of himself in public, he was probably worth more to the Kremlin alive than dead. Certainly, from this point on, L'Humanité, on Moscow's instructions, did regular dialectical battle with Bessedovsky whenever one of his articles appeared, a battle which it usually got the better of. Again, there is a significant contrast with Bajanov, whom, as Stalin knew only too well, was an antagonist of a totally different caliber. L'Humanité never so much as mentioned his name, let alone debated with him over his anti-Soviet writings. It was thought prudent not to draw attention either to his defection or to his opinions.

But though he failed, on the whole, as a publicist (at least during this first phase of his career), Bessedovsky's defection was, nonetheless, of considerable significance to the West. There was, to begin with, the immediate information he revealed to the French authorities about the OGPU network which operated under diplomatic cover from the Rue de Grenelle. He named Vladimir Yanovitch, who masqueraded as a cipher clerk, as its chief, and Comrades Ivans and Ellert as his two principal aides. The last-named, under the cover of a Naptha Syndicate official, maintained liaison with Soviet agents in London. These gentlemen did not wait to be formally expelled. A great exodus from the Paris Embassy, with batches of officials and bundles of documents being rushed off by air to Berlin, was observed in the wake of Bessedovsky's escape.

The renegade diplomat also had at least one juicy item of interest to sell to British Intelligence. At the beginning of July 1929, an Englishman had called at the Rue de Grenelle, giving his name as Scott and offering to sell, for two thousand American dollars, what he claimed was the code then in use for secret communications between London and New Delhi. When Yanovitch, the head of the OGPU section, heard of this, he had devised a scheme to get the code for nothing. He asked the Englishman to call again, and then requested the loan of the code so that it could be "verified" before payment was made. The Englishman, who, if the story is true, must have been a woeful tyro at the game, agreed to hand it over for a few hours. It was promptly photocopied and passed to Moscow for examination. When Mr. Scott came for his money, he was told that the merchandise, which was given back to him, was regrettably "of no value." According to Bessedovsky, however, it was a very satisfied Yanovitch who later declared that they had, in fact, got "the real thing," and without losing one American cent from the Embassy's hard currency funds.[8]

But whatever intelligence dividends of fine detail Bessedovsky's defection brought with it, his main value was the broad picture he could paint of a diplomatic service not merely penetrated and monitored by the Soviet secret police in all their various guises, but actually controlled and directed by them, on a worldwide basis, in the prime task

---

[8] No confirmation is available in present-day records about this story.

of subverting the capitalist world. As the Arcos raid showed, the Western democracies already had their suspicions about the activities of Soviet missions abroad. Bajanov had warned of this international Communist network, both at Simla and in Paris; and, as we shall see, senior OGPU defectors were soon to add to his story with inside accounts of how the campaign was operated. But Bessedovsky was the first man who could describe what the process looked like from within the Soviet foreign service itself—in Vienna, in Warsaw, in the Far East, and in the heart of western Europe.

The uneasily intertwining threats of subversion and diplomacy had, after all, followed him throughout all these stages of his own career. In October of 1922, for example, soon after he had taken up his first post abroad as Ukrainian consul of Vienna, Manuilsky, one of the heads of the Third International, had descended on them with the news that the Austrian capital was to be made one of the Comintern's main centers of operations, with the Soviet diplomatic and trade missions as cover. Then there was Warsaw, where the Soviet ambassador, in Bessedovsky's time, had resembled a figure straight out of the pages of Tolstoy. This was Leonid Obolensky, a prince by birth and a former tsarist privy Councilor by profession, who, as a Bolshevik envoy, would never rise from his bed until two in the afternoon, and would then receive his officials in his brocaded dressing gown, gulping vodka as he signed documents without even reading them. Not surprisingly, the Cheka (secret police) was absolutely omnipotent in this embassy, and Obolensky, the titular head of the mission, lived in fear of them. The story was little different in 1924, when Bessedovsky returned for a second spell of duty to Warsaw. The Embassy then was effectively in the hands of Comrade Volkov, a lecherous, pompous, and theatrical drunk, whose sole claim to fame (and to Bolshevik gratitude) was that he had been one of the squad of assassins who, on July 18, 1918, butchered Tsar Nicholas II and his family in the cellar of the Villa Epatiev at Ekaterinburg.

After that, in 1925, had come Bessedovsky's assignment to America, as an authentic diplomatic official to give respectability to "Amtorg," the Soviet trading company in New York which was the base for all Soviet subversion activities in America. (With its 12 million Negroes and 2 million unemployed, the United States had been recently designated by the Politburo as the prime target in the capitalist world, following the spectacular failure of several Soviet-inspired Communist uprisings in western Europe.) As things turned out, difficulties over a visa prevented Bessedovsky from taking up his New York post, and he had gone instead to Tokyo. Here, his main task (as a Soviet diplomat accredited to Japan!) had concerned China: to aid the Soviet penetration of Manchuria and Mongolia, a task for which, he alleged, the Politburo had allotted the enormous sum (in 1926 values) of $25 million.

Finally, when passing through Moscow on his way from Tokyo to Paris, Bessedovsky had been given some impressive first-hand evidence of the OGPU's Intelligence service at work. Chicherin, his foreign minister, had produced for him the text of the telegram from the local French Embassy to Paris foreshadowing his own appointment. The OGPU had broken this, among many other French codes. It appeared that a certain Comrade Boyky was the head of this special cipher-cracking squad and his operations, as early as 1926, included the "bugging" of all foreign missions in Moscow, the hidden microphones connected to his central monitoring room. Chicherin himself had once been invited, as a demonstration, to listen to a live relay of the Afghanistan ambassador making ardent love to a Moscow light opera star. The young lady, needless to say, was herself picking up an extra fee as an OGPU informant.

In short, Bessedovsky, though not in the same political league as Bajanov and though not perhaps as important as a source of information as any of the senior Soviet Intelligence officers who were to follow him, could fill in many gaps because of the particular service he had fled from. Moreover, this first defection of a regular Soviet diplomat served, as the Kremlin feared at the time, as a contagious example to others.

After the excitement of his leap over the embassy wall had died down and his memoirs had been published, Bessedovsky's further career as an émigré makes sorry and sordid reading, at least as reflected in the opinions of the various Western experts who kept an eye on him. Within twelve months, they suspected him of having been "turned" by the OGPU to work for it as an *agent provocateur*. By 1938, however, he was reported to be in touch with Hitler's Intelligence service. During World War II he appeared to have switched loyalties again and was thought to have been active for a time in the French Communist resistance—for which activity he was subsequently "pardoned" by Moscow for his Nazi contacts.[9]

In view of this rehabilitation with Moscow, Bessedovsky's postwar activities came as no surprise. As early as 1945, he was reported to be gathering information about the American Army in France for the Russians; and the last known phase of his career, when he returned once more to the literary field, was thought also to have had Soviet sponsorship.

Bessedovsky had always been something of a split personality; but he seems to dissolve, in this final period, into fragments. Among the various *noms de plume* he now adopted for his books and newspaper articles were those of Ivan Krylov and Cyrille Kalinov. Though superficially anti-Soviet, the underlying trend of these writings is to present Russia and its dictator Stalin in a rather more jovial light than the true facts warranted. Now these were the years, roughly 1947 to 1951, when a certain Ivan Ivanovitch Agayants of the KGB was in Paris, stationed in the Rue de Grenelle under diplomatic cover. Agayants later became the first head of KGB's regular organization for such "disinformation" when in 1959, a special "Department D" was founded in Moscow for this purpose. The assumption in Western circles was that Bessedovsky was one of a group of Russian émigré writers who, whether they fully realized it or not, were being used by Agayants as Paris guinea pigs for a technique that, in a few years' time, was to be given worldwide application. Wherever the inspiration and the money came from, Bessedovsky seems for a time to have done very well out of it. He moved down, in due course, to the Riviera.

It is in the agreeable surroundings of the Côte d'Azur that his trail, blurred for so long, fades out altogether. The fate is known of

---

[9] According to Bajanov, Bessedovsky was arrested in the middle of the war as a resistance fighter, but, with characteristic aplomb, got himself transferred from prison to a comfortable internment camp reserved for Moslem detainees of the Gestapo in the Channel Islands. To achieve this, he claimed he was a Moslem himself, and started regular operations on a prayer mat to "prove" it.

every other major defector named in this book, whether he or she is dealt with at length or merely mentioned. True, it is not always clear whether those who died did so through natural causes or accidents, whether they committed suicide or were assassinated. The circumstances and real opinions of the important survivors (most of whom the author has met) are also sometimes hard to evaluate. But of all these Soviet storm petrels, Bessedovsky is the only one today of whom we simply do not know for certain whether he is alive or dead. An inquiry made early in 1977 at the Office of Russian Refugees in Paris produced the reply that, if he were dead, he had not died in France, as his file, dormant for some years, had not yet been officially closed. An announcement specially inserted in the November 1976 issue of the Paris paper *La Pensée Russe* asking whether any reader knew for sure whether Bessedovsky was alive or dead produced no response. It is a suitably ambivalent concluding note on which to move forward to another year and another case.

Chapter Six

GEORGES AGABEKOV: THE LOVE-SICK AGENT

There was, for Boris Bajanov, a sweet irony about the arrival of the next Soviet defector in Paris. The newcomer, who turned up out of the blue from Marseilles on June 26, 1930 was Georges Agabekov, the very man who, as head of the OGPU network in Persia in 1928, had been in charge of the hunt to kill Bajanov during his perilous three-month flight into British India. Now, only eighteen months later, Agabekov was on the run himself, and the hunter and the hunted found themselves fugitives together in the French capital.

Though each knew of the other's presence, the two men at first swirled uneasily around each other, like leaves in a teacup. Much as tea leaves however, a magnetic attraction brought them steadily closer together as, on both sides, curiosity gradually overcame hostility. Before the summer was out, a meeting had been arranged in the apartment of mutual friends.

Agabekov made the worst possible impression on his former quarry. "It was an ugly, and shifty figure, small, with the face of a criminal who came up to me," Bajanov recalls today. "His two eyes looked out in different directions, and each seemed to be scouring opposite sides of the room, as though looking for a trap."

The two men talked for about twenty minutes on the most important topic they had in common. Agabekov described how, on that New Year's Day of 1928, he had been about to go on tour in southern Persia when a priority telegram from Moscow about Bajanov's escape had stopped him. For the first time, Bajanov learned that it had been Agabekov himself who had conducted that first hunt for him in Meshed. He learned other details too: that a band of six trained Turkoman killers had been sent into northern Persia to aid the hunt being mounted there by the local OGPU; and that, even while Bajanov had been under close Persian guard in the Meshed police headquarters, another attempt had been made to get rid of him by poisoning his food with cyanide.

He was also told that, in the Soviet diplomatic offensive that had been mounted in Teheran (in tandem with the OGPU manhunt in eastern Persia) to get Bajanov back, Stalin had authorized the offer to the Persians of every inducement at his disposal: concessions over frontier demarcations, oil deposit disputes, and even over the perennial quarrel about fishing rights in the Caspian Sea.

It was because the Kremlin had been so convinced that these inducements would prevail that, at one point, he, Agabekov, had had his orders to kill Bajanov suspended. They were reinstated for the final stage of the escape from Duzdap, where, as we have seen, the OGPU were foiled largely by the efforts of the British consul. Listening to all this in a Paris drawing room, Bajanov must again have marveled that he had survived thus far.

The main interest of Agabekov, however, is not his vain pursuit of Stalin's secretary but the extraordinary story of his own flight and its aftermath. He himself described the reason for his defection as disillusionment over the failure of Communism in Russia, as shown most vividly by famine among the peasantry.[1] In fact, the immediate cause

---

[1] See Agabekov, *The Russian Secret Terror*, pp. 246–67. Apart from gross misrepresentations such as this, the book is full of factual errors. Thus the date of his ar-

of his defection was the most unlikely one imaginable for an OGPU chief, and especially one whose appearance was every bit as unattractive as his profession.

Stalin's secret policeman fled to the West because he had fallen hopelessly in love with a young English girl of a staid middle-class family; and she, despite the glaring contrast between their ages, backgrounds, and faiths, both religious and political, had fallen just as madly in love with him. The romance between Georges Agabekov and Isabel Streater is one of the most baffling and most tragic love affairs of their, or any other, generation. It is not as much mentioned in his own book. But the various government archives of the day speak, for weeks on end, of little else; and the passion that once linked this ill-assorted and ill-fated pair still manages to burn through even the bland prose of those bureaucratic files.

The story begins on October 27, 1929, when the Soviet vessel *Chicherin* anchored in Constantinople after a voyage from Odessa. Among the passengers it brought from Russia was a sallow-complexioned Armenian traveling under the identity of Nerses Ovsepian. His real name (though this is only official conjecture) was Arountunov, but he had last called himself, in Persia, Georgi Agabekov.[2] The reason for this alias was that he had been assigned to Constantinople to fulflll the same function he had held at Teheran, namely, head of the "illegal"[3] or underground OGPU network in the region.

There was more than one paradox about this particular posting. Agabekov, as we shall continue to call him, took over in Turkey from Jacob Blumkin, whose brief but eventful career in the OGPU had ended, as already described, before a Moscow firing squad. Thus the two top-level assassins ordered by Stalin to try to liquidate his runaway secretary occupied the same foreign desk in succession. Moreover, twelve months before setting out for Turkey, in October of 1929, Agabekov had been summoned to Trilliser, the head of the OGPU's Foreign Section, and ordered to stand by for a different

rival in Paris is given as January 1930, while the police records show it conclusively to have been in June of that year.

[2]   He adopted the westernized style of "Georges" after his flight.

[3]   Quite distinct from—and indeed often a rival to—the "legal" network, which operated in parallel under local diplomatic cover.

assassination mission in Paris—this time of Bessedovsky. The treach-
erous diplomat, Trilliser said, had to be "finished off at all costs," as
there were signs that his treason might prove "contagious."

However, the next day, Agabekov was summoned again and told
that the murder assignment had been canceled, now that the Politburo had decided that more harm than good would be done by an
attempt to kill the renegade. So, in due course, Agabekov alias
Ovsepian arrived in Constantinople, where his "cover" as illegal
OGPU chief was that of a merchant running an agency for the sale of
bicycles and typewriters.

This innocuous-looking livelihood concealed an espionage and
subversion brief which extended throughout the Near East. Whatever
Agabekov was to claim a few months later about falling out with his
superiors, there can be no doubt that he enjoyed their full confidence
when he set sail from Odessa. His area of operations comprised Syria,
Palestine, the Hejaz, Egypt, and all of Turkey except the city of Constantinople itself, which was reserved for the "legal" OGPU "resident," with his office in the Soviet Legation.

Within this territory, Agabekov had been entrusted with a number
of delicate and important missions. In Damascus, for example, one
of his tasks was to explore the possibility of a Soviet-sponsored
union between the Syrians and their neighbors, with the long-term
objective of founding a large independent Arab state, looking to
Moscow, rather than to London and Paris. As part of the same general scheme, the aim in Egypt was to split the ruling Wafdist party
and create, from its ranks, a left-wing group radical enough to cooperate with the Egyptian Communists. These were already receiving
a small but regular monthly subsidy from Berlin, the OGPU's main
financial center for operations in western Europe and the Arab world.

Agabekov was given the same assurances about the British High
Commission in Cairo as Blumkin had received before him. There was
no need, he was told, to waste time trying to penetrate it because
other branches of the OGPU had penetrated it already. Moscow had
been regularly furnished with copies of Lord Lloyd's reports, and was
now being similarly served as regards the secret correspondence of
Sir Percy Lorraine, his successor. Agabekov's task was to be not so
much espionage as the laying of the foundations for subversion on a

scale ambitious enough to weaken the hold of both the British and French, the twin imperial masters of the region.

All these plots and plans were to be brought to nothing, so far as Agabekov was concerned, by an item which he inserted in the Constantinople papers soon after his arrival. In it, he advertised, under his alias of course, for someone to give him English lessons.[4] Whether this was a perfectly genuine request by Ovsepian the merchant or whether it concealed just another attempt by Agabekov the agent to make useful contacts is not known. At all events, it resulted in a contact which transformed his life, for the teacher he acquired was Isabel Streater.

Miss Streater was the youngest daughter of an Englishman who worked in the Constantinople offices of the Blair and Campbell Shipping Company. Neither rich nor remarkable in any way that is apparent from the records of the case, the Streaters appear almost as the prototype of the middle-class expatriate businessman's family of the day. They were solid, patriotic, respectable; and also determined, in an age where commerce was still not regarded as an ideal career for gentlemen, to hang on to the status they had deservedly won for themselves as long-standing local residents of unblemished reputation. It is difficult therefore even to imagine the force of the shock wave which hit this unsuspecting family[5] when, by Christmas of 1930, it became clear that the twenty-year-old English girl was having a love affair with her thirty-four-year-old pupil and was, in fact, completely besotted with him.

The impression made by Isabel before she met her lover—that of a nice, quiet girl who was even shy for her age—might help to explain why the encounter with this wild and mysterious man had had such a traumatic effect on her. At any rate, that character now seemed transformed as her parents tried desperately to break up the liaison. They were especially backed in their efforts by the girl's elder

---

[4] He was also making diligent inquiries to the same end through his landlady.

[5] These shock waves do not appear to have subsided nearly fifty years later. The only surviving member of the Streater family who could be traced was Jasper, younger brother of Isabel's. He told the author in December 1976 that he could not bring himself even today to discuss his sister's "tragic romance." In view of his youth at the time, he learned little anyway, and was forbidden by his parents even to raise the subject.

sister Sybil, who was employed at the British Embassy, where, indeed, Isabel herself had been working as a temporary typist.

But what none of them could have known or have believed was that the ugly Agabekov had fallen just as deeply in love with his Isabel. If the affair had, for him, begun as an exercise in casual philandering combined with espionage, it had soon blossomed into the romance of his life. This is not to say that infatuation was the entire story on his part. However skeptically one judges his later tales of developing a sudden revulsion against the Bolshevik system, there is some evidence that, during these same months, he began to have doubts about his career. One or two of his own closest colleagues and friends in the service were being demoted or dismissed, and this caused him to feel uneasy about his prospects, though not, as yet, in any fear for his life.

Matters came to a head all round on January 15, 1931. A Soviet steamer was anchored in Constantinople and there was a free passage home on it for him, if he chose to return to Moscow to discover just what his situation was. (He had not, it seems clear, been officially recalled.) He decided on that day to make a clean breast of everything to his young English girl by telling her exactly who he was and what work he was doing. What he did then would depend on Isabel's reaction. If she recoiled in horror at the discovery that her lover was, in reality, a Soviet secret police chief, with a good deal of blood on his hands already, then he would catch that steamer to Odessa. If she stood by him, he would stay in the West, break with Moscow, marry her, and start up a new life. Isabel evidently passed the test, for the steamer sailed away without Agabekov, who was soon heading instead for the British authorities in Constantinople, to prepare for the defection he had promised her to make.

This proved rather more complicated than he had expected. Not knowing the back door to the British Intelligence Service (which, in matters like these, is always the main entrance), Agabekov knocked first at the front door, and approached the military attaché at the Embassy. He gave the British officer his real name and identity and, without revealing too much about his knowledge at once, did offer to reveal the methods by which the OGPU were tapping all correspondence between the Foreign Office and its embassies and legations in the Near East. The military attaché replied politely that he personally was not interested in this sort of thing, being a regular officer under the War Office; he would, however, report his visitor's offer to those whom it might interest. Nothing, however, happened. After a few weeks of puzzled waiting, Agabekov tried another, smaller, front door, and tackled a Commander Rogers, who was serving at the British Consulate, with the same disclosures and the same offer. But once again, precious time passed and there was no reaction.

It was not until some three months after his initial approach that Agabekov felt he had made an impact. He was asked to prepare a curriculum vitae in which, for the first time, he set out a full summary of his career right down to his present post as chief of illegal OGPU operations throughout the Near East. It concluded:

> For personal reasons, I have no intention of returning again to Russia. . . . Now I apply to you again, and am prepared to leave for London or any place you indicate for final negotiations, and if my services appear to be uninteresting I will only ask for travelling expenses.
>
> I remain in anticipation of a reply
>
> N. Ovsepian.

But the response still did not come, for it was still not decided whether this was a genuine top-level agent who had decided, in the courtroom phrase, to turn "King's evidence" and tell all; whether he was an agent provocateur planted by the Russians; or whether he was merely a shady adventurer after money. Though Agabekov had not as much as mentioned Isabel Streater's name, the connection had been established by the British, who only drew the natural, though incorrect, conclusion from it. Ruling out at this stage all thoughts of a supreme passion, they assumed that Agabekov could only be paying court to Isabel in the hope of getting access to the documents which she and her sister Sybil were typing out every day in the British Embassy.

So winter passed into spring, and spring into summer, with London making no sign of opening its arms to the would-be defector. He was, by now, frantic as well as nonplussed. The scenario which the two lovers had planned for themselves in that crucial talk on January 15 seemed to be collapsing around their heads. He could scarcely hope to begin a new life with an English girl until he himself was accepted by England. But despite six months of his applying, appealing, and importuning, England remained unresponsive. In the meantime, his Isabel, guarded like the Crown Jewels (and even, occasionally, locked up like them), was under the severest family pressure to break all ties with him. So far, she had held completely steadfast; but could any inexperienced young girl be expected to go on resisting much longer? In his desperation, Agabekov even contemplated defecting, not to the West, but to the Far East, traveling on his bogus Persian passport and taking his beloved with him, despite the extra hazards.

But Isabel was shifted first, and that move was to settle everything, including their own fate and, eventually, the action of those undecided authorities in London. Isabel's distraught parents, hoping that one way to break this appalling romance would be to put a thousand miles between the pair, suggested a visit by Isabel to their eldest daughter Joyce, who was married to a Mr. Charles Lee, and was then living at St. Germain near Paris. Mrs. Lee was only too glad to help out in this family crisis, and so her wayward young sister was packed off on the Orient Express, to arrive in the French capital on Sunday, June 22, 1930.

But the parents had underestimated both the strength of feeling between the two lovers and their ability, despite the strictest precautions on the family's part, to keep in contact. As soon as Isabel told Agabekov of the proposed trip, he rebuilt his own plans around it. He had always contemplated going to Paris on a brief visit, to ask the advice of his ex-diplomatic colleague Bessedovsky, who had caused such a stir with his own defection the previous autumn. Now he determined to go there for good and start up his new existence with Isabel in France while the British were making up their minds. The upshot of this was that, when Isabel Streater boarded that Orient Express, she was carrying, concealed in her clothes, a copy of the manuscript of Agabekov's memoirs, and also a sum of £200, which, he had told her, was the proceeds from selling up his stock of bicycles and typewriters. It was a strange basis on which to plan a marriage; but then, this was no ordinary courtship.

As for the parents' fond hope of separating the couple, there was barely a moment when the two were not heading for the same rendezvous. Agabekov left Constantinople by sea on the same day that Isabel left by train. He arrived in Paris, via Marseilles, only four days after her, and immediately headed for the Lees' house at 35, Rue de Lorraine in St. Germain-en-Laye.

From this point onward, the British government starts to get involved willy-nilly in the affair, to end up in a new role altogether, that of the reluctant matchmaker. At first, the Lees tried to cope with the situation by themselves, and refused point-blank to let their visitor take Isabel away. Mr. Lee had formerly worked as an accountant for the delegate of the League of Nations at Constantinople, where, presumably, he had met his future wife, the eldest Streater girl. Though a man of some international background, therefore, as well as a one-time subaltern in the British Army, he was a bit out of his depth when coping with a formidable opponent like Agabekov, who, at the age of only twenty-six, had supervised the liquidation of the great rebel warrior Enver Pasha himself in the wilds of Turkestan.

Agabekov now disclosed his real identity in an attempt to break the deadlock. But this had only the opposite effect. Mr. Lee, learning that the importunate suitor was an OGPU chief on the run, understandably started running himself, in search of official advice and reinforcement. He called first on M. Fopabidé, the director of the Political Section of the Sûreté Générale, and then on the British passport control officer in Paris, whom he believed to be in some sort of contact with British Intelligence. Agabekov countered these moves by turning up on his next visit to the St. Germain house accompanied by a French detective as his bodyguard. The French authorities, he told the Lees, had received him courteously as an important Soviet official seeking asylum, and they were now insuring his personal protection.

Having established what he hoped would be accepted as his political bona fides, Agabekov then tried to interest Charles Lee in a business proposition. Would Mr. Lee like to take charge of the manuscript Isabel had brought with her to Paris, and negotiate its publication in London? His "cut" would be £1,000, representing a 20 percent commission on the £5,000 advance that Agabekov required. Isabel's brother-in-law indignantly refused to entertain the idea. (A day or two before, the Lees had forced the wretched Isabel to withdraw £150 with which Agabekov had opened an account for her at the Place

Vendôme branch of the Westminster Bank, and hand the notes back to her lover in their presence.) Having seen that these Paris guardians of Isabel's could not be bribed, Agabekov withdrew in a threatening mood. He would clearly be back in the Rue de Lorraine soon.

It was more than any sister and brother-in-law could manage on their own. On Wednesday, July 2, the Lees, accompanied by Mr. E. R. Cawdron, an English solicitor working in Paris, paid a formal call on the British consul-general. The lawyer explained that he had taken this step in the government's interests as well as those of his clients, and that they were now, as British subjects, seeking whatever help could be given by official sources to end this impossible situation. This call started up a long and tangled bureaucratic chain of events which was to span four capitals before it ended. On the private front, the Lees had meanwhile summoned Isabel's mother from Constantinople to take charge of the family battle in person. Isabel had apparently guarded her terrible but precious secret so well that it was only through Charles Lee's urgent telegram from Paris that Mrs. Streater had learned, for the first time, that her would-be son-in-law was not just a repugnant Armenian but a Bolshevik agent to boot. Smelling salts, followed by the most drastic rescue operation, were clearly indicated.

The rest of July appears to have been a time of long-distance bombardment between the family, gathered in the Rue de Lorraine, and the suitor, whose headquarters were in Room 19 of the Hotel d'Angleterre in the Rue de la Böetie. But by the end of the month, it was clear that the family, for the moment, had won hands down. To begin with, Isabel had been shipped back, tearful and protesting, to the parental cage in Constantinople (as she was not quite twenty-one, she was not yet in those days legally independent). Then, at the beginning of August 1930, Agabekov was expelled from France and forced to take up residence in Brussels, further away still from his beloved.

One factor behind the expulsion order may well have been that French Deuxième Bureau, who had interrogated Agabekov during July, found him evasive and uncooperative. This, at any rate, was what the French security authorities told their British colleagues afterward. Furthermore, Agabekov was something of a political embarrassment.

Soon after arriving in Paris he had, indeed, contacted his old friend Bessedovsky and had picked up a few tips in the arts of the political refugee from the renegade Soviet diplomat. One result had been a virulent anti-Bolshevik article by Agabekov in the White Russian newspaper *Dernières Nouvelles;* and the French government can hardly have welcomed the prospect of having yet another high-level Communist defector on the rampage in the Paris press.

But all this is only part of the explanation. The rest is to be found in the marathon struggle between Agabekov and the Streater family, and it is here that the real impulse behind the French move probably lies. Indeed, an official French report dated August 18 to London on the affair stated categorically that Agabekov had been expelled "chiefly as the result of a request made by the British Consul-General in Paris, who had intervened on behalf of Miss Streater's mother."

The British government was soon to change sides as the whole case performed a somersault. Yet in mid-August things looked gloomy indeed for these oddly assorted lovers. Isabel was back where she had started from, and with even less freedom than she had enjoyed in Paris, since her passport had now been impounded by the family and locked up in her father's safe. Agabekov, who had taken rooms at 87, Rue Potagères, Brussels, was forced to start all over again to win the protection, or at least the tolerance, of yet another foreign police force and Intelligence service. It was no easy matter: he had been arrested briefly at Liège on August 14 and released under the surveillance of the Belgian police. Meanwhile, his only remaining links with Isabel were by letter, and, as the family censored her ordinary mail, they were precarious contacts.

The British Intelligence service, which he had first approached through intermediaries fully six months before, remained his only hope. He now resolved on publicity to try to stir them into action, despite the extra provocation that such a bold step would give to his Soviet enemies. On August 26, in an interview with the Paris edition of the *Chicago Tribune,* he revealed his identity and his plight as a "homeless" refugee from Bolshevism—denied entry to Britain, expelled from France, and accorded only a three-month visa in Belgium. This "unkind treatment," the interview continued, was only dissuading other important OGPU men from following his example and deserting with their secrets. He claimed to know at least three such former colleagues who were itching to do so, provided they were given some indirect encouragement. Agabekov's lament was picked up the next day by the British press and echoed around Whitehall. It seems to have done the trick, for it is surely no coincidence that, only twenty-four hours later, the first preparatory moves were made in London to arrange for a direct interrogation of the suppliant runaway. On September 17, 1930, in an office of the Belgian Sûreté Publique in Brussels, this confrontation at long last took place. As a dramatic occasion, it was to prove worthy of the long build-up, so coolly cautious on the one side, and so anguished on the other.

The British had concluded, not unreasonably, that what he was mainly after in return for his disclosures was money, and plenty of it. Accordingly, his British interrogator, who was introduced to him as "Captain Denis," as pronounced in French, got down straightaway to what he imagined to be the brass tacks: how much?

Agabekov's reply must have shaken him. The OGPU chief replied that he would do nothing for money, no matter what sum was offered. Even £100,000 would not move him. On the other hand, he was prepared to tell the British all he knew, and to advise them on any future problems, provided only that they would help to bring about a reunion between Isabel Streater and himself. The British official collected his wits and started talking round the problem from the Belgian end. It might be possible, Agabekov was told, for the Belgian authorities to be persuaded to allow him to remain undisturbed in Belgium and for a Belgian visa to be issued to Miss Streater so that she could join him in Brussels and marry him. On the other hand, if he proved uncooperative, influence might be exerted in the opposite sense, so that Agabekov would find himself expelled from Belgium and Miss Streater denied entry. Then, as though incredulous that money really was no object, the interrogator repeated his offer to pay anything within reason for any useful information he could produce.[6]

Agabekov brushed aside both the offers and the threats. Money, he

---

[6] The British government was, by now, particularly interested in the identity—which Agabekov said he could reveal—of a Soviet agent known only as "B.3," who was gathering intelligence from inside the Foreign Office.

repeated, was no consideration. Neither was the idea of expulsion from Belgium, a prospect which did not alarm him unduly so long as he was alone. As for getting a Belgian visa for Isabel, that was tackling his problem from the wrong end of the stick. The real difficulty was to get her out of Turkey, and it was here that the British consul in Constantinople could surely help, either by persuading her father to return her existing passport to her, or by issuing her with a new one. He added a strong legal argument. Isabel Streater had now passed her twenty-first birthday, so her family had no right whatever to keep her a virtual prisoner any longer against her will.

The Englishman later reported that reunion with Miss Streater did seem to be a genuine obsession with Agabekov. The Russian, he said, was so distraught that his nerves went to pieces whenever he discussed the subject. Moreover, he seemed to be literally pining away with frustrated love. According to the Belgian police, he was steadily losing weight. For a matter-of-fact Anglo-Saxon who had been expecting to argue only about the number of ten-pound notes he should produce, this was a strange emotional vortex to be staring into. To ram home his point, Agabekov even produced some of Isabel's passionate love letters, and obliged his somewhat embarrassed interrogator to read a few of them.

It was all a very different world from the usual shabby traffic in informers. But "Captain Denis" was clearly a good professional who soon got his bearings. He decided that a close but secret watch should be kept on Miss Streater's movements, and tactful pressure applied on the British Embassy in Constantinople, in the matter of her withheld passport, emphasizing that the young lady had now come of age. He also felt that questionnaires on all subjects on which Agabekov might have useful information should be prepared at once, so that interrogation could start immediately Miss Streater had left Constantinople, and be completed before she had actually reached Brussels. Still under the impact of Agabekov's unrequited passion, the Englishman was clearly concerned that their man might well become non compos mentis the moment he had Isabel in his arms again.

Finally, Agabekov himself was assured that the matter would be put up immediately to higher authority, and, in return for this pledge, the Russian set down his terms formally in writing. This "contract," dated in September 1930, must be one of the strangest documents which even the varied trade of espionage and defection has ever produced. It reads, translated from the Russian:

> By the present, I, G. Agabekov-Arountunov, bind myself, if my bride[7] will leave from Stamboul by October 1, 1930 for Brussels, to disclose to the bearer of this note of hand—
> 1. In what manner, where, and through whom the Bolsheviks re-ceive documents by the Foreign Office (all detail and, if necessary, give personal assistance).
> 2. To reply to all questions which shall be put to me which I shall consider myself competent to answer.

The awkward thing about that undertaking was the date. October 1 gave the British exactly ten days in which to prize open the bars of the family cage in Constantinople, and let Isabel flutter safely away to Brussels. It was the only mistake the English official had made. A bureaucrat himself, he should have known that, in a matter of such complexity and delicacy—above all in a field where Whitehall could unearth no sacred precedent—the operation was going to take many weeks rather than a few days to accomplish. So it proved. The first of October came and went, and still Isabel remained pinioned down in Constantinople.

The day after the deadline had expired, "Captain Denis" went to Brussels to see Agabekov again, to plead for more time and to urge patience upon him. It proved no easy task. The moment the Russian, at 11:00 a.m., came into the room reserved for them in the Sûreté building, the Englishman saw that he had lost still more weight during the past fortnight and that he seemed to be breaking up under the strain and uncertainty.

More in the manner of a doctor soothing a patient than of one experienced agent bargaining with another, "Captain Denis" assured the distraught OGPU chief that his superiors in London were doing everything possible, "without infringing the laws of the British Empire," to bring about the reunion. First efforts, admittedly, had

---

[7]   The wish seems father to the thought in Agabekov's use of this word, assuming the translation to be correct. There was a report that he and Isabel had managed to go through a form of civil marriage ceremony at the Persian Consulate in Constanti-nople in May 1930, but it was never confirmed.

been unsuccessful; but "there was every hope that, sooner or later, a favourable solution would be arrived at."

Agabekov was grateful but unpacified. He was, he said, losing hope, and his despair had been fed by frantic messages from Isabel. For the first time, her courage appeared to be giving way too; indeed, she was contemplating suicide. There seemed nothing for it but for him to go back to Constantinople and try somehow to snatch her from her parents' grasp. He knew the difficulties and the dangers. He had little money, no valid passport, and only the faint prospect of a welcome from the Turkish police, let alone from the Streater family. Moreover, Turkey itself was far too close for comfort for the Soviet Union. But it looked to be the only solution. Would the British at least help him with a passage on one of their ships, and give him such protection as they could on the journey?

Baron Verhulst, chief of the Belgian Sûreté, was summoned by the Englishman to help him talk Agabekov out of such a wild scheme. By now, Verhulst had ample reasons of his own to be in Agabekov's professional debt and was himself anxious to keep the Russian on hand for further help.[8] He willingly joined "Captain Denis," therefore, in applying pressure. The upshot was that Agabekov finally agreed to another fortnight's grace. He promised "to do nothing rash" until October 15, in return for an assurance that "no stone would be left unturned" to get Isabel Streater out to Brussels. He was also assured by his English contact that, if he required any money in the meantime, he should not hesitate to ask for funds via the Sûreté.

This growing anxiety to placate Agabekov is explained by the growing potential of his importance. Not only were there crucial secrets like the identity of that Soviet agent planted inside the Foreign Office (who was still, allegedly, hard at work, oblivious to the perils brewing up for him in a Brussels police office). Agabekov had also by now emerged as a possible recruiter, as well as an unmasker, of spies.

He had received a letter, in the handwriting of a colleague in the Foreign Section of the OGPU, an Armenian called Kevorkian. The writer, who operated in Teheran under the cover of secretary to an Armenian prelate there, had sent this message to the Paris office of

---

8   See p. 116 below.

Dernières Nouvelles, the Russian émigré paper which had published Agabekov's articles during the summer, and the paper had added the Belgian address and forwarded it on. Kevorkian wrote that he was in Paris, where he was living at the Hotel d'Angleterre under an assumed name, and that he urgently wanted to see Agabekov. The whole thing might, of course, be a plant, or a trick designed to end with Agabekov's murder. On the other hand, Kevorkian could easily be the first of that batch of OGPU officials whom Agabekov had publicly declared to be itching to follow his example. It was a dazzling prospect, and "Captain Denis" accordingly strengthened his pressure for immediate steps which would give tangible results in the Isabel Streater affair.

But once more, the deadline came and went. Agabekov gave the British seven more days and then, on October 23, he launched a carefully hatched plot of his own to spirit his beloved out of Constantinople. The plan revealed the professional expertise of the senior secret service official. It also showed that Agabekov, though no Romeo in appearance, could play havoc with female heartstrings, especially over this romantic drama where his Juliet was stranded on such a very distant Oriental balcony. What he had done was to persuade his landlady at the Rue Potagères, Madame Banken, and her stepdaughter Silvia to risk certain imprisonment by attempting the rescue for him. The key to the rescue was that Silvia and Isabel were much the same in age and appearance.

On October 23, the two ladies set out for Constantinople, with Agabekov presumably paying their expenses. The scheme, on arrival, was to contact Isabel and hand her Silvia's passport. Miss Streater would then return to Brussels as Mlle. Banken, accompanied by her "stepmother," while the real Silvia, claiming that her passport had been lost, would get a new one from the Belgian Consulate and travel back later. But, alas, Agabekov's intrepid helpers found, when they got to Constantinople on October 27, not only that they could not get near Isabel, but that they were being shadowed themselves. Mr. Streater—as dogged as his daughter and no doubt just as genuinely motivated—was having her watched by the Turkish police as a possible Bolshevik spy, and everyone who tried to make contact with her also came under surveillance. Madame Banken's nerve (or money, or both) soon ran out, and, after forty-eight hours of this, she left for home. But Silvia gallantly hung on, hoping to complete this once-in-a-lifetime adventure single-handed.

It was perhaps just as well that her gallantry never had to be put to the test. The Lion and Unicorn came to the rescue, just in time. This timing may have been pure coincidence, though it is more likely that, hearing about this latest alarming imbroglio, the British authorities redoubled their efforts to "free" Isabel, before Belgian citizens became publicly involved in the scandal as well. At all events, while the Bankens were in the middle of their mission, Agabekov in Brussels was suddenly told, through the Belgian Sûreté, that the British consul-general in Constantinople had now been officially instructed either to recover Miss Streater's passport from her father or, failing this, to supply her with a new one.

On November 2, 1930, Agabekov at last received the message he had been pining for. The telegram read simply: "All is well. Happy. Isabel." The same day, at the insistence of both the British and the Belgian authorities, he recalled Silvia. One suspects that the young Belgian girl, though glad it had all ended so well for the two lovers, was a little disappointed at having to return so tamely herself.

If "Captain Denis" or Baron Verhulst were present at that long-awaited reunion on Belgian soil which they had done so much to bring about, they left behind no reference to it, let alone an eyewitness account, in the Agabekov papers. The same applies to the wedding which followed shortly after Isabel's arrival. Two guests who would certainly have been at that ceremony were Madame Banken and her stepdaughter. Two guests who, with even greater certainty, would not have attended were Mr. and Mrs. Streater. Indeed, for the next few years at any rate, Isabel seems to have been treated as a "nonperson" by her family, much as her husband was treated by his own country. Isabel's parents in Constantinople were prophesying disaster for their runaway daughter. Agabekov's masters in Moscow were threatening vengeance on their turncoat comrade.

This was the somber background against which, early in 1931, the two lovers, now "M. et Mme. Arountunov," started their new life in an apartment at 188, Grande Rue au Bois, Brussels. Both the threats and the predictions were soon to break over their heads.

Chapter Seven

RUNNING THE GANTLET

Before following the dark trail that lay ahead of the newlyweds, it is worth pausing a moment to ask what the British and Belgian authorities had got in return for all their efforts? How big a "catch" did Agabekov turn out to be when he was finally landed? The answer, which can only be a partial one, falls into two parts: the general information he produced about Soviet policy, and the specific disclosures he made about current Soviet operations.

Like Bajanov in Paris two years before, Agabekov drew up in Brussels, in the spring of 1931, a comprehensive picture of the OGPU's aims and structure, a condensed version of which was given as an appendix to the memoirs he published later that year. But whereas Stalin's secretary had described the OGPU as seen (and seen in his case with the utmost distaste) from the political viewpoint above, Agabekov provided his interrogators with the first top-level account of the working of that organization, as actually experienced by an official operating inside it. The two descriptions, when placed side by side, and focused properly, gave an exceedingly sharp image.

Thus, Bajanov had spoken of the Kremlin's grand strategic aim of penetrating the whole of the Near East in order to seize the bridge on which Britain—then the supreme enemy—depended for her hold on India. Agabekov now filled in how, during one of his first foreign assignments (with the OGPU group in Afghanistan) he had fallen in, when riding on the outskirts of Kabul, with another horseman who turned out to be one of the thirty thousand Bukharan refugees from Soviet Bukhara who had fled across the Afghan border. The old emir of Bukhara himself held his émigré court only a few miles away.

Agabekov first passed himself off as an attaché of the Turkish legation, for he was fluent in both Turkish and Uzbek. But, once he had gained the confidence of the emir's circle, he boldly revealed himself as one of the detested Bolsheviks, and, by playing astutely on the homesickness of the exiles, persuaded them to stop fomenting insurgencies inside the Soviet Union and return home. The Kremlin was delighted at the prospect, for the exiled emir and his followers were troublesome opponents—and useful allies for the Afghans and the British—in the case of any frontier war. Amnesties, restitution of property, and full compensation were all promised from Moscow, and the first batch of Bukharans duly left for Russia in the spring of 1925. Agabekov's grand design was dashed by the stupidity, or treachery, of the Soviet reception committee. The homecomers, instead of being welcomed, were arrested and robbed. They fled back across the border and their stories put an abrupt end to any further repatriation. But what the venture had shown was the enormous pull of nostalgia among these refugee communities which passed as solidly anti-Bolshevik.

Agabekov played on the same string the following year, when, as part of the OGPU team in Persia, he recruited most of his agents from the local White Russian émigrés, including a former general and a former colonel of the tsarist army. Here, too, Britain was the target, and an eventual war with the British Empire was the working assumption, especially after the return of the Conservatives to power in 1926. Soon after their victory, and the subsequent worsening of relations between Moscow and London, Agabekov received orders to foment revolt along the Indian border and even across it, in areas like British Baluchistan. Tribal chiefs were to be bribed into cooperating, and secret caches of arms prepared for their use, once the Kremlin gave the signal.

A year later still, in 1927, Agabekov was ordered to launch a similar campaign among the Kurds, that luckless people whose homeland was split between Turkey, Iraq, Persia, and the Soviet Union. In their case, the Russian plan was more ambitious: to found an "independent republic" on the soil of that part of Kurdistan which lay on Soviet territory to act as a magnet for the other fragments. Once again, war with Britain was the raison d'être for the scheme. According to Agabekov, the Kremlin hoped that, once hostilities had broken out, sympathetic Kurdish tribes, acting as Soviet allies, would attack the important British airfields in Persia. The British did not need anyone to tell them that Moscow's constant aim was to gnaw away at the approaches to the Himalayas. But it was from Agabekov that they learned how this operation was being mounted and conducted from the Kremlin end.

However, even this general information was surpassed in value by the sum total of the detailed disclosures Agabekov made on a wide variety of subjects. There was, for example, the matter of the interception of British official mail, which he had mentioned as one of his earliest "baits." This had been organized by Agabekov himself in Persia, through bribery of the local postal officials. It had worked particularly well at the regional center of Meshed, the town which had featured so prominently in Bajanov's escape. From 1926 onward, the OGPU had been reading, among other diplomatic correspondence, almost every British document intrusted to the Persian mail services between Meshed and Teheran, as well as most of the official mail sent in from India.

When this interception operation was in full swing, Agabekov and his OGPU team were being presented with over five-hundred items a month to read and copy. The tariff was two dollars per British or Persian letter and a flat rate of one dollar apiece for all the others. There were times when even the two-dollar tariff proved dirt-cheap. It was partly through this regular and reliable leak, for example, that the Russians had been able to monitor the progress of the crucial Anglo-Persian talks on oil concessions and on the use of Persian territory as a staging post for air flights between Britain and India. When the Russians read that the British were actually proposing to build special airfields and storage depots in Persia for this purpose, they mobilized every form of diplomatic pressure at their disposal in Teheran to frustrate the scheme.

Most of this official mail was, of course, sealed before being committed to the tender mercies of the Persian postal system. But, as Agabekov now revealed, that afforded little or no security protection. His men had perfected a method—in which they used, of all things, a pair of ordinary knitting needles—for detaching the original seal, melting it down after taking an impression, and then replacing it again so skillfully after the missive had been opened and read that it was impossible to detect any tampering.

When Agabekov and Baron Verhulst, who seem to have hit it off well personally, were chatting one day, the Belgian police chief remarked how relieved he was that a pouch of Belgian diplomatic mail, which had been missing for twenty-four hours, had now been found again, after a frantic search, with its contents quite intact.

Without a moment's hesitation, Agabekov had replied: "Intact perhaps, but not unopened; the Russians have certainly read everything in it." And when Verhulst protested the impossibility of this, as all the seals had remained undamaged, Agabekov asked the baron to write any letter there and then, seal the envelope as copiously as he chose, and let him have it overnight. This was duly done. The next day, Agabekov returned the envelope which, even to the police chief's expert eye, appeared to be still in its pristine condition. Nonetheless, the Russian was able to repeat for him word for word the message inside.[1] The Belgians, like the British after them, profited from this demonstration.

But what interested the Western Intelligence services the most were the cover names, real identities, and current assignments of the OGPU agents active in their midst. Bajanov had mentioned only one or two, notably the Persian minister Teimourtach. Bessedovsky could

---

[1] This little anecdote was related by Baron Verhulst to Boris Bajanov, who passed it on to the author.

only reveal, with any certainty, espionage operations based in the Paris Embassy, where he himself had worked as a career diplomat. But Agabekov, whose own career had been with the Bolshevik secret police ever since 1920 when, aged only twenty-four, he had joined the local Cheka at Ekaterinburg,[2] could "blow" entire networks of Soviet officials as well as local recruits.

Though, so far, mention has only been made of Russian intercepts of British mail and ciphers, the reverse process was, of course, also going on. It is from one such Western intercept made at this time that we know what a heavy blow Agabekov's defection had dealt the Kremlin. The coded telegram concerned was sent on July 2, 1930 (i.e., eight days after Agabekov went missing from his post) from Moscow to the Soviet Embassy on the Unter den Linden in Berlin, the OGPU's administrative center for Europe. It was marked for a Comrade Veresaiv of that mission and informed him that a "serious danger" had arisen as a result of Agabekov's treason. It continued:

> An especially dangerous situation has arisen for those comrades who were in touch with our office in Constantinople up to 6/24/30.

There then followed the names of ten such comrades who were to be recalled to Moscow at once. Three others were ordered to "change their places of residence forthwith and temporarily cease activity."

That telegram (and the dozens of other similar messages that must have flashed out of Moscow at the same time) gives the key, not only to Agabekov's importance, but also to the peril in which he now stood. Like Bessedovsky, from whom he had taken advice while in Paris, he too had rushed into print as a form of instant safeguard. Moreover, as the months passed, his former masters must have assumed that all the really sensitive "information" which the traitor had not published had, by now, been imparted secretly to the French, Belgian, or British authorities. Nothing could be gained in this respect, therefore, from stopping his mouth, because that mouth had already done the damage.

Yet there was no parallel here with the case of Bessedovsky twelve

---

[2] The town in the Urals where, two years previously, Tsar Nicholas II and his family had been murdered.

months before, when the Kremlin had called its executioners off once it was seen that they could do little good. Agabekov was the first comrade to defect from a top-level position within the OGPU itself. Quite apart from the natural desire among some of his former colleagues to get personal revenge, there was the strictly professional argument: if he were allowed to skip off to the West unscathed, how many more might try to follow? When Stalin ordered the murder of Bajanov, he was, basically, venting his own private pique against his renegade secretary. But when he ordered the liquidation of Agabekov, he was trying to shore up the pillar on which the whole of his terrorist regime rested. In order to set an impressive example, the operation ought, if possible, to be no sordid and politically embarrassing shooting on the streets of some Western capital, but something worthy of the organization which the traitor had betrayed. "M. and Madame Arountunov" had barely settled down in their Brussels apartment before, in Moscow, one such intriguing possibility presented itself.

What happened next became famous as the "Philomena affair." It is certainly a classic of the espionage history of these interwar years. It can also be seen as a classic of the entire Stalin era, as regards the elaborate and costly lengths to which the dictator was prepared to go in order to avenge himself on a henchman who had betrayed him. Incomplete or inaccurate segments of the story appeared, at various times during 1932, in newspapers all the way from Brussels to Constantinople. As far as is known, what follows is the first full account of the drama, based on the official records of the principal European governments concerned.[3]

The story begins in Paris early in 1930 with a certain Alexandre Auguste Lecoq, who lived in some style at the Hotel de Bretagne in the Rue de Richelieu, which belonged to his mother-in-law. Lecoq was a French citizen who described himself as an engineer, but who appears to have been also an international adventurer prepared to look at any proposition, provided there was money in it. It was in this latter capacity, rather than for any engineering advice, that he was approached by one Nestor Fillia, a Russian refugee living in the French

---

[3] In particular, Rumania, whose directorate-general of police prepared a twenty-two-page report on the affair which is still extant.

capital, with the following problem. Nestor's wife, Eudoxia, and their daughter Ana, were still living in the Soviet Union, at the town of Nicolaiev, and they had been striving for some time to get out and join the father in exile. All attempts by the two women to get travel papers had, however, been blocked by the Soviet authorities. The old lady was very rich and had managed to deposit a fortune of 100 million Swiss francs[4] at the Banque Fédérale in Geneva in a personal account which only she could draw upon. So if Lecoq knew of a way to get the wife out, he would be sure of a large commission once she reached Geneva.

Lecoq later claimed that he had begun in the orthodox way by approaching acquaintances in the Quai d'Orsay, in case something might be achieved through normal diplomatic channels. Be that as it may, he was soon off on a very different tack. In May of 1931, he put the matter before one Jean Paniotis, a Greek citizen then domiciled in Paris. The Greek had been born at Odessa, and though he had changed his nationality, he had kept his Russian loyalties. He was in fact an OGPU agent, though it is not certain that Lecoq knew this from the start.

Paniotis discussed the proposal with another "illegal" OGPU man in the Paris network, Serge Mintz, and the two agents decided that, before doing anything further, they would find out whether Madame Fillia's supposed Geneva fortune really did exist. This was eventually confirmed for them by one of their contacts in Switzerland and, in July, Lecoq was informed that the deal was on. On the twenty-fifth of that month, Paniotis left for Russia, where he visited Odessa, called on the two women at Nicolaiev, and spent some days in Moscow. Whether his motive had originally been, like Lecoq's simply to get his hands on some money or whether the OGPU had developed a professional interest in the matter from the very beginning is not known. But by the time Paniotis returned to Paris in August, this professional interest was very much on top. Lecoq was given the startling news that the Soviet authorities had agreed to allow Madame Fillia and her daughter to leave Russia provided that he would, in return, help the OGPU to lay their hands on their renegade colleague, Agabekov. If

---

4   In one version of the story, the sum is put at 400 million.

he had not realized it before, the Frenchman realized at this point that he was in deep and dangerous waters. However, as he was now offered a second reward from the Russians for his services, in addition to the commission payable in Geneva, he decided to play along. After all, what was an internal feud within the Bolshevik secret service to him?

The broad outline of the scheme, which had already been drawn up in Moscow, was outlined to Lecoq. Agabekov was to be approached with the genuine story of the Fillia family and asked, whether, as a former OGPU official who knew all the ropes, he would take personal charge of an attempt to spirit the two women out of Russia. Naturally, a substantial cash payment was to be offered. Moreover, a smuggling operation which would look entirely feasible to such an expert was to be suggested. As money was no object and an escape by sea seemed simplest, why not hire a steamer for the sole purpose of fetching the ladies from Odessa to, say, some safe port like Varna in Bulgaria? Nothing, surely, could appear simpler for a man like Agabekov, who must have plenty of contacts left up and down the Black Sea from his time as bureau chief in Constantinople.

It all sounded quite plausible. But the problem which faced the conspirators was how to put the proposal up to the wily professional so that he would be tempted by the money without suspecting the trick. Whether or not the steamer brought the Fillia ladies to Varna, the real purpose of chartering it was, of course, to lure Agabekov on board and then return with him—preferably alive—to Odessa, and to retribution. Even Lecoq, who had the most respectable credentials of any of the actors involved so far, did not seem respectable enough to present such a concealed double cross as that.

At this point, a highly enigmatic figure enters the scene in the person of Albert Stopford, a seventy-two-year-old Englishman living in Paris at 31, Rue de Valois. He was tall, distinguished-looking, seemingly with plenty of money, and certainly with wide social connections. Whether Stopford was a British agent, a Soviet agent, a double agent, or, just possibly, nobody's agent, he *was* a homosexual, and this was how the OGPU had got a certain hold upon him. Paniotis himself later admitted to a homosexual relationship with the Englishman, while the other OGPU man involved, Serge Mintz, is described in one police document on the case as actually working for Stopford as his "secretary." At all events, Stopford was now chosen as the all-important "front man," on the grounds that his appearance and standing as an English gentleman of means would impress the victim. The go-between either agreed, for money, to do the job or was simply drafted to the assignment by men whose orders he could not refuse.

The next phase is best told from the detailed accounts which Agabekov gave to the Belgian authorities. He was in Berlin, negotiating the German rights of his memoirs when, on September 23, he received an urgent summons from his wife to return to Brussels. Albert Stopford had turned up at their home and, disappointed at finding only Isabel there, had asked her to recall her husband at once, as there was a piece of important and lucrative business awaiting him. The English visitor added that, the moment he got a telegram in Paris saying Agabekov was back, he himself would return to explain everything.

In fact, when the first meeting between the two men took place forty-eight hours later, it left Agabekov with the uneasy feeling that there was a great deal that still needed explaining. There was, above all, the question of how the contact had been made.

"Who recommended me to you and how did you get hold of my address?" asked Agabekov.

"Oh, it was all from a White Russian general in Paris."

"What is his name?"

"I really cannot recall it for the moment. You know how hard it is for us foreigners to remember these foreign names."

That sounded much too innocent, and also improbable: émigré tsarist officers were not likely to know, let alone recommend, a recently defected OGPU chief. But his suspicions melted a little when the harmless-sounding problem of the Fillia family was explained, especially as, at this stage, Stopford asked merely for advice, for which he offered to pay. Agabekov declined the money but gave a few tips on how passports might be obtained in Moscow if one knew the right people and paid the right price. The Englishman profusely thanked him and departed.

That had been purely a reconnaissance to establish credentials. A few days later, Agabekov received a letter from Stopford saying that

Madame Fillia was afraid to approach the Soviet authorities yet again herself, but that she was prepared to make "every sacrifice" to leave Russia without their help. Would Agabekov personally supervise this, in return, of course, for suitable payment? If the two women were only brought as far as Bulgaria that would suffice, as, from there, they could easily make their own way to Paris. Though Agabekov did not like the sound of Bulgaria, he liked the sound of the money, and agreed to a discussion.

This took place, in the middle of October, at the Grand Hotel in Brussels, where Stopford had booked himself one of the most expensive rooms. The Englishman was accompanied on this occasion by the OGPU's contact man in Switzerland who had confirmed the existence, and the size, of Madame Fillia's bank account. He was introduced as Otto Jaeger, and produced a Swiss passport in that name. Being himself a banker, his function, he explained, was simply to arrange the financial side of the transaction: and he proceeded to offer very tempting terms. Agabekov was to receive 10,000 francs before leaving Brussels and a further 10,000 on arrival in Bulgaria. But this was only expense money. Once he had got the two women safely into that country, he would be paid a fee of £2,000—a very substantial sum in 1931 values and exchange rates, and one on which, for example, the Agabekovs could have lived comfortably for the next four or five years. It was hardly surprising that the ex-OGPU chief, now wed to his cherished Isabel but without any regular income to support her, agreed to take the job on, relying on his professional training to combat any dangers to himself.

A month later, he set out for Bulgaria, traveling via Austria and Rumania, as the Hungarians had refused him a transit visa. The only contact he had been given was a man named Dmitrov, who lived at 20, Nishka Street in Varna. He, apparently, knew all about smuggling people by sea out of Odessa. The OGPU, meanwhile, had obligingly moved Madame Fillia and her daughter down to that Russian seaport, and Stopford also handed over their address there.

This first run proved a flop all around, though a relatively harmless one for Agabekov. There was a ten-day delay in Vienna, where the Austrian police pumped him for some urgent information as the price of letting him travel further.[5] Another briefer but more disturbing holdup followed when he crossed the River Danube border from Rumania into Bulgaria. He was searched inside out by the Rumanian frontier guards. When they found nothing incriminating, the officer in charge apologized and, in confidence, gave the reason. An anonymous telegram had been sent from Paris, alleging that an important Bolshevik was about to cross their border, smuggling illegal literature. This made no sense at all to Agabekov, who was expecting no danger until he reached his destination. Yet it was troubling because, so far as he was aware, the only person who knew all about his journey was that silver-haired English gentleman in the Rue de Valois. Could this mean that Stopford was himself an OGPU agent; or was he being duped as well? The truth would doubtless reveal itself at Varna.

Agabekov never got that far. On his third day in Sofia, he was summoned to Prelawsky, the chief of Bulgarian Security, and told that it was in everybody's interests—and particularly his own—that he should get out of Bulgaria as quickly as possible, and without passing through Varna. Though Agabekov had a one-month visa, he knew that it was both useless, and inadvisable, to resist. The next day, he started back along the route he had come, arriving home in Brussels tired, empty-handed, and puzzled.[6]

Everyone now had to think again, not least the OGPU, who had planned everything for Varna. It was when Stopford learned from Agabekov how pleasant the Rumanians had been to him that the natural alternative presented itself. "Let's try the Rumanian port of Constanza, and get a steamer in there from Odessa instead," he proposed, outwardly unperturbed by the hitch.

Agabekov also had to think again. He decided to bring his power-

---

[5] The Austrian Communist leader and Soviet secret intelligence agent Semmelman had just been murdered there, and the Austrian security authorities wanted some authoritative background on the assassin, whom they had arrested. He had described himself as a Yugoslav named Pirkovich. But Agabekov immediately identified him as Schulman, the former head of the OGPU's so-called Black Cabinet in Moscow, and the very colleague who had prepared his own false Persian passport for the Constantinople assignment.

[6] It seems that the Bulgarian authorities had got wind of some spectacular plot against Agabekov's person on their soil and were anxious to avoid an international scandal.

ful patrons and protectors, Baron Verhulst and "Captain Denis," into the picture, murky though it was. On December 13, 1931, he wrote out for them a summary of the affair to date, beginning with that first call upon his wife nearly three months before and ending with the latest proposal to switch the Fillia operation to Rumania. Agabekov emphasized his own suspicions but, curiously enough, did not ask for any professional guidance about Albert Stopford. He did, however, attach to his report copies of all the letters received from the Englishman thus far. They make an unctuous, feline impression, calculated to put up the hackles of any normal fellow countryman of his straightaway, though perhaps Agabekov imagined this was all in accordance with good English breeding.

Thus the opening letter to Agabekov's wife begins, in impeccable Russian style:

> Dear Madame Arountunov,
> I think *Madame* goes better with a Russian name than *Mrs.*? . . .

Writing on September 28, after his first visit to Brussels, it is already: "My dear Friends, if I may call you so?"; and the dear friends are told that his telegraphic address is "Stoppy Paris," two words which somehow conjure up a picture of the man even today. Three days later, when he is arranging the money transfers with "Zurich" (who is presumably the so-called banker, Otto Jaeger) the greeting has swiftly progressed to "My dear kind friends." So it goes on, Levantine in tone rather than Anglo-Saxon, and rather too good to be true for any breed.

But one thing emerged clearly from this sheaf of a dozen letters. "Stoppy Paris" was the junction through which all communications passed on their way to Brussels, even messages of despair (written, of course, at the OGPU's behest) from Madame Fillia herself in Russia. This was beginning to look so secretive as to be almost suspicious. At this point, however, the plotters were obliged, for quite different reasons, to bring someone else out of the shadows and introduce him to Agabekov. The reason emerged later on, after the scandal had been investigated by the police of half a dozen countries. At Varna, the OGPU squad detailed to seize Agabekov included people who knew him personally. But once the operation was switched to Constanza, arrangements had to be improvised and were much less water-tight. It was therefore necessary for someone in the conspiracy to accompany Agabekov quite openly on his journey to Rumania and, once they had arrived there, to keep a watch on his movements and also be ready to identify him to his kidnappers. Their choice fell on the Frenchman Lecoq, the man who, for personal gain, had set the whole plot in motion.

So, when Stopford arrived the next time at the Grand Hotel to finalize arrangements for this second attempt via Rumania, Lecoq, "a French businessman who is helping us and who happens to be in Brussels today on business," was presented.[7] There was a brief discussion about the best way of chartering a steamer "to get the Fillia ladies to Constanza" and detailed travel plans were made. Agabekov and Lecoq were to make their separate ways to Rumania, setting out from Brussels and Paris respectively. They were to leave on December 23 and to meet up on the morning of the twenty-sixth in the Athenée Palace Hotel at Bucharest. It was a strange way for the Agabekovs to mark what was probably their first Christmas as a married couple, especially for poor Isabel, who was left behind alone in Belgium.

Before following the two men to Rumania we have to reconstruct (again from international police records compiled some weeks later) what the Kremlin was up to, because it is at this point that the *Philomena* affair justified its name as well as its reputation. Toward the end of December, the OGPU had found the vessel they were looking for. She was a Greek cargo vessel, the *Helena Philomena*, and appears to have been located by the OGPU (acting through the cover of the Soviet shipping organization Sovtorgflot), while anchored at Marseilles. She had a Greek captain, Spiro Catapodis, and, initially, an all-Greek crew of some twenty sailors. But when she left, almost immediately, for Constantinople, seven of these sailors had been discharged and replaced by seven OGPU men. (The manifest revealed that the ship had also taken a young German woman aboard, one Fräulein Gaubler, but she appears to have been locally recruited, not for the kidnapping but to add to the coziness of Captain Catapodis's bunk en route.)

---

[7] The Greek, Paniotis, one of the real hatchet men in the operation, had also traveled to Brussels with the pair, but he kept well out of sight.

While the *Philomena* was steaming across the Mediterranean, Agabekov and Lecoq had been taking stock of one another in the Athenée Palace Hotel of Bucharest, where both had arrived on schedule. What Lecoq thought of the man who had become his victim we do not know, though, in his signed statement made afterward to the Rumanian police, he claimed to have felt pangs of remorse, and to have refused any part in the actual abduction or killing. For his part, Agabekov, in his private reports, made it quite clear he had not taken at all to this short, stout, fair-haired, and middle-aged Frenchman who had been wished on him as a traveling companion. He found him "shallow, inferior, and incapable of even lying properly" (a cardinal fault to any ex-OGPU chief). Moreover, he discovered that Lecoq was a complete coward. This, as it turned out, was to come in very useful.

The plotters had agreed that, once they had got Agabekov as far as Bucharest, they would make one last attempt to persuade him to go to Varna after all. Accordingly, Lecoq took the Russian's passport along to the Bulgarian Legation and inquired about a visa. Agabekov was not unduly concerned, for he was confident that his frank talks with the security authorities in Sofia a few weeks before would have left their proper mark; and why, after all, had the Bulgarians been so anxious to get rid of him? So it proved, and Lecoq returned empty-handed. But Lecoq himself still had to be talked out of the Varna project and Agabekov suddenly realized he could achieve that by playing on what he picturesquely described as the Frenchman's "white threads." He drew such a lucid portrait of wild happenings in Bulgaria where, he declared, innocent men were killed in broad daylight every day that, on December 29, Lecoq wired to Paris to say that there was no alternative but for the steamer to be sent to Constanza.

The Rumanian secret police, or "Siguranza," had put a close surveillance on the notorious Agabekov, and on his companion, from the moment the two men crossed the border. They accordingly read that telegram (which was addressed to Mintz in Paris) and all the other messages sent and received by Lecoq. This surveillance was to play a vital part in the drama later on. But what even the Rumanian Siguranza could not have known at the time was the scale of OGPU activity during those first days of January 1932, as the entire operation was recast.

On December 29, the day Lecoq's cable had been sent confirming the switch, he and Agabekov, on orders from Paris, had moved to Constanza. Lecoq put up at the Grand Hotel there. Agabekov, thinking of his own protection, but giving as an excuse the need for economy, installed himself in the cheaper Hotel Central. Stopford now sent a message to the Frenchman saying that a man was on the way to him at Constanza who would provide "all necessary help." All he had to do in the meantime was to stay put and make sure that Agabekov did not move either.

This proved no easy matter, for as the days went by, the Russian became more and more uneasy and less and less convinced that what they were all waiting for was merely the arrival of two women from Odessa. His suspicions were strengthened on the morning of January 7, when Lecoq introduced him to their "contact man with the Odessa steamers" who had just got in from Varna. Agabekov found himself shaking hands with a broad-shouldered, tough Bulgarian in his middle thirties called Tzonchev who, to his experienced eye, had secret policeman written all over him. When Agabekov discovered that the Bulgarian had arrived, not from Varna at all, but from Constantinople, and, moreover, knew nothing whatever of the Varna arrangements, his mind was made up. This was an OGPU man and, in all probability, his intended assassin.

He was right on the first point. Tzonchev (who was the man Stopford had indicated in his cable) was in the pay of Agabekov's own successor as OGPU chief in Turkey. But he was wrong on the second count. The Bulgarian's role was that of the "fingerman," who would, when the time was right, point the victim out. The real executioner arrived in Constanza the next day, January 9, on board the S.S. *Philomena*, which, to avoid suspicion and satisfy its greedy captain, had now been chartered for six months by the Soviet Union for the sole purpose of one sinister trip up the Black Sea. The newcomer, who was accompanied by a further miniature squad of OGPU agents put abroad the vessel at Constantinople, was another so-called Bulgarian national named Gregori Alexiev. He was, however, Russian by birth, and a Bolshevik by conviction ever since his desertion from the tsarist army in 1917. Indeed, he seems to have acquired his Bulgarian identity expressly for this operation for, in 1930, he was still active in Russia as a member of a local "Soviet of Electric Tramway Workers." His nickname was "Grisha," which we shall call him from now on.

It was quite a change from the trams to his present job. Grisha had been told, on arrival at Constantinople, that it was to him, as a dedicated party worker, that the task had been intrusted of "dealing with the traitor Arountunov-Agabekov." The renegade would be persuaded to board the *Philomena* at Constanza by two men he knew (one of these being Tzonchev). If Agabekov needed any extra persuasion, then or during the voyage to Odessa, Grisha was to subdue him with chloroform, which he was given for that purpose. On arrival at Odessa, he was to hand the traitor over personally to the Soviet Executive Committee of the town.

If, however, nobody succeeded in getting the traitor up the gangplank of the *Philomena* in the first place, then he had to be shot down in cold blood in Constanza. Grisha was also given a supply of dollars with which to purchase the murder weapon locally, and told to make for the *Philomena* himself—it was like a floating OGPU station—as soon as he had done the deed. The tidiness of this plan, which had been worked out with Moscow's guidance and approval, was that none of the principals in the game would be exposed. In particular, there was no open involvement of any member on the regular staff of the OGPU networks in either Turkey or Rumania. Grisha himself was hidden away happily overnight in the house of a prostitute.

The first step in the plan was achieved easily enough on the day the *Philomena* anchored. Agabekov had made a regular habit (an odd mistake for one of his training) of lunching either alone or with Lecoq at the Jubilee Restaurant in Constanza. Over that weekend, Tzonchev joined the party, and was able to point the victim out to Grisha. But nothing would induce Agabekov to go near the vessel which, allegedly, had arrived to be put at his disposal to evacuate the two Fillia ladies. He smelt a whole shipload of rats on board and asked confusing, time-wasting questions whenever the *Philomena* was mentioned.

By the afternoon of Sunday, January 10, it was clear to the conspirators that it would have to be the gun rather than the chloroform. It would also have to be done soon, if only to save Lecoq from a nervous collapse. The Frenchman had already started sending telegrams to Paris complaining that he was ill and could not stand the strain much longer. Stopford also announced that he was about to leave the comforts of the Rue de Valois and come to Constanza to smooth things out—a sure sign that the Paris OGPU were getting concerned.

In fact, the elderly Englishman was not needed. On the Sunday evening, Lecoq and Tzonchev made their first attempt to lure Agabekov to his doom. The setting chosen was a ball that night at the Hotel Regina. Why, they suggested, should not all three of them go together, and spend a merry evening forgetting about Madame Fillia? It promised to be a gay affair, with dancing beginning at 10:00 p.m. and going on until the small hours. This sounded a particularly ominous proposal to Agabekov, as 10:00 p.m. was the latest time by which the haggard Lecoq always insisted on being in bed. Clearly, Agabekov concluded, they were hoping to get him drunk or drugged, and then, helped by the jostling crowd, either abduct him or put a knife in his back. He pretended to accept, but locked himself in his room instead. When, around midnight, the two men knocked on his door to ask what had happened, he merely apologized for having "taken a nap and overslept."

It was at this point that they told him that they would both be leaving Constanza the next morning. Lecoq explained that he had to get back to Paris on urgent business and, with Stopford on the way, he was no longer really needed. Tzonchev said he was going to Bucharest, but probably "just for a couple of hours." Agabekov was at the railway station at dawn, to make sure that the Frenchman was really going. That part of the story turned out to be true. Lecoq arrived with Tzonchev but departed alone, and Agabekov stood with the Bulgarian to watch the train pull out. They spent part of the day together and arranged to dine at the Jubilee at 8:00 p.m.

Agabekov was not surprised, when he got to the restaurant, to find he had the table to himself. He had already discovered that Tzonchev was not catching any train to Bucharest. Instead, he was booked on a ship leaving Constanza for Constantinople at 9:30 p.m. that same evening. This meant that he would be late and in a hurry, if he turned up at all. To Agabekov, the almost simultaneous departure of these two "front men" signified only one thing. Their services were no longer needed, and the whole Odessa deception plan had been abandoned. The OGPU were now going to try to kill him on the spot. The denouement is best described in the words of one of his unpublished reports:

> By 8:00 p.m. I was in the restaurant. I sat down at one of the tables by the window, overlooking a narrow courtyard. A thin, laced curtain covered the window. There was a draught from the window and I decided to move to the other end of the table, facing the window. Tzonchev arrived in a few minutes' time. We ordered some vodka and supper. Tzonchev ordered very little, and all ready dishes. He told me that he would probably be leaving for Bucharest with the night train, but before that he had a meeting with somebody. I drank my vodka in silence and watched him. In fifteen minutes' time he paid and left without having finished his supper.
>
> "If you will still be here in half an hour's time, then I shall come to see you after the meeting," he said to me on parting. I replied that it was dull at the hotel and I should probably remain at the restaurant.
>
> After Tzonchev had left, I sat alone smoking and waiting for my Turkish coffee. Suddenly, I saw a shadow on the other side of the curtain looking straight at me. The right hand of the shadow, gripping something, rose slowly. Before I had time to think or decide what to do, other shadows appeared and I heard the sound of voices outside the window. I immediately rushed to the nearest door and saw several men holding another man, who was handcuffed, by the arms. Immediately I understood what had happened. . . .
>
> The men who, at the last moment, had handcuffed the would-be assassin, were agents of the Rumanian political police, who had taken matters into their own hands. The same evening, Tzonchev was arrested while going on board the steamer. Lecoq was detained at the Hungarian frontier on the Orient Express. Cursing the Rumanian police and not knowing why he was arrested, Lecoq was then brought back to Bucharest. Samurakis, owner of the steamer, was seized two days later in Bucharest, where he had gone to find out where his clients had disappeared to. After him, the captain of the steamer, *Philomena*, and his German "wife," were also arrested.

In fact, as Agabekov discovered shortly afterward, the Rumanian police had made an even cleaner sweep. That shadow behind the lace curtains did indeed turn out to be the hired assassin, Grisha, who had dressed himself in a brand-new suit for the occasion, doubtless bought out of his OGPU dollars. After pretending for a while that his real name was Stoianov, he eventually broke down under Siguranza questioning, and revealed exactly how the murder had been planned. In the process, he disclosed many of the top names of the OGPU networks in Bucharest and in Constantinople—the latter, of course, having only recently been built up from scratch again after Agabekov's own flight and disclosures. Nor would it have helped Grisha had he managed, as instructed, to scamper aboard the *Philomena*. The vessel had been promptly confiscated by the Rumanian government, and everyone on board taken into custody. One after the other, the mixed bag of prisoners—French, Greek, and so-called Bulgarian—made their confessions. If he had set out for Constanza only twenty-four hours earlier, the elegant Albert Stopford too would also have been caught in the net. As it was, the elderly Englishman was the only front-line operative to escape.

Though nobody with a Russian passport had landed in jail (thanks to the precaution of providing Grisha with a Bulgarian identity), this first attempt to liquidate Agabekov had backfired so badly that the OGPU's hands had been scorched in the process. Even worse than the "blowing" of so many of their agents was the public exposure, which proved, not a nine days' wonder, but a two-year scandal. There was a certain poetic justice about the fact that it was the *Philomena* herself which caused Moscow the most prolonged embarrassment. The Rumanian police archives show that, of all those arrested, it was the Greek Captain Catapodis who had held out the longest under questioning. Indeed, he was only forced into a sulky confession when confronted by the incriminating testimony of everyone else in the plot.

He turned out to be just as stubborn a customer with regard to his Soviet employers. They had talked him into the adventure with the guarantee of a lucrative time charter, and he was determined somehow to extract the money out of them. For six months he could do nothing, for the *Philomena* and all her crew, including himself, were placed under six months' arrest at Constanza. When he put out to sea again, the captain bided his time until he could get his hands on a Soviet cargo. This he managed to do in January 1934, almost two years to the day after the Constanza fiasco, when he loaded a shipment of Russian timber for Alexandria. When he docked there, on February

1, 1934, instead of handing the shipment over to the local merchants who had imported it, Messrs. Bassili and Co., Catapodis seized it himself and declared his intention of selling it off by public auction. In 1932, he declared, he had been promised the equivalent of £8,100 by the Soviet Union for his part in the attempted kidnapping of their former agent, and had got nothing but the six months' internment and loss of earnings instead. This Soviet cargo, worth about £3,000, would at least make partial amends, if paid into his pocket. The Soviet government had no option but to hire the best Egyptian lawyers they could find and take the matter to court. There it rumbled on for weeks, with all the dirty linen of the 1932 abduction conspiracy being hung out on the line yet again.

Reasonably enough in all the circumstances, the one man who had profited, in some respects at any rate, from the scandal, was its intended victim. The crucial benefit to Agabekov was that he had now won something of a reprieve on his own life. Surely, the OGPU, who stood publicly exposed and condemned for this blatant bid to murder him, would hesitate, and think very carefully, before mounting a second liquidation attempt.

Another, more modest, dividend was that Agabekov could now present himself as something of an expert on the Rumanian security service. He had made himself very useful to them during the aftermath of the Constanza drama, and had won the confidence of the chief of the political police, Vetilla Ionescu, and his senior assistants. Indeed, one of these, a man named Pravco, had even tried to recruit Agabekov to work for them against the Russians. He had stalled on that proposal, but had departed for Belgium on the best of terms with the Siguranza, with mutual promises to keep in touch. These were useful contacts, especially to his Whitehall patrons. At that time, there were about half a dozen British agents in Rumania, engaged, among other activities, in ferrying infiltrators across the Dniestr River border into Russia. A new link with Ionescu was not, therefore, to be despised.

But the *Philomena* affair also produced one major setback for Agabekov. Soon after he arrived back in Brussels, he was told by the police that the revelations which had come to light about his own activities—trying, on his admission, to smuggle Russians out of the

Soviet Union—had violated the understanding on which he had been granted conditional asylum. He was therefore required to leave Belgium, though the ban was not to be considered as permanent, and his wife could, meanwhile, remain on at their home. Baron Verhulst, of the Sûreté, had done his best to prevent the temporary expulsion order, but had been overridden by higher authority. There was no denying that Agabekov had been indulging in political escapades and, even if the motive had been financial, this nonetheless contravened the pledge he had made on being admitted to the country eighteen months before. Thus the wretched Isabel, after barely a year of marriage to her OGPU man, welcomed him back after their anguished Christmas separation, only to learn that she was to be left alone again.

However, her husband was nothing if not resourceful. He had picked up some old professional threads in Germany while on his visit there to see his publishers, and he now decided to transfer his center of operations temporarily to Berlin. But who was he going to work for: and how were he and Isabel going to exist?

"Captain Denis" (or one of his colleagues) stepped willingly into the breach. At a hurried meeting—again arranged by the faithful Verhulst—on the eve of Agabekov's departure, a working arrangement was improvised which turned him, in effect, into an ad hoc agent on the British payroll. Agabekov could pursue two useful lines of intelligence in Germany. He had friends in the Reichsbanner organization, which was thought to be trying to subvert the French republic as well as combat Communism. Moreover, there were about a thousand Soviet agents active on German soil and, as he put it, it would be very odd if he could not manage to "turn" one or two of them.

His great concern was for his wife, even though he expected to be able to visit her from time to time. Could it be arranged for her to get a British visa, so that she could visit the United Kingdom in the difficult months ahead and stay with her aunts who were domiciled there? Even more important, could it also be arranged for her to receive some regular supply of money while he was absent? The upshot of this was that Agabekov agreed to regard the British as his "principals" in his new theater of operations. They, in return, would advance him £60 to get settled in in Germany and would also pay, at least for the immediate future, £20 a month to his wife in Brussels. "Captain Denis" and his colleagues seemed satisfied that this rather tenuous arrangement would keep him tied to them. One reason may well have been a rather touching revelation that Agabekov had let drop. His wife, he said, was always pleading with him to work for the British, even at this frightening espionage business of which she understood so little. Only that way, Isabel felt, could she ease her conscience and justify their marriage. If he remained a spy, but became a British spy, then that solid middle-class patriotism of hers would be satisfied. A strange glimpse into a strange and tortured private world: yet, given the context, it fits.

In the years that followed, Agabekov never quite seems to have made the grade, for reasons which are not recorded. Twelve months later, he made a proposal to go back to Kurdistan and recruit some of his old cronies there to work against the Russians, and asked for the substantial sum of £10,000 to finance the operation. Nothing more is heard of Kurdistan, and when money comes into the picture again, it is on a much more modest scale. In 1933, he received a sum of £15, apparently in remembrance of past services.

Whether it was the strain of this precarious and somewhat unsavory existence; whether it was because that physical and emotional blaze which had once consumed them had turned to ashes; or whether it was a combination of both, after three more years of this nerve-racking marriage, Isabel could stand no more. In April of 1936, she separated from Agabekov and returned to England. As though to emphasize that she intended the break to be a final one, she reverted to her maiden name. There were, fortunately, no children to complicate the metamorphosis. Later that year, we find an Isabel Streater enrolled for a six-month secretarial course at Pitman's College in London. Aged twenty-seven, she was trying to build a new life for herself alone, and on the prosaic foundations of 120 words of shorthand and 60 words of typing per minute.

Left to his own devices in Brussels (where, by now, he was reestablished), Agabekov went from bad to worse. With no worthwhile commissions to be got either from publishers or Intelligence services, he was desperate for money; and with the responsibility (and perhaps the restraining hand) of Isabel removed, he became even more reckless over methods. That was what the OGPU, very patiently, had been waiting for. In 1937, they set their second trap.

The setting was the Spanish Civil War, then raging at its peak, with Stalin heavily committed in political and military support to the Republican side. The dictator was, however, determined that his Spanish protégés should somehow be made to pay, as far as was possible, for the "fraternal aid" being sent to them. The Kremlin's most spectacular coup in this respect—the seizure of the entire gold stock held by the Spanish National Bank—we shall come to later, in dealing with a subsequent and more prominent defector. What Agabekov now found himself drawn into was the more modest but nonetheless lucrative operation of the looting of Spanish art treasures. The Russians had helped to organize a system whereby, whenever a church, monastery, or castle fell into Republican hands, it would be stripped of pictures or any other valuables likely to find eager purchasers on the international market. These were then smuggled across the border into France, and so up to dealers in Paris and other centers, including Brussels. An OGPU agent named Zelinsky was running the operation from the Belgian end and, early in 1937, it occurred either to him, or his superiors in Moscow, that profit might now be combined with long-delayed revenge.

Agabekov was accordingly approached by intermediaries with the proposal that he should join the Brussels syndicate, in return, of course, for a fat slice of the profits. The Russian caught a faint whiff of danger in the idea, for he refused point-blank to cross over into Spain, where, he knew, he would almost certainly be facing another abduction or assassination attempt at the hands of those OGPU agents who swarmed in the Republican areas. However, tempted by the pickings, he did agree to act as general supervisor of the traffic from the French side of the frontier. For this, his basic "salary" was fixed at 10,000 francs a month, and he was paid cash down for several months in advance.

As he was still officially banned from France, there was some delay while he was equipped with false papers for the journey; but at the beginning of July, he was known to have passed through Paris on his way to the Pyrenees. And that Paris contact was the last living trace of Georgi Sergevitch Agabekov-Arountunov.

According to one version of his death,[8] he was twice allowed to remain on the French side of the border and collect his share of the spoils for the relatively simple and safe work of dispatching the loot received up to Paris and other reception centers. But on the third run, with his suspicions either partly lulled or swamped by greed, he was tempted to go high into the mountains to take charge of the next consignment directly from Republican hands. Here, where the terrain is wild and the border often hard to define, he is said to have been set upon by a team of thugs specially assembled for the purpose, butchered, and his remains thrown down a ravine. By the time they were found, certain identification was not possible.

According to another version, Agabekov's suspicions were never even lulled. Indeed, suspecting an OGPU trap from the start, and calculating that they would, in fact, allow him at least one safe trip as an inducement, he planned to "rob the robbers" as well as foil the assassins. His scheme was to hang on to one really valuable picture from the first consignment, and simply disappear with it to start up a new life yet again in somewhere like South America. But if this had been his plan, his thoughts had been read by his former professional colleagues. Toward the end of August, this account goes, he was shot close to the frontier by OGPU agents. The murder was staged as though it were part of a wider execution program of deserters attempting to flee the Republican lines. Uncertainty also intervenes in this second version. The corpse, it is said, fell into the hands of the local police authorities, but, because of the false papers in the pockets, it could never be established beyond doubt whether the victim was Agabekov or not. Both accounts agree, however, that Agabekov did walk into a trap on the Spanish border—eyes wide open or half-open—and that the trap was sprung. One way or the other, the trail of his life peters out somewhere in the Pyrenees.

That of Isabel's, as far as it can be traced, pursues a humdrum, but probably, at heart, an equally desolate course. After five years back

---

[8]   Given by Agabekov's loyal Belgian protector, Baron Verhulst, to Boris Bajanov, who passed it to the author in July 1976.

in England, she regained the British nationality lost on her marriage to the Russian. Almost immediately afterward, in the middle of the war, she joined the Women's Auxiliary Air Force as an ordinary recruit, serving initially with H.Q. 24 Group at Hindlip Hall, Worcester. The war's end finds her with the rank of corporal and the job of confidential clerk to the senior Air Staff officer at H.Q. 28 Group in London.

For twelve months after the war, she worked as an indexer with the United Nations War Crimes Commission. Finally, in 1949, the wheel of her life turned full cycle and she became again what she had been in that fateful autumn twenty years before, a Foreign Office secretary. Throughout the fifties, she served as a shorthand typist, either in Whitehall or at British embassies abroad—Lisbon, Saigon, Mexico, Tokyo—reaching, on at least one occasion, the extra dignity of personal assistant to the ambassador. She was extremely competent in her work, but grew more withdrawn in her nature as the years passed.

Colleagues who served with her recall only one attachment which seemed to have brought a touch of late romance. It was to an American Army officer whom she met at one of her Far East postings. An easy extrovert, typical of his race, he treated this remote, fragile little woman "like a piece of Dresden china," and was clearly devoted to her. But nothing came of it, and when "Miss Streater's" assignment ended, they went their separate ways.

Her friends from the diplomatic world also remember one eccentricity of hers. Wherever she was posted, she traveled only with one small trunk, about three feet long and half as wide, which contained everything she possessed in the way of both clothes and personal belongings. She always stood out from the rest in refusing to accumulate any works of art, trinkets, or even souvenirs of the countries she worked in. When asked about it, she would shrug her shoulders and say simply that she did not want to be bothered with "a lot of clutter."

This was, perhaps, as significant as it was unusual. The only time she had stepped out of her plain English mold into an exotic foreign setting, everything had ended in disaster. But she never mentioned that episode in her early life; nor indeed did this former wife of a senior OGPU chief ever express any political opinion about the East-

West conflict that was raging over every embassy in which she served. It was as though she had sealed herself off inside from the world and its problems.

The gray-haired widow of Georges Agabekov died in New York City on November 29, 1971, still in harness at sixty-two as an employee of the British Mission to the United Nations.

Chapter Eight

WALTER KRIVITSKY: A PURGER PURGED

Two distinct clusters merge when a time chart of the early defectors from Stalin's Russia is drawn up. The first spans the years 1928–30 and covers, as far as western Europe is concerned, about half a dozen cases, the three most important and interesting of which have just been described. If these defections have any common political factor, it is that final victory Stalin had won over Trotsky and the sense of disillusionment and danger which this battle of the titans left in its wake. Yet, as we have seen, the personal circumstances of these pioneer cases varied widely from individual to individual, as did their professional careers.

The second cluster comes nearly a decade later and also covers a period of roughly two years, running from 1936 to 1938, when Yagoda had been supplanted by Yezhov as Stalin's police chief. Here, the common background is, by comparison, overwhelmingly strong:

Stalin's great purge of all his rivals, real, potential, or imaginary—
purges which struck at the old Bolshevik guard in the party, the
army, and even the secret police itself. The common professional links
were also much stronger in this second batch. The most important
among them were all members of the NKVD, as the old OGPU now
called itself, and they were fleeing from an organization at war with
itself. On the personal plane, there was, however, one contrast. All
except one ran to save their lives. The exception was an agent stationed in western Europe called Ignaz Reiss, the man who started
everything in motion. When he ran, on July 17, 1937, it was to save
what was left of his self-respect.

The onslaught against the old "Chekists" inside Russia had started
in earnest that spring, directed by Yezhov and the three hundred
handpicked officials he had brought in with him. The real purpose
of the changeover and of the wave of persecutions which duly followed, was not, as proclaimed, to track down genuine conspirators,
but simply to silence everyone within reach who had a veteran's
inside knowledge of how Stalin had maneuvered himself into supreme
power.

To cut down the risk of purge candidates trying to escape abroad,
Yezhov had placed the department which issued passports to NKVD
officials under the direct control of his own secretariat. To reduce
their chances of seeking safety literally by flight, he had replaced the
officers commanding all the special aviation squadrons of the secret
police. But none of those precautions was of any use for those old
guard Chekists who were already stationed abroad. They could only
be blackmailed or cajoled into returning home to Yezhov's net; and
this, the trickiest part of the great purge, was not started until the
summer of 1937.

The operation was launched with elaborate cunning. The first to be
recalled were those with families left behind in the Soviet Union,
wives and children who would be hostages in Yezhov's tender care
in case of a refusal by the husband. When the official did return, he
was usually duped into helping deceive subsequent victims. He
would be given a friendly reception at headquarters, and then sent,
with his family, to holiday in one of the party's best Crimean resorts.
After he had written a few reassuring letters to his colleagues still

abroad, explaining how nonsensical all these rumors of persecution inside the service were, his usefulness was almost over. His last unwitting contribution to the conspiracy was to be seen off by friends when leaving Moscow's railway station—duly equipped with his newly forged passport—to all appearances happily bound for his next "foreign assignment." The assignment, in reality, was with his jailers; and it was no nearer the border than a stop or two outside the capital.

One of Ignaz Reiss's own immediate superiors, the NKVD "resident" in Paris, Nikolai Smirnov,[1] had been one of more than thirty officials to fall victim to this trick. He had been recalled to Moscow that same summer to "make a report," and he had nervously followed the summons, leaving his equally nervous wife behind. All seemed well, however, when a week later she received a cheerful letter in what was undoubtedly her husband's handwriting. In it, he told her to pack up immediately and rejoin him in Moscow, as they had been given a new posting with the NKVD's large underground organization in China. Off she went—only to disappear into the same oblivion which by now had swallowed up her husband.

As self-preservation was all that his other colleagues—duped or not—were thinking of at this time, it may be wondered what reasons there are to suppose that Ignaz Reiss had any other thoughts in his mind during these dreadful months. However, there is one of his former subordinates still alive (and very lucid) in America today who can testify that Reiss was indeed driven by more altruistic motives.[2] Hedda Massing was, in the thirties, a vivacious and attractive Viennese woman who, like her German-born American husband Paul, had joined the Communist camp basically because it was the strongest of the underground antifascist camps and, later and more importantly, of the anti-Hitler ones as well. She had already worked on a number of assignments in Europe for Reiss (to whom she was evidently devoted, both as a chief and as a person) when, in 1934, President Roosevelt opened diplomatic relations with the Soviet Union. This was the chance, which the Kremlin had long awaited and prepared for, to build up a full-scale, legally camouflaged espionage network

---

[1]   An alias, of course. His real name was Glinsky.
[2]   What follows are extracts from a long talk the author had with Mrs. Massing in New York on December 16, 1976.

in the United States, operating quite independently from its "illegal" organization. Hedda Massing was sent ahead to America that same year with her husband to lay the administrative foundations for this new network—courier systems, liaison officers, "safe" houses, financial channels, and the like. She was thus the advance scout for the whole system. When everything had been prepared, it was intended that Reiss himself should follow her across the Atlantic and take charge of the whole operation as NKVD resident. The fact that he was being groomed for such a key post showed the faith that the party leadership had in him. Long before he was due to take up that post, however, Reiss was losing faith in that party leadership, and in everything it represented.

Hedda Massing has described him as a deeply cultured, sensitive, and humane person (which is about the closest rendering of her German phrase, "ein echter Schöngeist"); and she was not surprised to see such an individual grow progressively more disillusioned as the sordid, brutal farce of the political show trials unfolded in Moscow. Even so, she was hardly prepared for the envelope which arrived at their New York apartment toward the end of July 1937, stamped earlier that month with a Paris postmark. In it was a letter from her chief, enclosing a copy of a message he had just dispatched to the general secretary of the party's Central Committee in Moscow, that is, to Stalin. The message to Moscow expressed what thousands of old Bolsheviks—or idealists of any brand—were thinking and feeling but which, until now, not one of them had dared express in public to the dictator himself. Reiss began by saying that he reproached himself for not having written these words twelve months before, when sixteen veteran leaders of the party had been "murdered in the cellars of the Lubianka at the command of the Father of Nations." He went on:

> I kept silent then. I raised no voice of protest at the subsequent murders and, for this, I bear a heavy responsibility. My guilt is great, but I shall try to atone for it—quickly, to ease my conscience.
>
> Up to now, I have followed you. From now on, not a step further. Our ways part. He who keeps silent at this hour becomes an accomplice of Stalin, and a traitor to the cause of the working class, and of Socialism.

From the age of twenty, I have battled for Socialism. Now, on the eve of my fifth decade of life, I do not want to exist by the grace of Yezhov. . . .

No. I cannot continue any longer. I am retaining my freedom—back to Lenin, to his teachings and his cause.

The language was stinging enough. But, as though to rub salt into the wound it would inflict, Reiss, in a postscript, said he was enclosing the Order of the Red Banner awarded him in 1928.[3] "To wear it in the company who have hanged the best representatives of the Russian workers is beneath my dignity."

The personal letter made the same points, but addressed in very different language to two dear friends, who, the writer was convinced, would agree with him. "I know," he wrote, "that you would both join me if you could." Though Reiss was never to learn it himself, he was right. Forty years later, Hedda Massing still recalls with emotion the instant effect the letter had upon both her and her husband:

An overwhelming sense of joy and relief swept over us after we had finished reading it in the hall. Tears came into our eyes and, spontaneously, we embraced each other. We suddenly felt that a yoke had been lifted from our shoulders and that we, too, were free at last.[4]

Mrs. Massing also recalls the tone of that last message from her chief. "Complete disgust and moral revulsion were what it practically trembled with. There was no question of Ignaz acting to save his life. Indeed, as he made clear, he knew full well that he was probably signing his own death warrant."

That premonition of Reiss's was fulfilled all too soon. On the night of September 4, 1937, his dead body was found across the border in Switzerland, lying in the road which runs from Lausanne to Cham-

---

[3] There is something of a puzzle about this claim. Normally, officials like Reiss were strictly forbidden to take their Soviet decorations abroad with them.

[4] Hedda Massing did free herself ultimately from the Soviet grip; but it was no swift or easy matter. As the closest colleague of the defector, she was summoned to Moscow for questioning, and, relying on the protection of her American passport, she decided to risk it and go. As an added precaution, Hedda got in contact with a large group of foreign journalists who happened to be staying at the same Moscow hotel. After weeks of interrogation, she was allowed to return to the United States. From then on, she gradually broke with the NKVD, though she did not finally denounce them until just after the war.

blandes. There were five bullets in his head and seven more in his body. A strand of gray hair still clutched in his fingers seemed the only clue; but gradually the Swiss police managed to reconstruct the crime by tracing and interrogating the Swiss woman, Renate Steiner, who had hired the American car used by the murderers. It emerged that Reiss's hideout had been betrayed to Moscow by one of their agents in Italy, a German woman named Gertrude Schildbach. She was not only an old friend of Reiss and his family; he was aware that she, too, had recently been wavering in her loyalty to the Stalinist regime. When, therefore, she took the decision to go on serving that regime, she proved the perfect decoy. It was on an after-dinner stroll after eating with her at a restaurant near Chamblandes that, at a pre-arranged point, a murder squad of two men from Yezhov's Paris staff bundled him into the hired car and emptied the best part of a sub-machine gun magazine into him. The strand of gray hair was thought to be Gertrude's; she must have been helping to hold him down.

The assassins escaped after what, from Moscow's point of view, had been a copy-book revenge killing, designed to stop the rot in the NKVD from spreading any further. Yet because that killing had not been accomplished until some seven weeks after Reiss had gone underground, the rot had already done harm enough, at least among the members of foreign missions, for whom asylum was tantalizingly close.

It was surely no coincidence, for example, that only a day or two after the defection of Reiss in Paris (an event that would have been signaled instantly to all NKVD stations abroad), Alexander Barmine, a senior employee of the GRU who was masquerading as a diplomat at the Soviet Embassy in Athens, finally decided that the moment had come for him, too, to make a run for it.[5]

By far the most important of the other NKVD defections which were either influenced or triggered off by the example of Ignaz Reiss

---

[5]   Indeed, Barmine was chargé d'affaires at the time. His only published work, mis-leadingly entitled *Memoirs of a Soviet Diplomat,* contains relatively little of interest. His main value to the West was in government service, as an American citizen, in the United States, which he reached in 1939 after a stay in France. He served with the American Army and OSS during the war, for example, and later headed the Russian section of the Voice of America network. He is still (January 1977) alive, but uncommunicative and with a failing memory.

was that of his old friend and close collaborator, Walter Krivitsky. Though not the highest in rank nor in status of these prewar defectors, this man, who had been coordinating spy operations in half a dozen Western countries, was to deal a heavier series of blows than any of them to the Soviet espionage system, blows that did most damage after the war with Hitler had broken out.

Though Krivitsky later claimed that it was a sudden upsurge of moral repugnance which had prompted him to defect, there is in fact little doubt that the motive was rather a sudden upsurge of panic.[6] There is even less doubt that it was Ignaz Reiss's dramatic exit which had left him no choice in the matter. An additional complication (and fascination) of the affair was the particularly strong personal bond which existed between the two men and the question whether, in those tense July days in Paris, Krivitsky had done all he could to stand by it.

The two men were both Jews from southern Poland, and it had been Krivitsky, the older man, who had sponsored Reiss, first as a Communist party member and, later as a recruit to the secret police. They had kept in close touch ever since, often working together in underground assignments. It was in this joint capacity that they met up again in The Hague on May 29, 1937. Krivitsky's nerves were already in tatters, which was hardly surprising. He had just arrived from Moscow, via Sweden, and, as we have seen, Moscow at this time was a capital which precious few veteran Chekists were allowed to leave. Krivitsky himself had abandoned all hope of returning to his post as "illegal" NKVD resident in Holland when what had been intended by him as a brief liaison visit was dragged out by his evasive superiors at headquarters into a stay of more than two months. But finally he was given his forged passport back and put on the train north. There was a last-minute scare at Bielo-Ostrov on the Finnish border, where the local Soviet frontier guards commander had come running up to his compartment, brandishing a telegram. But it turned out to be an order from Moscow to help him on his way, not arrest him, and Krivitsky thankfully rejoined his wife and family in Holland on May 27. He now became again Dr. Martin Lessner, an Austrian art

---

[6]   See his *I Was Stalin's Agent,* p. 279.

dealer, of Celebes-Straat 32 in The Hague, which was his cover for the Dutch operation.[7]

Two days later, his old friend Reiss had called on him to discuss the terrible times they were passing through, and to get the latest first-hand information on the turmoil in Moscow. Krivitsky wrote later that Reiss, whom he described as "a thorough idealist," was so deeply shocked by the purge and treason trials which were rocking the Soviet Union that he had already decided to break with a system which "appeared to him more and more obviously an evolution towards fascism."[8] Up to this point, however, on his own admission, Krivitsky was still "determined to continue to serve the Soviet Government"—despite the arguments of his old comrade, and despite what he had just seen and experienced for himself in Moscow.

The next meeting between the two men was in Paris at 7:00 p.m. in the evening of that fateful July 17. It had only been a hurried conversation in the Café Weber, and Reiss was very anxious to arrange for a longer talk the following day. But that was to be their last meeting. The promised telephone call from Reiss to fix a safe rendezvous never came. Krivitsky received a very different summons instead. It came from the deputy chief of the NKVD's Foreign Division, a man whose name, Shpiegelglas ("mirror glass"), was just as droll as his reputation was sinister; and the order was to come to meet him immediately in the exhibition grounds of the World's Fair which Paris was then staging. Without ado, a very agitated Comrade Shpiegelglas (a Jew and a veteran Bolshevik himself, and therefore terrified for his own skin) produced out of his pocket two documents which Reiss had handed in that morning at the office of the Soviet Trade Delegation in Paris, for immediate dispatch to Moscow. Instead of being forwarded, however, they had been opened by a woman NKVD agent attached to the mission. They turned out to be Reiss's formal letter of resignation and the original of that blistering message to Stalin. Shpiegelglas was touring NKVD missions throughout western Europe at the time to sniff out

---

[7] The passport in this name had been handed back to him at the Soviet Embassy in Stockholm, where he had deposited it on the home journey. Forged papers under another alias—Edward Miller, an Austrian engineer—were always used for the Moscow–Stockholm trip.

[8] See *I was Stalin's Agent*, p. 275.

more candidates for Yezhov's purge; unluckily for him, he had landed in Paris just when this particular candidate had both revealed himself and escaped.

In his book, Krivitsky claims that it was only now, when hints were dropped that he should prove his "loyalty" by helping to recapture or eliminate the renegade, that he realized, in a flash that his "life-long service to the Soviet Government was ended."[9] Indeed, he lays such stress on his moment of truth that he has the relevant sentence of his memoirs printed in italics. Somehow, the claim seems weakened by all this special emphasis. Repugnance Krivitsky certainly would have felt at the thought of delivering up his old friend into Yezhov's hands, and he did what he could to alert Reiss without exposing himself. After midnight, he telephoned the secret hideout whose number Reiss had given him, only to drop the receiver the moment the runaway answered. This procedure was repeated two or three times in the early hours of the morning of July 18, in an attempt to warn Reiss that his defection was already known about and that he was in imminent peril.

Whether Reiss received other danger signals we do not know; at all events, by breakfast time he had vanished, heading for his Swiss haven. For a professional, his last act in Paris was appallingly indiscreet. He sent a letter to Krivitsky at the Hotel Napoleon (an establishment regularly used by the NKVD and therefore subject to their own internal surveillance) bidding him a fond farewell and explaining again why he had felt compelled to act as he had done. One can only account for such a blunder by the numbing influence of severe emotional stress. The same explanation could apply to the equally clumsy reaction of Krivitsky, who neither destroyed the letter nor reported it. Sure enough, the porter in the hotel had done his police duty, and, at 3:00 a.m. the following morning Krivitsky was aroused from his slumbers and confronted by an indignantly hostile Comrade Shpiegelglas demanding to know all about that letter from Reiss.

If Krivitsky's position two days before in the World's Fair grounds had been desperate, it was now, in the context of what was happening in Russia in the summer of 1937, as good as hopeless. From being

---

9   Ibid., p. 279.

a senior official still sufficiently trusted to be allowed to return to his foreign post, Walter Krivitsky had become, within less than forty-eight hours, the lifelong patron, and now, it seemed, the protector and confidant, of a traitor. Whatever high moral tone Krivitsky was to strike in print, it seems clear that, from July 19 onward, his mind turned to defection because he knew full well that he was under a suspended sentence of death himself. Indeed, he admitted as much later on.

What he badly needed at that moment, however, was time to plan his escape. That meant postponing the inevitable summons to Moscow for as long as possible and allaying the suspicions of Comrade Shpiegelglas as best he could. Though there is no evidence to support the theory (advanced by Hedda Massing, for example) that, during the next few weeks in Paris Krivitsky actually helped to "finger" Reiss for the Swiss murder squad, he was clearly obliged to discuss all manner of theoretical assassination schemes as "proof" of his "loyalty." One scheme reportedly advanced by Shpiegelglas, for example, was that, when they had located Reiss, Krivitsky would call on him, as an old friend, and then simply bash his head in with a flatiron which had somehow been concealed from the victim. (When one recalls that Trotsky was to be hacked to death three years later with an icepick, also hidden by the visitor on his person, the plan appears less outlandish than at first sight.)

All this while, Krivitsky was quietly preparing his own flight. He called his wife and child back from their holiday in the French countryside and they established themselves, under his alias of Lessner, at a pension in the fashionable Paris district of Passy. He still functioned, however, as an NKVD officer (though under increasingly close shadowing by his colleagues); indeed, toward the end of August, he even went obediently through the motions of returning to Moscow—a summons which, fortunately, was canceled at the last minute. It was when he opened the *Paris Matin* on the morning of September 5 and read the dispatch from Lausanne reporting the gruesome murder of "a Czechoslovak citizen, Hans Eberhardt," that he realized the hourglass was almost empty. Hans Eberhardt, as he well knew, was the bogus passport name under which Ignaz Reiss traveled. With the traitor disposed of, the last usefulness, as a possible

NKVD decoy, of his old friend and colleague in Paris had disappeared.

Krivitsky and his wife Tanya (a dedicated Bolshevik revolutionary from Leningrad whom he had married in Moscow in 1926) now talked of nothing but escape; yet they still needed a week or two more to find a safe hideout and also, if possible, to procure some legal identity papers. He turned for help to Paul Wohl, a Russian Jew by origin, an American by citizenship, and a writer by profession who lived in Paris with his mother. Wohl was an old friend and, it seems, a close contact of Krivitsky's, and he now stepped into the breach. He left promptly for the south of France and rented a small villa for the intending runaways at Hyères, near Toulon. To throw Moscow off the scent, Krivitsky had meanwhile proposed himself that he should return home for consultation. This gained him a little more time, especially as he had also suggested traveling on a Soviet vessel, a matter which needed some arranging. Eventually, his headquarters picked one for him, the *Zhdanov*, due to sail from Le Havre on October 6.

He duly made all arrangements for his passage at the Soviet Embassy and, when the day arrived, deposited some advance baggage for the ship at the appropriate railway station. But when the hour for departure arrived, he and his wife, traveling in a car hired by the indispensable Paul Wohl, left the Gare d'Austerlitz severely alone and headed southward instead, bound for Hyères. As soon as they reached the outskirts of the capital, Krivitsky stopped at a café, rang his office number, and announced to his secretary, Madeleine, that the NKVD now had another defector on their hands, her own boss. No reply came back along the line. He was told later that the poor creature had fainted clean away at the telephone.

Chapter Nine

THE MAN WHO TALKED TOO MUCH

It was when the Krivitskys arrived in New York City in December 1938 that the significant stage of their exile began. This choice of America,[1] which Walter Krivitsky had never even seen before, as a place of asylum, was to establish a completely new trend in prewar Soviet defection. Hitherto, the runaways had nearly all made for Paris, center of the largest and most variegated Russian community in exile. From now on, they were to head across the Atlantic, using the French capital only as a transit stage in their journey.

One reason for this change of pattern was, of course, the steadily worsening political situation in Europe as a whole. By the end of 1937, the shadow of Adolf Hitler loomed far larger over the continent

---

[1] Visas had been arranged for them at the American Embassy in Paris by that same friend, Paul Wohl, who had helped them in their escape to Hyères.

than the more remote presence of Stalin; and, for Jewish fugitives like Krivitsky, the purely racial menace of Nazism was much more blatant. Compared with an enfeebled and already demoralized French republic it was now the United States which spelled stability, security, and tolerance. In Krivitsky's case, there was another and more compelling factor. His fourteen months' stay in France had coincided with the high-water mark of NKVD violence against Soviet émigrés in the country. He himself survived at least two traps set by Yezhov's killer squads—one at midnight, on the platform of Marseilles railway station, and another, in broad daylight, at a café off the Place de la Bastille in Paris.

Indeed, after his bold decision to return to the French capital in December of 1937, he had only survived unscathed thanks to a close police guard which the Socialist minister of interior, M. Dormoy, had provided for him and his family.[2] They had deliberately chosen a hotel (the Hotel des Académies in the Rue Saint Pères) which was next door to the local police station, and from then on a guard of three gendarmes, working in eight-hour shifts, occupied the adjoining room, while the inspector kept his eye on the hotel entrance.

After this special surveillance, the casual atmosphere of New York, with no police supervision of any sort, must have come as a violent contrast. At first, the change in the local authorities' attitude seemed not only agreeable, but understandable. During the first month or two, while the family were finding their feet in this concrete forest of a city, with Krivitsky busy putting out feelers to magazines and publishers, the only worry on the horizon was their rapidly dwindling savings. Yezhov and his killer squads might have been creatures from another planet, let alone another continent. Then, at lunchtime on March 7, 1939, that other planet came right into Times Square.

Krivitsky was eating that day at a restaurant just off the Square with David Schub, editor of a New York Jewish daily and the author of a biography of Lenin. They had barely started their meal when three

---

[2] Krivitsky was fortunate in that Theodore Dan, the leader of the Russian Socialist émigrés in Paris, who befriended him, had close links with the Socialist government of Leon Blum. It was through this connection that Krivitsky was also issued with a proper carte d'identité, on which he traveled to America.

men came in and sat down at the next table. Two of them were strangers to Krivitsky; but the sight of the third put him off all thoughts of lunch. He had recognized Sergei Basoff, a veteran agent of his own Soviet military intelligence, who had been sent to America some years before as a long-term "deep cover" agent, and who had succeeded in acquiring the deepest cover of all—American citizenship. Either the instant recognition was mutual, or, more likely, Basoff had been trailing his quarry from the start. He immediately followed suit when Krivitsky, pulling Schub with him, got up to leave, and a strange conversation ensued at the cashier's desk. Krivitsky asked his former colleague point-blank whether he had come to shoot him down. Basoff assured him that, on the contrary, his presence was quite "unofficial" and that all he wanted was "a friendly chat." There was little comfort in those words. The assassination of Ignaz Reiss had begun with the friendliest of chats.

That, however, had been in a lonely forest in Switzerland. Here, they were in a bustling American city center, and less than a hundred yards from the offices of the *New York Times*. Krivitsky and Schub headed straight for it and, once inside the building, made for the third-floor newsroom. They were still accompanied by Basoff, who was talking amiably away about old acquaintances. Though there was little danger of having a gun pulled on him in these surroundings, Krivitsky realized that his life might well depend on shaking his former colleague off before Basoff got the chance of following him home to his apartment. A miniature melodrama went on for the next six hours in the waiting room of the unsuspecting city editor. Schub telephoned around New York for reinforcements, and these, in the shape of friendly journalists and fellow Russian émigrés, began arriving in relays during the afternoon. Basoff departed when the first of them turned up, but only to rejoin the two companions he had left on the street outside. However, by waiting until early evening, when Times Square was packed with a throng of theatergoers, Krivitsky managed to make a swift getaway in a friend's car and shake off his unwelcome company.

This incident transformed Krivitsky's whole attitude toward his American asylum. The lack of police protection in New York had not mattered so long as there appeared to be no danger from which to protect him. But now, the contrast with the Hotel des Académies and its twenty-four-hour guard of gendarmes was disturbing and ever-present. Nor was it only police protection that was missing. Krivitsky was also discovering, to his dismay, that it was seemingly impossible even to make contact with an American intelligence organization of any sort. This almost total lack of official American interest in his case might have been excused as a temporary oversight when he had first entered the country—quietly and unobtrusively, and traveling on normal French identity documents—in December 1938. But it becomes, in retrospect, more baffling from April 1939 onward, when Krivitsky started bursting into print with a series of widely discussed revelations about Stalin's sinister aims and unsavory methods. These began with a series of articles in the *Saturday Evening Post*, and the same material was then expanded into his book of memoirs, which was published later that year. Both the articles and the memoirs proclaimed, loudly enough, that here in New York was a former general of Soviet military intelligence, and a man who, until recently, had been in charge of the Kremlin's espionage network throughout western Europe.[3] Though the publicity was, in one important detail at least, inaccurate, it was clear, to anyone interested, that a unique source of information about the Communist world was now living in their midst, and more than willing to talk. The extraordinary thing was that, in the America of 1939, there was only one official who did seem to be interested; and he sat, not in the FBI, but in the State Department.

Raymond Murphy was a classic case of the prophet being both before his time and without honor in his own country. As the memoirs of his distinguished colleague Charles ("Chip") Bohlen were to show many years later, there were hardly any diplomats in the Washington of the mid-thirties who were prepared to concentrate their minds, and their future careers, on the Soviet Union, as viewed in its ordinary political context as a world power. There was only

[3] Walter Krivitsky was never a general in the GRU, as Soviet Military Intelligence was styled. He had for many years held lower ranks in that service, but had been transferred from it in 1933 or 1934 to the NKVD. It was as NKVD "resident" in Holland, with liaison responsibilities for other western European countries, that he had defected in 1937. He himself is known to have been embarrassed by being labeled with the false title of general, which seems to have been simply part of the publicity buildup in America for his writings.

Murphy who devoted the same energies to studying it in its far more crucial context as an implacable subversive threat to the entire Western ideology and way of life. And, for his pains, Raymond Murphy, and the small anti-Soviet research section he headed at this time, are said to have been considered almost pariahs by all the conventional branches of the department. There seems to have been an Ivy League consensus of opinion among the earnest, high-minded, and somewhat naive American diplomats of the day that there was something ungentlemanly as well as unprofessional about this obsession of their colleague with his arcane and sordid subject.

Murphy did not exactly help things along. He was a loner, pursuing a lone cause. Openly contemptuous of the insensitivity which surrounded him, he tended to keep his files and his visitors very much to himself. Though, perhaps significantly, most of those files were dispersed and destroyed beyond recall when Murphy retired soon after the war, we do know that Walter Krivitsky was among those visitors during 1939 and 1940. The two men had three or four sessions together, and it can be assumed that the Russian elaborated on the themes he was setting out in his memoirs.[4]

Central to all Krivitsky's revelations, both public and private, was the thesis that, whereas in the twenties Stalin had done everything in his power to disrupt and even destroy the German republic (a campaign that Krivitsky himself had taken part in by trying, for example, to form underground cadres for a German Red Army), Hitler's seizure of power in the early thirties had transformed the Kremlin's attitude completely. Krivitsky even gave the critical date for this transformation—June 30, 1934, when Hitler staged the first purge of his bloody reign by eliminating Captain Roehm and his SA followers. That same night, Krivitsky disclosed, Stalin had summoned a special session of the Politburo to evaluate the upheaval in Berlin. It was not, of course, surprising that Stalin should secretly admire his neighboring dictator for eliminating rival centers of power, even if this did mean the

---

[4] According to his lawyer, Louis Waldman, Krivitsky also had two meetings with the head of the Passport Division in the State Department, a formidable woman called Ruth Shipley. As all he was asked to do, however, was indicate any "undesirables" he could recognize among the photograph files—without any expert discussion or interrogation—he soon backed away.

murdering of old comrades. The Soviet leader, after all, was about to apply the same ruthlessness and brutality to the same problem inside his own country himself. But the Kremlin's directive, which, according to Krivitsky, was issued that night, came nonetheless as something of a shock to the inner ranks of the party faithful. Stalin had concluded that, by this resolute purge, Hitler had demonstrated that he was there to stay and that he was, moreover, a leader to be reckoned with. From now on, the Soviet Union, while concealing its true objectives in a welter of antifascist propaganda, must spare no effort in secret to reach the supreme goal of an understanding with Nazi Germany.[5] The two great dictators should be clasping each other's hands, not reaching for each other's throats.

Though the American public may have found this hard to swallow just from Krivitsky's magazine articles (and perhaps even Raymond Murphy was dubious at their private talks), the *Post* series had only been finished for three months when, on August 23, 1939, confirmation on a spectacular scale arrived. On that day, the foreign ministers of the Soviet Union and the German Reich, Molotov and Ribbentrop, announced to a flabbergasted world the conclusion of the Nazi-Soviet friendship pact. This event transformed Walter Krivitsky's standing as an analyst of international affairs; from being just another anti-Communist polemicist he had become something of a political soothsayer. It also doubled his potential value in the Intelligence field.

During the mid-thirties, the FBI had been intrusted by President Roosevelt with the additional task of countering foreign subversion in the United States. As, however, it was Hitlerite Germany which was then making all the running on the world scene, the bureau had concentrated on the internal Nazi threat to the United States, as posed, in particular, by Fritz Kuhn and his so-called Deutscher Bund. Until August of 1939, the FBI thus had an argument, though not a valid excuse, for ignoring what was, in fact, the older and far graver problem of Soviet subversion, a problem that went right back to the

---

[5]   Krivitsky pushed this argument so far (and probably too far) as to claim that even Stalin's intervention against the Axis powers in the Spanish Civil War was basically just another attempt to secure bargaining leverage in Berlin.

underground activities of bodies like Amtorg soon after World War I. But the Russo-German pact had invalidated even this explanation for the bureau's masterly inactivity on the Soviet front.

Yet neither this diplomatic bombshell of August 23 nor the military earthquake of the war in Europe which followed twelve days later seems to have shaken America's intelligence apparatus into moving any closer to this great professional prize in their midst. At any rate, no record of any FBI contact with Krivitsky—official or unofficial—has survived; and if Raymond Murphy ever passed any names or cases mentioned to him by the Russian along to the bureau, no evidence of any FBI response or action could be traced when, a few years later, Washington started constructing the most massive Intelligence organization in the Western world. As they then discovered, it was an edifice built virtually on no base.

It is those almost nonexistent prewar foundations of intelligence work which explain what, at first sight, seems a case of crass negligence in the Krivitsky affair. Throughout the thirties, the United States government simply did not have the professional infrastructure, let alone the political impetus, for dealing with the steadily growing problem of Soviet subversion. Hedda Massing is an authoritative living witness to this phenomenon. When she finally broke with Moscow and with Communism in 1949, and contacted the FBI, she said to the bureau, apologetically:

"How much better it would have been for both of us if I had come to you straightaway in 1937, instead of obeying that summons to Moscow."

An FBI official, equally apologetically, replied:

"Mrs. Massing, back in 1937, we just wouldn't have known what to do with you. In those days, we could not have produced a single agent capable of a proper interrogation."[6]

Fortunately for the Western world, however, the Second World War did bring out some of Krivitsky's intelligence secrets, though only just in time, and to two very different audiences. The first of these audiences was the part-public, part-private one of the House Committee on Un-American Activities, which summoned Krivitsky

---

6 Conversation with the author, November 16, 1976.

to give evidence on October 11, 1939. Unlike the FBI, this body had a long and continuous pedigree in the investigation of foreign subversion, starting with the Hamilton Fish Committee of 1919 and then moving through the era of Samuel Dickstein to its wartime chairman, Martin Dies. Yet, as the *procès-verbale* of the Krivitsky testimony shows all too clearly, its members possessed barely a kindergarten knowledge or understanding of Soviet affairs.[7]

Krivitsky had to spend some time explaining to them, for example, that the Politburo was the most powerful organ of the Soviet state; that it was Stalin who really ruled Russia through that body and in its name; that the Communist party of Russia "controls the Russian government" (a point the chairman had to have repeated twice so that he could grasp it); that, through the Comintern, Stalin controlled Communist parties throughout the world, including the American Communist party, led at that time by Earl Browder. It was only during the closing minutes of his day-long testimony that, after a fairly general discussion of Soviet Intelligence methods, it occurred to the committee to ask their witness whether he knew of any Soviet agents actually working in the United States. Krivitsky promptly named the chiefs of the GRU network in America from 1924 onward, including its current head, Boris Bykov. What seems extraordinary is that, according to the record, the committee's questioning was wound up there, without any further probing, or any motion to renew the proceedings in closed session. And what is equally strange is that—as with the Raymond Murphy interrogations at the State Department—there is no evidence that any material from the House hearing testimony of Krivitsky was ever passed for information or action to the FBI or anyone else in authority. Six weeks after the outbreak of a major war, these hearings ambled on in a leisurely limbo of their own. Krivitsky might have been a history student appearing for his oral examination before a board of faculty professors, and not a key witness in a world crisis that was eventually to engulf America herself.

Yet Krivitsky's struggle to get someone, somewhere, in the Western world to listen to, understand, and act upon what he had to tell

---

[7] See U.S. House of Representatives records (Washington, D.C.), vol. 9, no. 5719/ 5742.

was not lost. Indeed, it was about to be crowned with spectacular success on the other side of the Atlantic. If his defection—and with it the message of his whole life—was to have any meaning, that significance stemmed from what now took place in wartime London. Seven days after the House wound up the inconsequential interrogation in Washington, one of the most dangerous of all Soviet spies so far uncovered in Britain was tried at the Old Bailey by Mr. Justice Hilbery and put away for ten years' penal servitude. Though Krivitsky never knew it at the time, the original tipoff for that case had come from a name he himself had mentioned in a private conversation in New York a few weeks previously.

The trial of Captain John Herbert King had been conducted in complete secrecy, and it remained a secret for the next seventeen years. Only on June 7, 1956, after the spy's name had been mentioned, as a fragment of wartime history, to a later congressional investigative committee in Washington, was an official admission smoked out of London. This stated baldly that King, "who had worked in the Communications Department of the Foreign Office," had indeed been sentenced on October 18, 1939, under the recently enacted Emergency Powers Regulations, for "passing information to the Russian Government." The statement added that King had been arrested "after information had been supplied to the Foreign Office by the United States." That was all.

How this information came to be supplied in the first place is an episode typical of the hit-or-miss story of Krivitsky's exile. It was passed, not to an American official at all (not even to Raymond Murphy), but to a fellow Jewish Russian émigré, Isaac Don Levine. Levine was already a well-known writer on Soviet affairs and a highly enterprising journalist with several resounding coups to his credit.[8] His memoirs, *Eye Witness to History*, which were only published in 1973, have a self-defeating tendency to suggest that he either saw, or was right about, almost every important happening of the century. But there can be no doubt that, in September of 1939, Levine turned out to be very much the right man in the right

---

8   On a visit to the Soviet Union shortly after the revolution, for example, he had been the first reporter to uncover in the tsarist archives the notorious "Willy-Nicky" correspondence between the former German and Russian rulers.

place, and that, by his actions, he put the British government greatly in his debt.

Levine had been functioning for many months as one of Krivitsky's three principal literary advisers,[9] and the two men had often discussed the worsening world situation during that tense summer. During one of these talks, Krivitsky, who was normally extremely cagey on such matters, suddenly unburdened himself of a disclosure he was evidently dying to get off his chest to somebody. He knew, he said, of at least two Soviet agents who were operating from within the innermost sanctums of the British government. One of them he described as "a code clerk in the Cabinet" and he remembered only the man's surname, which was King. The other London spy, whom he did not name, was working in what Krivitsky called the "Imperial Defence Council." Levine was given this information in the strictest confidence and, at the time, there seemed no desperately pressing reason why he should, in fact, inform anyone else. But a very different situation developed over the next few weeks, when Hitler first concluded his pact with Stalin and then plunged Europe into battle. It struck Levine forcibly that, now, those spies in London were not only operating out of a capital at war but were also serving a regime allied with Nazi Germany. The thought, in his own words, "gave me no peace" and he determined, as a private citizen, to do something about it.

Sensibly, and characteristically, he went straight to the top. Through Adolf A. Berle, an assistant secretary at the State Department, whom he had contacted before on security matters affecting his own department,[10] Levine arranged to call on the British ambassador in Washington, Lord Lothian. If Krivitsky himself was invited by Levine to accompany him and tell his own story, or even consulted about the step, Levine does not mention it. At first, it seemed as though this personal breach of confidence, if such it had been, was not likely to be justified by events. Lord Lothian listened attentively to what his visitor had to say but appeared plainly skeptical of the idea that the Kremlin had managed to plant two spies in the very heart

---

9 The others were two former Communist sympathizers, Nelson Frank and Ed Morrow (not to be confused with the famous broadcaster Edward R. Murrow).
10 The beginnings of the famous Whittaker Chambers espionage case.

of Whitehall and what was more, in two crucial centers of policy-making, Levine left the Embassy building on Massachusetts Avenue feeling relieved but not exactly hopeful.

Only a fortnight later, however, he was rung up in New York by Lord Lothian's secretary, and asked if he could come to Washington and see the ambassador again as soon as possible. Never a man to tarry over a summons like that, Levine promptly set off. When he arrived, a somewhat chastened British envoy told him that word had just been received from London "confirming the unbelievable," as Levine later put it. A cipher clerk called King had indeed been identified as a Soviet agent. Would Krivitsky, as a matter of the greatest urgency and importance, now cooperate with the British authorities in unmasking any other Russian spies he believed were at work in London?

Before going on to that fateful cooperation, the story of Captain King needs to be told. That very brief, factual Foreign Office press communiqué of June 7, 1956 came, as we have seen, seventeen years after the event, and it remains to this day the sole official statement made about the case. It is only now possible, two decades further on still, to give an authoritative and detailed account of how King was enlisted by a Kremlin agent, to be trapped, years later, by a Kremlin defector.

John Herbert King can fairly be described as the archetypal prey for any sophisticated recruiter of spies. In his mid-thirties at the Armistice (he was aged fifty-five when arrested), King was one of those desolate figures for whom the status and the excitement furnished by a wartime officer's commission (he had been a captain in the Artists Rifles) were to remain the high point of life's achievements. When peace came, he could find no better employment than that of a Foreign Office cipher clerk at a salary, to start with, of a meager £100 per annum. One of the highly significant factors in his case was that he was not earning a great deal more than that at the time of his arrest twenty years later.[11] Among several lessons which Whitehall learned from the affair was that government cipher

---

[11]   The salary scales for Foreign Office cipher clerks in 1939 were in the range £85–350 a year and, as King was then still only listed thirteenth out of the sixteen clerks in the department, his pay cannot have been at the top end of the scale.

clerks, whose high security importance was out of all proportion to their relatively humble grade, should not be exposed to avoidable temptation by being asked to exist on the wages of a groom. An extra complication in King's case was that he remained a temporary official throughout his service, with no right to a pension, and no security to look forward to in his old age.

Temptation duly came King's way in May of 1935 in Geneva, where he was working on temporary duty with the British delegation to a League of Nations meeting. By now, he was in an unhappy state anyway, a frustrated middle-aged man, separated from his wife, Gertrude, at a dead end in his occupation, and with hardly any friends among his colleagues. He had, it is true, found a British girlfriend, Helen Wilkie, but on his pay and allowances he could barely afford to buy her one good meal a week in any of Geneva's excellent restaurants. Almost inevitably, therefore, money was the bait, and the man who first got him on the hook with that bait was a Dutchman named Pieck, an artist by profession and a Soviet agent by persuasion (the persuader having been none other than Ignaz Reiss).

Pieck, an apparently wealthy man whose paintings (much of it risqué nudes) brought him into Geneva's diplomatic swim, soon identified King as a likely looking loner, thirsting for the good life he could never afford. The Dutchman started splashing him with lavish invitations, and even took him and his girlfriend away on holiday in Spain, with all expenses paid. The bait, when it came, was presented in a most plausible way. Pieck mentioned to the Englishman that he had an extremely wealthy friend, a financier who liked to make his money by acting on advance knowledge of forthcoming international developments. Would King who, as a Foreign Office official, saw so much that was going on in the world, consider providing such tips, strictly for private and commercial use and in return, of course, for a suitable fee from this grateful business client? Whether the aging cipher clerk felt the hook straightaway, or only bit on it later on, is impossible to say. But he nibbled first time and, from then on, a regular flow of secret information came from King to Pieck and, eventually, after the spy had returned to London, from King to a certain Theodore Maly, who took over as his "controller." This remarkable individual merits a paragraph to himself.

By the mid-thirties, Maly, alias, among many other names, Paul Hardt, had won himself a reputation in Moscow as one of the NKVD's most daring and dedicated officers. He was, without any doubt, also one of its strangest recruits. During the First World War, he had been a true son both of God and of His Apostolic Majesty, the Emperor Francis Joseph, having served as chaplain to a regiment of the Austro-Hungarian army. When, just after the Bolshevik revolution, he went over to Communism, the Soviet secret police soon picked him out. Unlike the usual run of their early agents—primitive, uneducated people with little or no knowledge of the world—here was an intelligent and charming European who could pass for a citizen of several Western countries. This was the formidable NKVD officer, now stationed in England, who took over the running of King for two years from 1935 onward. Then, in July 1937, Maly himself fell victim to that same purge which had felled Reiss and driven Krivitsky into flight. He obeyed one of those summonses to report to headquarters and returned, first to Paris and then to Moscow, and disappeared for good in November—leaving King, and the other British spies he had been running, in something of a limbo.

Now when, shortly after the outbreak of war, Lord Lothian's message arrived in London stating that a cipher clerk called King had been reported to him as being a Soviet agent, the British security authorities probably placed, at first, little more faith in the story than the ambassador had done. John Herbert King was immediately identified as the only person with that name and job in government service. Yet nothing was known to his detriment. His sound war record appeared to have been followed by nearly twenty years of obscure but equally sound service in the Foreign Office Communications Department. However, the task in light of British Counterintelligence, unlike that of Lord Lothian, was to investigate and to suspect; and, about a fortnight after that Washington message came in, something happened in London which more than doubled their suspicions. Quite independently of the American warning, a British source came forward with additional evidence. This new informant was a businessman who, in 1935, had been a partner of Pieck's in setting up a small interior decorating firm in London. Pieck, though still living in Switzerland, would come over from time to time. As the months passed, the businessman (who appears to have been quite innocent in the affair) noticed some very odd things happening. Packages and letters which had absolutely nothing to do with interior decorating were collected and delivered, and, on one occasion, Pieck, without mentioning King by name, said that he had a great friend at the Foreign Office. In peacetime the business-man had not thought it necessary to voice his suspicions. Now that the country was at war, he felt obliged to speak out.

Two unconnected leads changed the picture entirely. Deeper in-vestigations soon confirmed the worst fears. On September 25, 1939, King, who had been allowed to go on sick leave, was confronted in the London bed-sitter where he lived. His modest home was searched and, as it was known that Helen Wilkie, the woman friend from his Geneva days, was now in London and still closely associated with him, her apartment was searched as well. To begin with, King denied even knowing Pieck. But four days later, apparently in an attempt to keep Helen, the one precious thing in his drab life, out of trouble, he made a partial confession. Yes, he had known Pieck, and yes, he had passed information on to him. But it had been purely of a financial and commercial nature, for Pieck's banker friend. No polit-ical secrets had been divulged, he claimed. Moreover, with a rather bizarre touch of departmental pride, King insisted that he had never handed over that most precious of all his professional tools, the Foreign Office code book.

By now, the evidence collected against him was overwhelming. It was also ironic. The very money he had started his spying for had, in the end, betrayed and destroyed him. These were the days when sterling was unchallenged as the banking currency of the world. They were also the days when one single pound represented a solid sum of money, so much so that all notes above £1 (and that meant big leaps to denominations of £5, £10, and upward) had their movements recorded by their serial numbers from the time they were issued to the time they were called in for pulping. This proved King's final undoing. When safe deposits under his name were opened at the Chancery Lane firm where Helen Wilkie was work-ing, they were found to contain £5 and £10 notes which, the records showed, had originally been issued straight to Soviet banks. From there, evidently, they had been transferred to the NKVD's treasury. Others, totaling altogether nearly £500, could be traced to a source which by now had been identified as an NKVD channel in the East End of London. This was a waste rag company called "Gada," run by a certain Bernard Davidovitch, an "illegal" Russian agent who had been sent to England and set up "in trade" for the specific purpose of helping Maly run King and his other British recruits.[12] One of the last of the many disguises of this former Hungarian army chaplain had thus been that of a rag trade representative, visiting his "business colleague," Mr. Davidovitch, in the heart of London's dockland— though it was the collection and disposal of precious scraps of information and not of humble scraps of waste linen they had been concerned with.

Now, on October 18, 1939, the central figure in this elaborate espionage structure had been removed and put behind prison bars. It was, of course, a horrifying thought that a steady stream of secret information about British foreign policy intentions had been passing to Moscow more or less as it was being passed to British missions abroad, and by the very person who was handling the transmission. Nor was it that much of a consolation to reflect that, for more than two years before his arrest, King had been a "sleeper," that is, an agent who had been temporarily switched off by the Kremlin following the recall of his controller, Maly, and the defection of his original master, Reiss. That sleeper could, at any moment, be reawakened, and by 1939 King was so totally in the NKVD's hands as a blackmail victim that it is doubtful whether even the outbreak of war would have caused the former British army captain to withold his services to Moscow.

It is here that we touch on the potential significance of King's exposure, which arises out of the enormous potential damage he might have inflicted on Britain and the whole Allied camp during the first eighteen months of the war. For had King indeed been "switched on" again in October of 1939, his secrets could have been passed, not merely to Moscow, but from Moscow to Berlin. That

---

[12]   Davidovitch was a relative of one of the "legal" NKVD agents stationed in London, a "second secretary" at the Soviet Embassy, named Shuster.

such collaboration had extended to the Intelligence field long before the conclusion of the Nazi-Soviet pact had just been confirmed by none other than Krivitsky, with his experience of more than twenty years an officer of the Soviet Military Intelligence organization. In his testimony of October 11, 1938, to the House Committee in Washington he had stated:

> Co-operation between the Soviet Red Army and the German Reich began before Hitler came into power. There were occasions when they co-operated in espionage and exchange of military information through the two Army commands. Inasmuch as Stalin's pact with Hitler is really an *alliance of the two armies,* operating in specified zones, I have no doubt that such exchange of military secrets and information . . . is indispensable to both Hitler and Stalin.[13]

It was not until June of 1941 that Hitler launched his surprise attack on Russia (Stalin, at any rate, was surprised, despite the variety of high-level warnings he had received). A year before that, Hitler had been planning an invasion of quite a different sort—that of England. Had he gleaned via Moscow, and ultimately via John Herbert King, any hint of the unbelievably parlous state of Britain's defenses after Dunkirk (the mere handfuls of serviceable tanks, heavy artillery, and so on which were available to defend the country that summer), he might well have pondered further before finally abandoning "Sea Lion," the projected crossing of the Channel. The foreign power that King had begun by spying for was merely an unfriendly one in peacetime. The power he could unknowingly have ended up betraying his country to was a wartime enemy, and a deadly one at that.

This, admittedly, is speculation, and speculation in retrospect. The hard fact which British security authorities had to go on in October of 1939 was that this first tipoff from a Soviet defector in Washington proved totally and swiftly accurate. What mattered now was to get him face to face, to solve the mystery of that second, "Imperial Defence Council," spy he had referred to, plus any others he could confirm or reveal. And this brings us back to that urgent telephone summons which Isaac Don Levine had received in New York from Lord Lothian.

---

[13] Author's italics.

Krivitsky is said to have shown reluctance to make the hazardous journey to London when the idea was first put up to him through his lawyer and personal adviser, Louis Waldman. One suspects that the hazards he had in mind were not merely the German U-boats which, in this first winter of the war, were tearing great holes almost at will in the shipping lanes of the North Atlantic. He was probably even more concerned with the Soviet threat to him which, he well knew, lay submerged under the surface of London itself. But eventually, encouraged no doubt by promises of the stricted safeguards, he put aside any reservations. He left New York in December of 1939 and arrived in London on January 19, 1940.

From the point of view of actual military operations, the British capital at that time may well have been stuck in .the doldrums of the so-called phony war. But, seen as a center of Intelligence, there was nothing at all inactive or phony about it, as Krivitsky rapidly learned, to his professional satisfaction. Unlike Washington, which had hardly begun to tackle the problems of Russian espionage and Intelligence, London had been locked in this particular silent battle with Moscow for upward of a century. Indeed, its beginnings—the conflict between tsarist Russia and the Indian Raj along the length and breadth of the Himalayas—might be called the precursor of the Cold War of today. Nor had the British government lacked experience in this field when dealing with the tsar's successors in the Kremlin.

In 1927, as we have seen, the security authorities had amassed enough evidence—and even more in the way of suspicions—about the undercover subversive activities of Soviet trade organizations in London to mount the spectacular police raid on the Arcos Company. That could, at best, be counted only a partial success. On the other hand, the breaking up of a Soviet spy ring operating inside Britain's armament industry—the so-called Woolwich Arsenal case—had been a resounding victory for British Counterintelligence, and it had been scored only two years before Krivitsky's arrival in wartime London. It was on January 21, 1938 that the arrest was announced of one Percy Glading, a former employee at the arsenal, together with three other men still working there at the time. From the Russian end, it had been mounted as a classic espionage operation: what the Kremlin were after were photocopies of production blueprints from the arsenal, and especially those for a new top-secret 14-inch British naval gun.

Equally classic and, in this case, more effective, had been the way the ring had been broken up from the inside. As early as 1931, a British woman agent had joined, on orders, a society known as the "Friends of the Soviet Union" with the object of keeping a long-term watch on an organization that was suspected of harboring some very extravagant notions about friendship. Sure enough, she was soon asked to fulfill various minor tasks of espionage for the society and, by 1937, had gained the confidence of its controllers to such an extent that, in February of that year, she was the person approached by Glading and asked to hire a flat in Holland Park for the specific purpose of photographing the arsenal blueprints. From that point on, it was a short, uncomplicated step to the laying of a police trap and the arrest of almost the whole of the group. One who escaped (because by now he was no longer in the country) was a "Mr. Peters," whom Glading had introduced to the woman agent, indicating that he was the man from whom the orders came. He was described to her as "an Austrian captain who had served in the Russian Army." By NKVD standards of deception, it was a surprisingly accurate label. As Krivitsky was now to confirm, "Mr. Peters" was none other than our Hungarian friend, Theodore Maly, wearing yet another of his numerous masks.

The point to note about all this was that when Walter Krivitsky sat down in England to begin his extensive interrogation, he was dealing, for the first time since his flight to America, with experts who knew not only what questions to ask but also how to evaluate his answers. It was, in fact, a woman official, Jane Archer, who conducted the actual "debriefing." Apart from a deep knowledge of the subject, she must also have possessed the right human qualities and the psychological insight to gain the confidence of this tense, slightly built Russian who, with his domed forehead, pale face, and bushy eyebrows, might have been a timid schoolteacher rather than a top Soviet agent on the run. The results, at any rate, spoke for themselves.

It is now known that, during three weeks of skilled and sympathetic debriefing, Krivitsky listed a grand total of nearly a hundred Russian agents working in various parts of the world. Of these, no fewer than sixty-one were named by him as operating either in the United Kingdom itself or directly against British interests elsewhere. Of these sixty-one, six were "legal" spymasters, Soviet citizens who had the cover of officials serving in the Embassy or state trading organization. Krivitsky next identified twenty "illegal" so-called apparatus workers also at work in Britain. Their task was to provide the administrative infrastructure on which any espionage network must depend— couriers, photographers, providers of "safe houses," and so on. The origins, as well as the aliases of these undercover helpers, were almost bewilderingly varied. Their nationalities comprised three Americans, three Germans, three Austrians, two Dutch, one Pole, and eight Russians of assorted backgrounds. Nine gave themselves out as businessmen, three as artists, one as a journalist, one as a secretary, one as a student, one as an ice skater, while the occupations of the remaining four were uncertain.

But the most critical group were the thirty-five people named by Krivitsky as being no mere apparatus workers but Soviet agents, fully engaged, that is, on espionage for Moscow. They included sprinklings of Poles, Indians, Czechs, and other foreign nationalities. But sixteen of those suspected spies were British subjects, and the names on this part of Krivitsky's list included eight people active in politics and the trade unions, six in the civil service, and two in journalism. Only about half of all the names produced by Krivitsky were new to the British authorities. The other half were already on watchlists.

The whole band of suspects, familiar and unfamiliar, were of course quietly "neutralized," so that they would be in no position to do damage. But none of them was ever prosecuted, let alone convicted, which is why their identities cannot be revealed here. What, on the other hand, of that trio of upper-class Britons who did eventually emerge as archspies for the Kremlin, Messrs. Burgess, Philby, and Maclean? Was any breath of suspicion ventilated against them in January 1940—by which date all three had, in fact, already been operating for some years as Soviet agents?

Krivitsky did not actually name any of them during this wartime interrogation. This may have been because their recruitment was such a closely guarded secret that even he, as a very senior western European agent, had been unaware of their precise identity. It may, on the other hand, have been because he was either afraid to "blow" Moscow's top spies and invite certain retribution or because he had decided to "play it long" on this first trip to London and reserve other information for a later date. Whatever the real explanation at the time, it can be said now, with the benefit of much hindsight, that, in January of 1940, Krivitsky pointed a finger toward the most senior and distinguished member of the trio, Donald Maclean.

This happened during the search for that second highly sensitive spy he had mentioned to Lord Lothian, the one said to be operating in the "Imperial Defence Council." While in London, Krivitsky was shown copies of various secret Imperial Defence Committee (IDC) papers and asked whether any struck him as being already familiar, from his work on the other side. Without hesitation, he identified several that he had indeed read himself in Moscow, in the form of photocopies provided by Soviet agents in London. The ones he picked out were mainly surveys or analyses of international problems. In all cases, several copies had been passed for internal distribution to the Foreign Office, where Maclean was already working as a junior secretary.

Another lead (though also only discernible with hindsight) came when Krivitsky revealed the identity, and the assignment in Britain, of a top Soviet agent called Arnold Deutsch. Deutsch was a Viennese who had arrived in the country in 1934 for postgraduate studies at University College, London. He had remained until 1937, when he too was withdrawn in the aftermath of the Reiss defection. But during those three years he was known to have specialized in penetrating the British student scene. It is now thought that it was Deutsch who either recruited or controlled (or both) Burgess, Maclean, and Philby, all of whom were being transformed from Cambridge undergraduates into Soviet spies during this period.

Faint and blurred though such traces were, perhaps, given time and top priority, something could have been made of them. But time was the one thing which, in 1940, neither the security authorities, nor the nation as a whole, was to be given. Only four months after

Krivitsky's interrogation, the Germans brought the "phony war" to an abrupt end with their offensive in the West. The fall of France and the trauma of the Dunkirk evacuation followed a few weeks later. From June 1940 onward, with a victorious Wehrmacht crouching barely twenty miles away across the Channel, priority in security matters, as in all other defense fields, was switched to likely German agents and saboteurs, as key figures in the invasion of Britain which everyone now feared. In the expressive American phrase, Soviet spies were "put on the back burner." A year later, when Hitler made Stalin the West's wartime ally with his onslaught against Russia, the gas on that burner was turned down lower still.

Nonetheless, there is a particular significance, and a particular irony, about the fact that Krivitsky, among the many other disclosures he made in London in January of 1940, should also have given what turned out to be the first lead to Maclean. The irony is that, although Krivitsky had failed to expose Maclean, it could easily have been Maclean who now proceeded to expose Krivitsky. The interrogations had been conducted in the deepest secrecy, and their detailed results were probably only familiar to the specialists involved. But it is now known that, in April of 1940, a secret Foreign Office report on the Krivitsky case was circulated, drawing attention to the many important political issues which his visit had raised, as well as mentioning some of his revelations. Once that got into Donald Maclean's hands[14]—and there was precious little to stop it, given the small, cozy, and confiding place the Foreign Office was in those days—there would have been panic both among his tiny nest of traitors and in the Kremlin.

Seen from Moscow, it was not only probable from such evidence of Krivitsky's visit that, for the first time, the West had now been furnished with an authoritative picture of the vast depth, breadth, and sheer elemental force of the Soviet thrust against it. The Russians must also have feared that the general picture had been filled in with the names and aliases of dozens of the agents recruited so patiently over the years to discharge that program in Britain. Many of the fish that had been caught in the net spread by Krivitsky were

---

[14] He was serving at the Paris Embassy until the fall of France in May–June of 1940, when he returned to the Foreign Office.

only medium-sized, and some were little more than industrious minnows. The three killer whales operating for the Kremlin, of whom Maclean was one, could assume that, so far, they had not been detected. But if this defector were given another chance to talk, what guarantee was there that even they would not be pushed up to the surface?

With his London debriefing in January 1940, it is likely that Walter Krivitsky drew up his own death warrant; and, in that case, it is even more likely that it was Donald Maclean who signed it for him in the summer of that same year.

Chapter Ten

A MYSTERIOUS END

At 9:30 a.m. in the morning of Monday, February 10, 1941, Thelma Jackson, a chambermaid working at the Bellevue Hotel Washington (a modest establishment near the Capitol), decided she must do something about the occupant of that fifth-floor room. No one, surely, could sleep as heavily as that; the guest must be ill. Though the door of Number 532 was locked from the inside by a throw catch, she opened it easily enough with her passkey. What she saw made her run down the corridor for help. The silent occupant was more than just ill. He lay on his bed in a pool of blood, with a pistol close by.

When the police arrived half an hour later, they were told that the dead man, who had not been known at the hotel before, had registered there at 5:49 p.m. the previous Sunday afternoon, and had taken the $2.50-a-night room in the name of Walter Poref. But when they searched his belongings, they found, among other documents, a Canadian affidavit in the name of Samuel Ginsberg. This was not, at the time, considered either very strange or very significant. Even when traveling alone, hotel guests often used fictitious names, or professional ones. And, in any case, Ginsberg meant as little to the Washington policemen as Poref. Then, that same afternoon, their headquarters received an urgent telephone call to say that Samuel Ginsberg was, in fact, Walter Krivitsky, the former Soviet agent whose writings and testimonies to the Dies Committee had created such a stir.

The caller was Louis Waldman, the prominent left-wing attorney who had acted not only for the dead man but also for Leon Trotsky, who had been assassinated just six months before. Waldman's plea to the police was to think again if they were about to get the coroner to issue a verdict of suicide. The attorney was convinced that the man in the Bellevue Hotel had met his end in the same way as the great Bolshevik exile in Mexico—in other words, he had been done to death by Stalin's henchmen.

That telephone call started a debate which rumbled on for a week or so in the newspapers, and which has never been satisfactorily settled down to this day. Was Walter Krivitsky another victim of that great wave of Stalinist revenge killings that had decimated the ranks of Russian émigrés and defectors in the West, as well as almost obliterating the old Communist party cadres inside the Soviet Union itself? And, if he had been murdered, how had the deed been done? Or had he, on the other hand, taken his own life? If so, why here, and for what motive?

As Waldman, backed by Krivitsky's family and friends, argued it over with the police during the next forty-eight hours (the FBI promptly disclaimed all knowledge of the dead man, and, to their shame, this was almost certainly true), it seemed that a persuasive argument for either version could be made out. The death of Walter Krivitsky would, in fact, have presented a classic mystery case for some great detective of fact or fiction to solve. As it was, the riddle was allowed to fade away unanswered after only routine police investigations. If it is revived here, it is not only because it forms part of the victim's personal story. It is also because the answer may emerge a little more clearly today, when related to the general history of all these early Soviet defectors. There are, after all these years, no fresh police clues on a case long since closed. But what can be done is to take another look at the original clues in the light of what had already happened—and what was to happen in the future—to Krivitsky's companions in exile. First then, the police evidence itself.

The bare, physical facts were that the hotel room, which was only some ten feet square, appeared to have no feasible entrance for an intruder, except for the door. There was no outside fire escape within reach, and the window, though open an inch or two, looked out on a ledgeless sill which even the most skilled of cat burglars could hardly have negotiated. The detective placed in charge of the case, Inspector Bernard W. Thompson, acknowledged that an assassin could, of course, have procured a copy of one of the master keys used by the maid to open the door. But he was to base his own conclusion of suicide on what he had actually seen inside the room. There was no sign of a struggle, or of anything having been disturbed. The body itself was clothed (apart from the shoes) and was lying on top of the bed covers. The death gun was on the bed, and not placed in the dead man's hand, as usually happens with fake suicides. A strange detail, however, was that all traces of fingerprints had been washed away, apparently by the blood.[1] The weapon was a .38-caliber revolver of a powerful high-velocity type. The clip contained hollow-nosed bullets, and was full except for the one shot which had been fired. This had passed clean through Krivitsky's head from the right temple (a "blast" or close contact wound) and had not merely buried itself but, apparently, also destroyed itself in the tile wall. At any rate, no trace of it could be found. Only the ejected cartridge case was retrieved.

In Inspector Thompson's mind (and reasonably enough, for he was an ordinary police official who knew nothing of the world of espionage), the conclusive evidence in favor of suicide was something else they had found in the room: three farewell notes which seemed to indicate beyond doubt that the occupant had intended to take his own life. The police handwriting expert, Ira Guillickson, had been called in and had stated that, in his view, they had in-

---

[1] Dr. Waldman claimed that the pistol butt was only partly smeared with blood, and reproached the police for not trying harder with the prints.

dubitably been written by the same person who had signed the hotel register in the name of Walter Poref. Yet even these apparently unequivocal clues contained a puzzle of their own. They were written, not on Bellevue Hotel notepaper, nor on any private stationery from New York, where Krivitsky and his family lived, but on sheets headed simply "Charlottesville, Virginia." Moreover, in two of the three farewell letters, the dead man had gone out of his way to explain that he had gone to Charlottesville the day before his death simply to get hold of a gun with which to kill himself.

The longest letter was in Russian, addressed to his wife and seven-year-old son. It read:

> Dear Tanya and Alek,
>   It is very difficult. I want very badly to live but it is impossible. I love you, my only one. It is hard for me to write but think about me and then you will understand that I must go. Don't tell Alek yet where his father has gone. I believe that, in time, you should tell him, because that would be best for him.
>   Forgive. It is very difficult to write. Take care of him and be a good mother to him and be always calm and never get angry with him. . . . Good people will help you, but not enemies. My sins are very great.
>   I see you, Tanya and Alek. I embrace you.
>
> > Your Vela.

Underneath came a form of postscript:

> I wrote this yesterday on Dobertov's farm. I did not have the strength in New York. I had no business to do in Washington. I went to see Dobertov because that is the only place I could get firearms.

The second note was written in English and addressed to Krivitsky's attorney. It was much shorter but also contained a reference to the death weapon:

> Dear Mr. Waldman,
>   My wife and my boy will need your help. Please do for them what you can.
>
> > Yours, Walter Krivitsky.

And the postscript in this case read:

> I went to Virginia because I knew that there I can get a gun. If my friends get in trouble, please help them. They are good people and didn't know what I got the gun for.

The last of these letters was a short message, in German, addressed to "Suzanne" (identified as Suzanne La Follette, a liberal writer from the well-known Wisconsin political family who had befriended Krivitsky, together with several other anti-Communist Russian émigrés living in America). It said simply:

Dear Suzanne,
    I trust that you are well. I die in the hope that you will help Tanya and my poor boy. You were a good friend.

Yours, Walter.

Despite the convincingly despairing and disjointed tone of these final messages, and the verdict of the police expert on their authenticity as far as the handwriting was concerned, it could be claimed that they raised almost as many questions as they were supposed to have settled. True, the owner of the Virginia farm was duly traced. He was a German named Eitel Wolf Dobert (which had been changed from Dobertov) and gave himself out to be a former officer in the Reichswehr who had been forced to flee Germany because of his anti-Nazi views. He and his wife Marguerite were, it seemed, good friends of the Krivitskys and Marguerite later confirmed that Walter had, indeed, spent that last weekend of his life with them. Moreover, she had also driven with him on the Saturday morning to a hardware store in Charlottesville and seen him purchase a gun which, he told her, he needed for his own protection. As he appeared calm and cheerful, she had accepted the explanation, though it seemed very puzzling. Why indeed go all the way from New York to Charlottesville to get a weapon which could be obtained anywhere, and then return to Washington to use it?

These were among the many points raised by Waldman himself after visiting the Hotel Bellevue and the Washington police headquarters on the afternoon of February 11. He succeeded only in postponing the formal issue by the local coroner, Mr. Magruder Macdonald, of the suicide certificate requested by the police. Yet that settled the matter in law only. Neither Krivitsky's attorney, nor his family, nor his friends, nor any of those who had had official contact with him ever believed that verdict. They all put the deed at the door of the Soviet secret police, in one form or another. A few thought Stalin's minions might have blackmailed their former NKVD colleague into taking his life, while the majority were convinced that those same minions had taken it for him.

Dealing first with the same bare facts, their arguments ran as follows. The locked door, as even the police had admitted, meant little or nothing: getting hold of a passkey would have posed no problem for an organized murder squad with ample funds at their disposal. It was a bagatelle, for example, compared with the chartering of a Greek merchant vessel and crew solely for the attempt on Agabekov. Moreover, professionals wishing to fake a suicide would obviously have left the room just as it was found, cleaning up any evidence of a struggle. They would certainly have avoided the blatant gimmick of placing the weapon in the dead man's hand. The farewell letters were, admittedly, a bigger problem to explain away. Yet, after all, Krivitsky's old organization would have been in possession of enough samples of his handwriting in various languages, and, in Moscow, they possessed one of the finest and most practiced band of forgers in the world, people who had fooled greater experts than Mr. Guillickson of the Washington Police Department. The rather labored references in two of the three letters to "borrowing a gun" also struck an artificial note. This was a detail which, surely, a genuine suicide penning his last lines to his dear ones would not have bothered to recount at such length. Nor was it at all like the ultracareful Krivitsky to implicate other people quite unnecessarily.

The assassination thesis has, of course, its own unexplained mysteries. Assuming that the Doberts were genuine friends who would never have betrayed him, how had a murder squad tracked him to Charlottesville and then back to a fairly obscure hotel in Washington? Moreover, if Stalin had been responsible for his death, why not kill him out in the countryside and try to hide the body, rather than fake a suicide in a hotel in the nation's capital, thus insuring instant and maximum publicity for the death? You *could* argue, of course, that the advance guarantee of such publicity had been, in itself, one of the main attractions to the NKVD of making the murder appear like a suicide. They had not, so far, risked an assassination on American soil, and the killings and abductions they had carried out in Europe had caused unpleasant political repercussions. A suicide in Washington would not only let them off the hook, it might even make a better deterrent. To any others in Russia wondering whether to follow Krivitsky's example, the thought that he had grown so disillusioned about his own defection that he had finally taken his life might, in some ways, be even more daunting to would-be defectors than the obvious dangers of long-range execution. In which case, however, why not insert something about disillusionment if you were faking the farewell letters?

But whatever uncertainties remain about the NKVD's supposed motivation and method, it does seem a safe bet to assume that, if the Soviet secret police were the real villains, they would have been obliged to do the deed themselves. The theory of "induced suicide" advanced at the time—the suggestion that Krivitsky had been somehow pressured into taking his own life—has never stood up to one fundamental objection. This was succinctly expressed thirty-five years later by the former Soviet agent Hedda Massing, the only fellow defector alive today who once knew Krivitsky. She commented:

> The only possible lever they could have tried to use against him was his family—threatening to kill his wife and son, and promising to spare their lives only if he took his. But Krivitsky would have known with absolute certainty that, even if the threats were serious, the promises were not. After all, he himself, as a senior official in the same service, had seen so many promises of clemency which had been made in the name of Stalin cynically broken the moment their aim was achieved. A professional like him would never for one moment have considered such a bogus deal.[2]

If that rules out the case for an "induced" suicide, the case for a genuine one seems to get weaker the further one moves away from Room 532 at the Hotel Bellevue and the physical facts of the on-the-spot findings. If the answer to the riddle is anywhere, it lies in the personal and political background which surrounded the case. To begin with, nobody was talking or behaving less like a potential suicide than Walter Krivitsky, right up to the day of his death. When he left New York on that last journey, he was in good health, happy in his personal life, and with no immediate money problems. Moreover, he was full of new plans for his family. One project, which

---

[2] Conversation with the author in New York on November 16, 1976.

he had enthusiastically discussed with his attorney only the week before he died, was to buy a farm and settle down in the country-side. Altogether, it was the talk of a man keen on living, not that of a tortured soul bound for imminent suicide.

Certainly, there were shadows in the picture, shadows to which he himself had drawn attention. Yet these, too, all pointed in the direction of an assassination attempt. Ever since Trotsky's murder, he had been warning friends about a secret influx into the United States of Comintern agents coming largely via Mexico. Many of these agents had served with the Republicans in Spain, from where they had been pulled out after the victory of General Franco's forces. Their new assignment, Krivitsky believed, was to set up a sabotage organi-zation designed ultimately to cripple America's war potential and, as an immediate target, to hamper the flow of American aid to an embattled Britain. (In February of 1941 Stalin was still, of course, Hitler's unsuspecting ally, and Britain was fighting Nazi Germany alone.)

A subsidiary target of these Comintern agents, Krivitsky thought, was Walter Krivitsky himself. He had begun to worry openly whether, after all that he had disclosed to the Dies Committee in Washington and to the British Intelligence authorities in London, his removal from the scene had not become, in his own deadpan words to a friend, "a practical necessity for Moscow." Indeed, only the previous month, he had expressed alarm at the reported arrival in New York of one particularly dangerous Communist assassin, a man he had identified in conversation only under the name of "Hans."

That was the background which he himself had painted at the be-ginning of 1941, and it was ominous enough as a general setting. What has emerged since then are certain specific reasons why the Kremlin might well have decided to eliminate him on or around the actual date of his death, February 10. Later that very same day, for example, Walter Krivitsky was due to testify before a New York State legislative committee which was examining the threat of Communist infiltration into the American educational system. He had had dis-cussions on the subject, only some forty-eight hours before, with Robert Morris, an official connected with this special inquiry.

That was not all; nor was it even the greatest threat which Krivitsky's continued existence posed to the Kremlin at the time of his death. We have seen the havoc that he had already wrought in London, twelve months before, on the Soviet espionage network in Britain. It is also known that, at the beginning of 1941, the British government was making preliminary inquiries in Washington with a view to having Krivitsky come over to London for a second extensive interrogation. There were, it seemed, additional names and cases on which they would have greatly liked his help.

In fact, only the Russians knew at this stage that, among their big fish who had so far escaped detection in London in 1940 were Maclean, Burgess, and Philby. But the Kremlin must have been keenly aware that this trio might also be exposed if British Intelligence were given the opportunity of another few weeks in Krivitsky's company. As we have seen, there are grounds for believing they had been alerted to that danger.

Fittingly, the last comment on the riddle of Krivitsky's death ought to come from the mouth of the dead man. Several times, in the weeks before he met his end, he said to his friends: "If one day, you should read that I am supposed to have committed suicide, whatever you do, don't believe a word of it."

Chapter Eleven

ALEXANDER ORLOV: "THEY WILL NEVER SEE THEIR EARS"

The last of these major prewar defectors, General Alexander Orlov, only just qualified as another Paris refugee. He arrived in the capital, with his wife and young daughter, soon after dawn on July 13, 1938, having traveled up on an overnight train from the south. That same afternoon, the three of them caught another train, bound for Cherbourg and freedom, with seconds to spare. But if the French connection in this particular flight was brief, it was also vital.

Only twenty-four hours before, Orlov had left his post in Barcelona a doomed man politically, and perhaps physically as well. Paris could be, at best, merely a springboard in the leap to freedom, and an exceptionally risky one at that, since, by now, Soviet agents were so active in France that no fugitive from the great Moscow purges was safe on its streets. And General Alexander Orlov of the NKVD knew that he was no ordinary quarry. Stalin was indeed about to lose the most senior Soviet secret police chief to defect to the outside world—up to that date and, for that matter, ever since. His potential value to the West on the Intelligence front was exceeded only by the significance, in the political field, of Boris Bajanov ten years before him.

Before following him across the Atlantic, however, the full story should be told of the greatest professional coup of his career.[1] He had pulled it off less than nine months before making this run for his life, and it was a feat that should have earned him Stalin's undying gratitude instead of a death warrant. Alexander Orlov was the man who took possession of the entire gold reserves of Spain and got them safely to Moscow, where they have remained to this day.

That was not at all what he had gone to Spain for in the first place. Orlov had been sent there by the Politburo at the height of the Civil War in September of 1936 (by which time he had behind him up-ward of ten years' loyal and varied service in the secret police), as the Kremlin's liaison representative to the Republican government. His basic job was to help that embattled regime to build up its Intelligence and Counterintelligence services against the Franco forces and their Nazi supporters. An important subsidiary task was to organize guerrilla warfare behind the enemy lines, something which had been a spe-ciality of Orlov's ever since September of 1920, when, as a young military officer, he had been given precisely that assignment when fighting with the Twelfth Red Army against the Poles.

On October 15, 1936, when Orlov had barely settled in at his Madrid office, his code clerk came in with a cipher message just re-ceived from Moscow. The clerk stopped decoding after a few words, and then handed both the message and the code book over to his puzzled chief instead. The one sentence deciphered was from Yezhov, whom Stalin had recently put in Yagoda's place as minister of interior and head of the Soviet secret police. It said simply: "I transmit to you the personal order of the boss." There then followed an instruction that the accompanying telegram was to be decoded by only Orlov

---

[1]   Orlov never revealed much of this episode in his own writings. Parts of it sur-faced nearly twenty years later, in Spanish newspaper stories printed in January 1957. What follows is the first complete account, based on Orlov's official testimony and on remarks made to his interrogators.

himself. The reason for this extreme "eyes only" security soon became uncomfortably clear. This is what Orlov found himself reading when he laid the code book aside:

> Together with Ambassador Rosenberg [envoy of the Soviet Union to the Republican government in Madrid], arrange with the head of the Spanish government, Caballero, for the shipment of the gold reserves of Spain to the Soviet Union. Use for this purpose a Soviet steamer. This operation must be carried out with the utmost secrecy.
>
> If the Spaniards demand from you a receipt for the cargo, refuse, I repeat, refuse to sign anything and say that a formal receipt will be issued in Moscow by the State Bank.
>
> I hold you personally responsible for this operation. Rosenberg has been instructed accordingly.

The cable was signed "Ivan Vasiliyevitch," which was Stalin's telegraphic code name.

It would have been a tricky order to carry out at the best of times. But these were about the worst of times, and in two respects. First, the military situation was becoming increasingly precarious for the Republicans. Franco's forces were within a day's march of Madrid. The civilian population was already beginning to abandon the capital, and the government itself was eventually to follow. But an even nastier threat than anything on the battlefield was the menace in those steely words: "I hold you personally responsible." Stalin had by now reached the stage in his blood-soaked career when thousands of his officials who were doing their duty to the letter were nonetheless facing firing squads. The prospects for someone who failed in a task specially selected for him by the dictator were hardly, therefore, cheering.

Orlov hurried immediately with the message to Rosenberg's offices, where he found the Soviet ambassador personally deciphering a similar telegram himself, the embassy code clerk banished to a remote corner of the room. The next day, the two men went with Stalin's order (suitably toned down as a fraternal suggestion) to the then Spanish finance minister, Dr. Juan Negrin, who was later to succeed Caballero as premier. This first hurdle—persuading the government to intrust the whole of its national treasure to Stalin on the grounds that it would be "safer in Moscow"—proved almost ludicrously easy to negotiate. After his defection, Orlov confessed that both he and Rosenberg had been "flabbergasted" when the finance minister immediately fell in with Stalin's proposal. The two Soviet officials knew well enough that the gold, once it had made the trip, would be all too safe in Moscow. But that was for future Spanish governments to worry about.[2] Orlov's problem, now that the diplomatic part of the operation had been so smoothly accomplished, was the practical side: how was such a precious and bulky cargo to be transported so far?

He came to a bold decision. When Negrin politely inquired how many Spanish soldiers would be needed to move out their country's gold, the Russian astonished him by replying that, in the first instance, he would use Red Army soldiers instead. Large shipments of Soviet tanks had recently arrived in Republican harbors; and, what was even more secret, Stalin had sent their own Russian crews with them to avoid the delays and complications of training Spanish crews. It was these Soviet tank men that Orlov proposed to employ. The solution offered the maximum in efficiency, speed, and security, provided that the operation went well. That was the big risk. If anything went wrong, Orlov warned Negrin (if, for example, the convoy were ambushed anywhere on Spanish soil), his men would have to fight it out to the last. The international scandal would be immense, to say nothing of domestic repercussions.

With the possibility of such a scandal in mind, Orlov now made what was, personally and professionally, a very shrewd move. Why not take precautions so that, if everything did go horribly wrong, it would be the British or the Americans, and not the Russians, who would be arraigned as hijackers? He himself spoke tolerable English, so what could be simpler than to equip himself with yet another set of bogus credentials, making him out to be an official either of the Bank of England or the "Bank of America"? This idea, too, met with Negrin's enthusiastic approval. So it was that Alexander Orlov set out on his expedition in the identity of a "Mr. Blackstone" of the "Bank of America [sic]," sent by President Roosevelt on a secret mission to Spain to transport the country's gold reserves to Washing-

---

[2]   As indeed they have been doing, incessantly. The return of the gold removed by Orlov in 1936 is still a bone of contention between Moscow and Madrid.

ton. Stalin would have been tickled by this touch, which had not even occurred to the master of deception himself.

That left the physical question of transport. The gold had long since been removed from Madrid and taken to the Republican stronghold of Cartagena, where it had been stored in a vast cave hewn out the mountains overlooking the port. "Mr. Blackstone" arrived there safely two or three days later. He was accompanied by Señor Mendez Aspe, the head of the Spanish Treasury, one of precisely five Spaniards let into the secret,[3] and now detailed to supervise the handover from the Republican side. What must have taken Orlov aback, when he entered that Spanish Aladdin's Cave, was the dazzling but daunting bulk of the problem. There was something approaching six hundred tons of the yellow metal in the hoard, worth, in 1936 values, anywhere between $600 million and $700 million.

Though his Russian tank crews could direct the move, Orlov realized that extra labor would be needed to shift and guard a consignment of that weight and size. He accordingly asked for, and was promptly given, sixty Spanish sailors to do the actual loading. There was no disguising from them what it was they were handling; but Orlov did nothing to discourage them in the belief that the treasure was merely being transferred, for greater safety, to another Spanish town. He had also decided, in view of the immense value of the load, to alter the strict letter of Stalin's instructions and spread it between four Soviet vessels, instead of putting it all on one. The extra ships were lying there at anchor, as a large Soviet convoy had just put in at Cartagena with arms and equipment of all kinds. The security problem was thus increased somewhat, but the risk of total loss, on the other hand, greatly diminished.

For three days and nights, the operation went on. The loading was done, in complete blackout, under cover of darkness, the trucks being driven right up to the winches of the Russian ships as they lay alongside the quay. During the day, Spaniards and Russians alike slept on

---

[3] According to Orlov's testimony afterward, these five were Azana, the president; Caballero, the prime minister; Negrin, the finance minister; Mendez Aspe; and, eventually, the defense minister, Prieto. On the Russian side, only Orlov and Rosenberg seem to have known the secret, making a total in Spain of seven in all.

what treasure remained in the cave. Things became critical halfway through when, on the second day, Hitler's bombers started heavy daytime air attacks on the port. The cave right next to Aladdin's was a Republican Army explosives store, filled with thousands of pounds of dynamite. Had a German bomb hit that, the gold and everyone guarding it, including Orlov, would have been blown to pieces.

His nerves stood the strain and he calmly ordered the operation to continue, arguing that, if they delayed, the four Soviet ships themselves could be in far greater danger waiting in the harbor than they were up on the mountainside. But Aspe, who had been in a shaky condition even before the German dive bombers arrived, now went to pieces altogether. He simply decamped, and produced a Spanish assistant to do the counting for him.

There was, in fact, something of a puzzle about that count when, on the third night, the cave was empty at last. Orlov's figures came to 168 truckloads, comprising 7,900 crates of gold in all. The Spanish total came to 100 fewer, 7,800 crates. Orlov, perhaps wisely, did not waste time arguing, but telegraphed to Moscow about the discrepancy. As his figures were the higher, he had little to worry about on that score. What did haunt him, however, now that the loading was finished, was whether the plans he had already laid to insure that those four cargo steamers reached a Soviet port intact would hold up. They had a long voyage ahead, part of it patrolled by warships of Franco's navy. Again, he took the law boldly into his own hands, even if it was only Spanish law.

A few days before, he had persuaded the prime minister, Caballero, to string out as many units as possible of the Republican Navy along the route the gold convoy would take and to issue each of their captains with sealed orders. These were only to be opened if a special distress signal, sent on a prearranged wavelength, was received. The SOS message had, of course, been given by Orlov to the four Soviet skippers before they sailed, and it signified simply that their vessel was under attack. If the Republican naval commanders should have cause to open their envelopes they would find inside orders to hurry to the rescue of the Soviet ship concerned, engage the enemy in battle, and save the merchantman and its cargo at all costs. Orlov realized that such an operation could only be mounted through Prieto, the Republican defense minister, who was also minister for the navy, so he now arranged for Prieto to hurry to Cartagena and issue the necessary instructions in person.

Everything possible to carry out the command of "Ivan Vasiliyevitch" had succeeded brilliantly thus far. Nonetheless, it was a very worried man who, on one night toward the end of October 1936, watched the four Russian vessels, with all Spain's gold on board, slip out of Cartagena harbor and head out into the Mediterranean, bound for Odessa. What might happen if they were intercepted en route, not by Spanish Nationalist vessels but by Italian warships belonging to Franco's other Axis ally, Mussolini, he hardly dared to think. In that event, the naval battle he had prepared for would cause plenty of sparks to fly inland as well. But the days passed without any special SOS message being transmitted. After a week of such blessed silence, Orlov could breathe again. By now, the gold would be on its way by armored train from Odessa to Moscow.

Orlov seems to have had not one word of thanks out of Stalin for his feat. But he received plenty of other professional tributes, as well as first-hand descriptions of how the great event had been greeted in the Kremlin. One such account (he revealed long after his flight) had come from a colleague and close friend of his who had actually attended a banquet given to celebrate the safe arrival of the gold. Stalin, who had invited, among the guests, all the members of his Politburo, was in excellent spirits, and cracked plenty of jokes. But one quip of his that was overheard turned out to be not only dead earnest but also prophetic.

"The Spaniards," beamed the dictator, "will never see their gold again, just as they will never see their ears."

Even in that ruthless age of purges, it seems almost unbelievable that, only a few months after rendering such an enormous personal service to Stalin, Orlov, through no action of his own, should have fallen under a cloud. Such ingratitude is, at first sight, even harder to fathom when one looks at Orlov's long record of unquestioning loyalty to the Bolshevik party and state before he even set foot in Spain.

The roots of this loyalty go right back to 1917, when Leon Lazarevich Feldbin, to give Orlov his real name,[4] graduated as a second lieutenant from the Third Moscow Military School. The twenty-two-year-old Leon, born on August 21, 1895 at Bobruisk near Minsk, was one of about twenty children of Lazar Feldbin, a fairly prosperous timber merchant of the town, and his wife Hannah. They were Jews and proud of it; indeed, ten years before Leon's birth, his grandfather had gone to Palestine in the so-called Aliy Rishona, or first emigration, to buy a patch of undrained marsh land, on the site of which the town of Petah Tikva stands in present-day Israel. It was a link which the later General Orlov was to recall with pleasure to his dying day. More to the point, that very Jewishness which had been such a perilous handicap under the tsars (driving many of his brothers, sisters, and cousins to the United States) proved, in his case, no barrier once the Bolsheviks had seized power. As a boy, Leon Feldbin had always dreamed of a military career; yet he was bitterly aware that, under the old order, a Jew could never aspire to an officer's commission. Now, the new regime had opened these doors for him, and his conversion to Communism after the revolution went hand in hand with purely professional gratitude.

It is important to remember that, in the case of Alexander Orlov—as we can resume calling him—the loyalty that sprang from this was total and unquestioning. Orlov is no moral hero of any inner ideological conflict, like Bajanov and Ignaz Reiss. If he ever had doubts about the increasingly repellent system he was serving, he suppressed them at the time and only gave vent to them later in the qualified form of a personal onslaught against the manipulator and absolute master of that system, Stalin. When, eventually, Orlov ran, it was mortal fear, not moral repugnance, which drove him. But either motive would have appeared equally incredible to the young and enthusiastic Red Army officer who, in April of 1921, married a beautiful girl from Kiev, Maria Roznetsky, and then settled down in Moscow.

The career that lay ahead of him for the next fifteen years was unusually varied. He had briefly studied law and now became an assistant prosecutor at the Supreme Soviet Court of Appeal, working also

---

[4] He only revealed this, like the rest of his personal biography, after his defection.

on the formulation of Communist Russia's first criminal code. The work was not only personally rewarding; it proved to be the stepping-stone to what, in the Bolshevik state, were much higher things. In 1924, Felix Dzerzhinsky, then head of the State Security Service, was so impressed by a fearless legal presentation which Orlov had made that he moved the young prosecutor into his own OGPU. After more than a year in Dzerzhinsky's Economic Directorate (where he super-vised, among other things, the handling of all foreign businessmen in the Soviet Union and the exploitation, for espionage purposes, of Soviet trade concessions abroad) Orlov returned to his cherished mili-tary field of action. In 1925, he was appointed brigade commander of the border guards in Georgia. It was a key post, given the unrest in Stalin's native province, and, from his headquarters in Tiflis, Orlov had control over six regiments totaling some eleven thousand men.

For a man who loved the soldier's life, it must have been a very happy time, though, had he and Maria but known it, this idyll at Tiflis was to bring in its train a terrible cloud over their future. One day, he took his wife, and their three-year-old daughter Vera, out rowing on a lake. It was cool, and the child got soaked, sitting with her mother in the stern of the boat. Afterward, she developed a shivery cold with temperature. When the shivers stopped and tem-perature went down, the parents thought nothing more of it. In fact, the little girl, who was to be their only child, had contracted the beginnings of rheumatic fever. It progressively weakened her heart and turned out to be incurable. She was to die of it, as a young girl, at the other end of the earth. The names of other defectors we have met with already now begin to flit in and out of Orlov's life. Thus, the man he handed over to in 1926, as Border Guards commander in Tiflis, was the ill-fated Jacob Blumkin, murderer of Count Mirbach and would-be murderer of Boris Bajanov. And when, later that year, Orlov was sent on his first assignment abroad, as head of the OGPU "Residentura" in Paris, his term of office there just overlapped with Bajanov's own arrival in the French capital. After Paris, where he used the alias of Leon Nikolayev, Orlov did a three-year spell in Berlin; and there then followed an even longer period of varied foreign travels, based on Moscow.

The first of these trips, which took him, in 1932, to the United

States, was, by secret police standards, surprisingly innocent. He genuinely wanted to see the country and look up all those relatives of his from Bobruisk who had emigrated there in the last years of the tsarist regime. So, through one of his Berlin business contacts, he got himself an invitation from General Motors, and traveled all round America as their guest, from September 26 to November 30, using his Paris alias of Nikolayev.

The journeys that followed were frequent and much less innocuous. From the beginning of 1933 until the autumn of 1935, he is always on the move throughout western Europe—principally in Germany, France, Czechoslovakia, Austria, and Switzerland. The main target seems to have been Germany (by now in Hitler's hands) and his principal aim the creation of long-term "illegal" OGPU networks, that is, "deep cover agents" who enjoyed no official status or protection. This was the most sensitive part of his work and, significantly for a loyal professional, it was the part he never fully disclosed in later years to his Western interrogators.

England lies at the center of this nebulous maze. That he had read many top-secret British documents which were being photocopied and passed to Moscow by Soviet agents working in London at the time became, eventually, all too clear. Yet, sometimes, his detailed knowledge, not only of this material but also of the exact location and appearance of various buildings in Britain, seemed to surpass what even the most privileged official, gifted with the most prodigious memory, could have retained just by perusing papers at a Moscow desk. Was it therefore, first hand experience? Did Orlov ever come to London himself during this darkest undercover period of his career, and help to set up and develop that famous top-level Soviet spy network which was to become the espionage sensation of the fifties and sixties? That riddle belonged to the future.

This, then, was the man who, in September 1936, had arrived in Madrid as Stalin's special liaison officer to the Republican government. Behind him lay twenty years of dedicated services to the Soviet cause—as Red Army subaltern and partisan fighter; as a criminal prosecutor and lawmaker; as a commander of frontier forces; and as "resident" and administrator of key OGPU offices in western Europe. Nor, after the exploit of the Spanish gold, did he do anything to blot his copybook in his subsequent activities in Spain. Indeed, he was so successful in organizing guerilla groups behind the Nationalist lines, especially among the miners of the Rio Tinto areas, that Franco was forced to divert two divisions from the front line to deal with this unrest in the rear. The Spanish post seemed like yet another brilliant step in the career of this trusty servant of the Kremlin; and, as though to mark it, he had taken, for the first time, this alias of Alexander Orlov.[5] Yet, though that name was to stick to him for the rest of his life, the new assignment, and with it the whole of his career, now began rapidly to crumble. The reason had little or nothing to do directly with Comrade Feldbin-Nikolayev-Orlov. It had everything to do with a major convulsion taking place within the Soviet security apparatus itself—a convulsion which was both propelled by, and in turn helped to escalate, the great political purges of the day.

For years, a rivalry had been growing within the OGPU between the so-called Georgian group of officials (who looked for patronage to their fellow Georgian, Stalin) and the Ukrainian group, which was largely Jewish. There is no reason to suppose that Orlov himself had been active in any conspiratorial sense with the Ukrainian faction, though, by reason both of nationality and race, he belonged emphatically to it. But one of his Bobruisk cousins, a certain Zinovy Katsnelson, was up to his neck in an anti-Stalin conspiracy before Orlov was even posted in Spain.

Orlov first learned of this in February of 1937 when he was in a Paris clinic, recovering from a sprained back caused by a car smash. Cousin Zinovy, who was at this time deputy chief of the OGPU in the Ukraine, called on Orlov and, in the safe surroundings of a private French hospital ward, confided something that must have made the patient start up violently enough to wrench his injured back in the process.[6] The Ukrainian opposition group, said Katsnelson, had had enough of the dictator and his purges. They were mounting a "legal" coup to dethrone him. He went on:

---

[5] He had chosen this particular alias out of admiration for the eighteenth-century Russian writer of that name.

[6] What follows was described by Orlov many years later in several of his interrogations.

Like good Communists, we are going to remove Stalin through the party, and we shall do so by denouncing him as a one-time agent of the "Okhrana" [tsarist secret police]. We now have conclusive proof of this. Three copies of all the evidence are stowed away in separate hiding places. After such an exposure he will have no option but to stand down.

Katsnelson then added two significant things. In the first place, he indicated that the military would support his "Ukrainian group." But he also voiced fears that the entire plot may have been leaked.

The truth of this claim that some Red Army leaders had made common cause with the OGPU Ukrainians in a bid to remove Stalin was never objectively established. But, assuming there was anything to it, it casts a new light on the most startling of all Stalin purges—the arrest, made public on June 11, 1937, of Marshal Tukhachevsky and seven other leading generals, on charges of treason. Before the Russian people had caught their breath after this announcement, there came another communiqué, issued only twenty-four hours later, to say that the legendary war hero and his accomplices (who, between them, made up the best military brains in the Soviet Union) had already been tried, found guilty, and executed. That the evidence posthumously produced against them, "spying for Hitler," was a ludicrous fabrication has never been doubted. But, as Orlov interpreted the charade when he heard the news, these charges had only been invented because, though there had been a genuine plot, Stalin was afraid to reveal its true nature.

This remains partly hypothetical. However, Cousin Katsnelson's second comment in that Paris clinic came all too true, all too quickly. He, at any rate, had already been discovered, for, when he returned to Moscow in March, it was to face a firing squad. At one stroke, Orlov's own position and prospects were transformed. From being one of Stalin's most trusted henchmen, he had become the inevitably suspect kinsman of one of the principal plotters against the dictator. Moreover, there was no knowing what Katsnelson had been tortured into revealing before his execution. If he had disclosed, for example, that Alexander Orlov now knew the whereabouts of two copies of the incriminating "Okhrana" dossier, then Stalin could be expected to strike at once. It was with some trepidation therefore that, in the spring of 1937, Orlov noted the arrival in Republican Spain of a certain Comrade Bolodin. The newcomer was wearing the uniform of a Red Army tank general. But, as Orlov well knew, he was one of the NKVD's top assassins. Had he come, not to command tanks, but to liquidate the Soviet liaison officer to the Republican government?

Everything went on normally until the political avalanche, already described, which was set in motion by the defection in Paris of Ignaz Reiss in July of 1937. From his post in Spain, Orlov heard all about the dozens of NKVD men recalled from foreign assignments by their new chief, Yezhov, and liquidated in the aftermath of the Reiss-Krivitsky affair. He must have wondered when his turn was coming. In August, sure enough, came the first ominous sign.

A message from his immediate superior, Sliutsky, the head of the NKVD's Foreign Department in Moscow, warned him that Franco's agents, with Nazi help, were planning to kidnap him on Spanish Republican territory to extract information about the Kremlin's involvement in the Civil War. To ward off this danger, the telegram continued, an NKVD bodyguard of twelve specially selected men was being sent to Spain to accompany him wherever he went. There were two queer things about this message. First, Orlov was virtually the head of the Republic's Intelligence and Counterintelligence service. It was, to put it mildly, strange that he should not have picked up a whisper of such a plan on the spot himself. Then, the very idea of sending such a large bodyguard all the way from Russia struck a false note. Its purpose, surely, was not to protect him, but to liquidate him. He knew all about the secret "mobile groups" which Yezhov, the new head of the NKVD, had organized to carry out the assassination of émigrés or suspect colleagues (operations known colloquially in his service as "wet jobs").

Orlov decided to bluff it out. He wired back to Sliutsky saying that, as his office was guarded twenty-four hours a day by Spanish soldiers, and as armed Spaniards accompanied him on all his travels, no extra reinforcements were necessary. However, alerted by that telegram, Orlov provided some extra reinforcements of his own. His choice was instructive. He had ten Communists, all serving with the German International Brigade, secretly relieved from duty at the front and seconded personally to him to provide an all-German security screen against Stalin. Orlov's emphatic reply kept the Foreign Department quiet, but not for long. In October of 1937, Sliutsky's deputy, Shpiegelglas, fresh from his triumph of organizing the murder of Ignaz Reiss in Switzerland, suddenly turned up in Republican Spain. This, again, was a disturbing development, for he had no business in the country, as Orlov was in the best position to know. His anxiety turned to alarm when he heard that the visitor had been conferring in Madrid with Bolodin, the bogus Soviet "tank general" on whom Orlov had been keeping a wary eye for some time.

It was from this point onward that Alexander Orlov started, not merely to think about defection, but to plan for it. He tried to put himself as a fellow professional in the quaking if menacing boots of Comrade Shpiegelglas. He and Bolodin would have weighed up the two protective rings—of Spanish soldiers and German Communists—which always surrounded their quarry. They would have come to the conclusion that it would be too difficult, and too politically complicated, to break through them and murder the Kremlin's official liaison officer at his post. So what, to the epert, would be the alternative? Obviously, the kidnapping of Orlov's wife and daughter, who were now living with him at a country house near Barcelona.

The thought grew larger and larger and gave him no peace. He took a day off, collected his family, and drove them over the mountains into France, where he installed them in a villa close to the frontier. He left behind his chauffeur, who was a trusted Spanish police agent, to guard them, and then drove the car back himself to Barcelona. They had considered making a dash for it there and then to North America but had held back, hoping, in the meantime, to make some arrangements for the safety of Orlov's mother and mother-in-law, both of them vulnerable hostages in Moscow. Yet, from now on, it was only a matter of time.

Zero hour finally came on July 9, 1938, when Orlov received another personal message from Moscow, this time from Yezhov himself. General Orlov was ordered to proceed to Paris and to contact Comrade Birukov, who was the Soviet consul-general there. Birukov would then drive with him in an Embassy car to Antwerp, where the Soviet vessel *Svir* lay anchored. He was to board her by July 14 at the latest for "important discussions." It was Agabekov and the *Philomena* all over again; and, like Agabekov, Orlov knew he was being invited by his colleagues to walk up the ship's gangplank into a floating prison. He knew also that, to have any prospect of survival, he and his family would need to have not merely severed all links with Moscow by the time the deadline arrived but to have already placed themselves beyond the reach of Yezhov and those mobile assassination squads of his which swarmed all over western Europe. It was a tall order, and had Orlov not begun to plan his flight nine full months before, he would never have fulfilled it.

Realizing that any hint of prevarication would be dangerous, he immediately wired back to Moscow saying that he would arrive at Antwerp by the prescribed route and at the appointed time. That left him forty-eight hours to make his final arrangements while appearing to carry out his orders. On July 11, he took leave of his staff at Barcelona and drove with his German bodyguard to the French frontier. So far, his movements, duly reported to Moscow, would have aroused no suspicion, as he was traveling in the right direction, and traveling, moreover, alone. But the moment he was across the border (having left the German bodyguard on the Spanish side) he started to follow his own trail. He made for the Grand Hotel in Perpignan where, by arrangement, his wife and daughter had been brought from their French villa the day before. From there, the trio went by night train to Paris, where they booked in at a hotel never used by Soviet personnel and where Orlov himself had never stayed before.

It was July 13, and the eve of the great French national holiday, Bastille Day. Orlov could not be expected to have thought of everything; but the fact that he had not considered that particular date might have doomed them. The usual preholiday exodus from the capital had begun, and when he went to his chosen haven, the United States Embassy, he found, to his dismay, that Ambassador Bullitt had already left Paris for two or three days. It was Maria who suggested that they should try the Canadian Legation instead. It proved an almost miraculous alternative.

When Orlov presented his diplomatic passport and asked to see the head of mission, he was doubtful whether he would even be received, for the Soviet Union and Canada had no diplomatic relations. But he was admitted and the minister proved, in Orlov's words, to be "a friendly sort of man." Moreover, he was a former Canadian commissioner for immigration and was therefore both familiar with the question of asylum and in a position of personal authority to do something about it. Quite how much Orlov told him of their plight on the spot is not quite clear; but within the hour, the Canadian diplomat had not only issued them with entry visas (ostensibly for a holiday in Quebec) but had also provided Orlov with a letter of introduction to his former subordinates in the Immigration Office.

That bit of good luck was followed by an even greater stroke of fortune. A Canadian priest, who happened to be visiting the Legation at the time, got into conversation with them, and, hearing about their urgent travel plans, produced the information that a Canadian passenger ship, the S.S. *Mountclair*, was due to sail home from Cherbourg that very evening. What is more, the priest had also heard that there were still some cabins free. Never, in his long professional career, can General Orlov have had such a timely piece of intelligence as this, which came just as that career was closing. He rushed to a travel bureau to get tickets while Maria literally ran to their hotel, which was nearby, to collect Vera and the luggage. They all met up at the railway station and caught the boat train with seconds to spare. Four hours later, they boarded the *Mountclair*. It weighed anchor, on schedule, that evening.

It was now approaching midnight on July 13. On board another ship, the *Svir* at Antwerp, Yezhov's assassination squad would be looking again at their watches, shrugging their shoulders, and consoling themselves with the thought that their victim still had another day's grace to report.

Chapter Twelve

THE DEFECTOR WHO VANISHED

Still traveling on their Soviet diplomatic passports, Orlov and his family entered the United States from Canada at Rouses Point, New York, on August 13, 1938. Exactly one month before, he had been due to keep a rendezvous at Antwerp which would almost certainly have meant his wife and daughter never setting eyes on him again. Now, the three were together in freedom; free, moreover, in the country he had chosen for his asylum when he had begun to sense Stalin's hands at his throat in Spain some eighteen months before. He had been helped by almost miraculous good fortune during those crowded hours in Paris. Yet, after allowing for that, it had been, as befitted a three-star general of the secret police, the smoothest and best prepared of all those prewar Soviet escapes. Orlov followed this up with further plans which were devised to safeguard the family's future now that they had crossed the Atlantic.

The first of these concerned Stalin himself and was already being

put into operation. Both Orlov's own mother and Maria's mother—
the two hostages back in Russia whom they had worried so much
about while mulling over their own flight—were now at the dictator's
mercy. Orlov knew his former master well enough to realize that
only one thing might stay his vengeance: blackmail on a bold, grand
scale. During his three-week stay in Canada, he had unsheathed a
weapon specially fashioned for this purpose. One of his many New
York cousins, Nathan Koornick, had been summoned to Montreal
and handed two copies of a thirty-seven-page document in Orlov's
handwriting. The top copy was addressed to Stalin personally; the
duplicate to his state security chief, Yezhov.

The main text wasted no time on rhetoric, recriminations, or self-
justification. It stated bluntly that if either Orlov's mother or mother-
in-law were harmed in any way, he would publish all that he knew of
Stalin's hidden crimes—and especially those ugliest secrets concerning the dictator's personal cruelty and perfidy throughout the great
political purges and Moscow show trials which had rocked the world.
Just to demonstrate that the writer knew what he was talking about
(not that either recipient could have doubted it), Orlov attached, as
an appendix, a long and detailed catalog of the principal misdeeds he
had in mind. He added that, should anything happen to him in exile,
provision had been made for the disclosures to be published automatically at his death. There was also one very nasty job aimed directly
at Yezhov. The police chief, Orlov informed Stalin, had been guilty,
the year before, of the most heinous offense in the security book: he
had allowed an "illegal" undercover agent, one Nikolai Skobline, to
take refuge in the Soviet Embassy while on the run from the French
police after a Paris street kidnapping.[1] Orlov knew that Yezhov had
lied to Stalin about the manner of Skobline's escape to cover up his
own professional blunder. Orlov also knew that this revelation would
deliver up the police chief once and for all into the palm of the dictator's hand.

The problem of how to deliver these warnings had been as carefully thought out as the messages themselves. With his passage to
Europe paid for by Orlov, Cousin Nathan had been told that, on land-

---

[1]   Of the Russian émigré leader, General Miller, on September 21, 1937.

ing, he was to make straight for the Soviet Embassy in Paris. He was given a precise description of that building in the Rue de Grenelle which Orlov knew so well from his two years as OGPU "resident" within its walls. Then had followed a minute-by-minute, and almost second-by-second briefing as to how, exactly, the documents were to be passed on. Nathan was to take a taxi; keep the taxi standing outside the Embassy with its engine running; press a certain bell; thrust the papers firmly into the hands of whomever answered it; and then, without a word of argument or explanation, dart back to the taxi and drive off. By the time the Orlovs crossed at Rouses Point, Nathan had carried out his instructions to the letter, and was on his way back.

The family thus entered America knowing that everything humanly possible had been done to protect the two most precious and most vulnerable people they had been forced to leave behind. The problem now was how to protect themselves. The general was under no illusions about his own safety. He knew that, even if his blackmail succeeded in dissuading Stalin from any profitless acts of retribution in Russia, the dictator would stop at nothing to get even with the insolent blackmailer, however long it took. The deepest cover was therefore called for in his life in exile, deeper than any he had provided himself with during his years as a foreign agent. He had already selected his principal new alias for America. The surname would be Berg, the Christian name alternating between Leon and Alexander. The question was how swiftly and completely Mr. Berg and his family could melt away into the American landscape.

He could never have imagined, as he arrived in New York and started to make contact with the American authorities, how much gratuitous help they were to give him in this respect, and how much careless damage they were to inflict, in the process, on themselves and the democratic cause as a whole. To the seasoned agent, trained under a regime when every footstep of every foreigner was shadowed and reported on by an all-embracing, all-powerful security network, this must have seemed like a land of unbelievable openness, innocence, and folly.[2]

---

[2]   The account which follows of Orlov's long underground existence in America has never been published. He himself wrote nothing of this period of his life. This

His first move was to find a lawyer to advise him. There were several of his childhood relatives from Bobruisk living in New York, notably an aunt married to a Mr. Koornick, who seems to have been a reasonably prosperous and knowledgeable American citizen. With their aid, he selected a Mr. John F. Finerty, who had come into prominence as the attorney serving on a congressional committee set up to examine a subject very close to Orlov's heart—the bloody chain of Moscow trials. Mr. Finerty, who was an influential member of the Democratic party, declared himself very happy to handle the distinguished newcomer's case, and decided to go right to the top on his behalf. The result was that, within a week or two of entering the United States, Orlov found himself invited to Washington for a private appointment with Mr. Francis Biddle, then the attorney general.

He gave Biddle only the barest facts of his rank and status (producing his Soviet diplomatic passport as credential) and made a purely verbal request to be allowed to stay in America. The attorney general could see no objection, but brought in his commissioner for immigration and naturalization, James A. Houghteling, just to make sure. All that Mr. Houghteling required was a formal assurance that the refugee could produce sponsors, if need be, and that he had some funds of his own to start his new life on. Orlov named various American relatives for his referees. As regards the money, he now revealed that he had brought with him into exile $22,800 in cash, a sum which, he said, represented "an accumulation of salary and savings" made while serving as a senior Soviet official.

That was the end of the matter. The American attorney general and his commissioner simply assured Orlov, on the spot and on the nod, that he was free to settle in the country if he chose. He was given nothing in writing—no formal entry certificate, not even an informal letter on government notepaper. Nor, which is even more extraordinary, was anything requested of him in return. It never occurred to either of these top-ranking Washington dignitaries that some of their colleagues in the State Department, the War Department, the FBI, or the Moscow Trials committee itself might conceivably profit from the presence in their midst of a three-star general of Stalin's secret

---

reconstruction is based largely on details he provided many years later to personal friends and to one or two U.S. government officials who won his trust.

police service, a man who could clearly untangle many current riddles, if suitably induced. In August 1938, a time when the world was already locked into the conflict of Europe's rival dictatorships, and sliding ever closer to war, this unique inside witness from that tyrannical order was not as much as asked for Stalin's size in shoes, in return for being granted immediate and unconditional asylum for himself and his family.

Even if he could scarcely believe his luck, Orlov did not trifle with it. He walked out of that Washington office, becoming Mr. Berg as he crossed the threshold, and then vanished completely, inside America, for the next fifteen years.[3] When he did surface—entirely of his own volition—a World War had been fought and won, and the Cold War was at its chilly height. It was not surprising that, when he did reappear, the political and intelligence establishments of Washington, by this time committed to an obsessive study of the Soviet menace, were both aghast and incredulous. We have seen how General Orlov was let off the hook. How did Mr. Berg manage to swim so totally submerged for so long?

One key was that $22,800 in hard cash, a very tidy sum in prewar and wartime values, and one which he was able to pad out a little further by loans totaling another $4,000 from his various relatives. He and Maria (they later told the authorities) set this capital aside, buying themselves only the barest essentials in clothes and furniture, and drew on it from 1938 onward at the rate of $1,500 a year, which they had made their annual expenditure target. This target had been fixed by Maria after an exhaustive examination of American prices for food and rents. The latter averaged about $75 a month for them over the whole decade and a half, their first and cheapest apartment costing them $45, and their last and most expensive $80. As for the food, that was kept as Spartan as everything else in their life, and they never once allowed themselves the basic luxury of a car, even in this land of mass motoring.

---

[3] His only contact with any authority in Washington during these fifteen years was on December 19, 1940, when he and his wife were registered and fingerprinted in compliance with the Alien Registration Act. Even then, however, he was allowed to register in care of Mr. Finerty, without giving his own address. And even then, with Europe already at war, not the slightest step toward interrogating him was undertaken.

It was an austere existence; but it had one great safety factor built into it. Orlov never had to register for employment, which protected him against chance discovery in factory or office by that bureaucratic machine he had been allowed to elude. Another safeguard was the routine one of frequent changes in both names and addresses. Even the trusted Mr. Finerty never knew exactly where he was or what he was calling himself at any given time. Orlov had placed his Soviet passport—his only identity document—in a safe-deposit box before leaving Washington, and, for a long time, communicated with his lawyer only by coded inserts in the *New York Times*. Apart from Leon Berg and Alexander Berg, his two staple aliases, he also called himself, as he moved from house to house and town to town across the United States, Alexander Feld, and Leon Koornick, after his aunt's American husband. Maria, while using as a rule whatever style Orlov adopted, had at least one alias all of her own: Maria Roznetsky, her maiden name.

Their changes of domicile were just as complicated. From Washington and New York, they moved first of all to Boston and then, after a short stay, to various addresses in the Pittsburgh area. The year 1940 finds them in Los Angeles, where they had to face the greatest tragedy ever to afflict their personal lives. Vera, whose health had been getting steadily worse, died there, aged only sixteen, of the long-delayed effects of that rowing boat outing on a lake in far-away Tiflis. Though they survived the blow, the parents never surmounted it. It was not merely that both of them had always doted on this, their only child. Two years of exile in America, even in an underground labyrinth of their own construction, had more than convinced them that this was the country, and this the form of society, for their daughter to grow up in. They, after all, could only grow old in it. Her death had robbed them, in a very special sense, of the future.

The Orlovs recrossed the continent with their child's ashes. They returned to Massachusetts where, at Cambridge, they opened a family crypt with permanent service at a local cemetery. In the circumstances, they must have been very loath to leave this town; but two things forced their hand. The first was the lurid spotlight suddenly turned on Soviet defectors and Soviet espionage in general by the discovery of Walter Krivitsky's body in a Washington hotel in February of 1941. Orlov was in little doubt himself as to how, and why, his erstwhile colleague had died, and Washington seemed rather too close for comfort. A second major factor was that, while in Cambridge, Alexander Berg (or whatever Orlov was calling himself at the time) was served with a draft card for military service with the American forces, which were now being placed on a war footing. This was something to be avoided at all costs, not because he would not have made a good G.I., but because the callup might have revealed that he was, in fact, a lieutenant-general in the Soviet KGB.

So, in 1941, the Orlovs moved on to what was to become the nearest thing to their American home town: Cleveland, Ohio. They rented modest rooms in an apartment house and used these as their base throughout the war and immediate postwar period. They lived the quietest of existences, going out little, cultivating no friends, and making only the necessary minimum of local acquaintances. Nonetheless, it was in Cleveland that Orlov underwent his Americanization. Like everything else in his life, the process was deliberate, unhurried, and well mapped out.

He began with the language which, with future plans in mind, he knew that he would need to master much more thoroughly than the average immigrant. He registered as a student at the local Dyke and Spencerian College and gradually perfected his English as he worked his way through the full graduate course. (It later transpired that the Cleveland FBI had an office in the same building; so, unbeknown to each other, the former Soviet agent and American security officials must have brushed shoulders on scores of occasions during these war years.) By the time the war was ending Orlov had earned his degree (in the name of Berg) and he now embarked on the next stage of his project, quietly and systematically, as though Cleveland, Ohio, were the self-contained center of the universe, and the convulsions shaking Europe and Asia were reverberating from another planet. The project was his memoirs, or rather, one small part of them, namely the enlargement of those blackmail letters to Moscow into a full-scale book about Stalin's reign of terror.

For the next five years, he could be seen, on almost any weekday, seated at his desk in the White Memorial Library of Cleveland (a branch of the main public library) researching the general background of the interwar period, checking his facts on the Soviet Union itself whenever his excellent memory left him in any doubt, and putting pen to paper on the actual manuscript. Despite the good command of English he had acquired by now, he wrote the original of his book in Russian, with Maria typing out the draft each evening in Cyrillic.

By the time he wrote the last words in the White Memorial Library, early in 1951, the great ideological conflict of the Cold War was at its height, the two camps led respectively by Orlov's native land and the country of his adoption. He decided to try for immediate publication, despite the fact that this would bring an end to their anonymous underground existence and might pose all sorts of awkward questions about their personal future. There were several factors in this decision. To begin with, he and Maria had to assume that, by now, both their mothers were dead and that, in all probability, therefore, there was no longer anyone left behind in Russia to protect by his silence. Moreover, with the East-West propaganda debate at its height, it seemed a telling moment to break that silence with a book that would put paid to so many of Stalin's lies.

But the most pressing reason to act was, almost certainly, much more prosaic. The last of that KGB dollar nest egg they had been living on so carefully since 1938 was almost spent. As Orlov later told his American interrogators, while those final chapters were being typed, he and Maria had been reduced to a diet of cheap breakfast cereals, eaten all round the clock. One after the other, they had pawned their valuables. The last—their daughter's camera—was now used to raise money for their fare to New York with the precious manuscript.

In New York, he contacted Max Eastman, a distinguished American writer with a personal history which made him very suitable for Orlov's purposes. In the early days of the Bolshevik revolution, Eastman had been a man of extreme left-wing views and an ardent champion of Communism. He had paid frequent visits to the Soviet Union, had become a confidant of Trotsky's, and had even married a woman from the Bolshevik hierarchy—the sister of Nikolai Krylenko, under whom, in 1921, Orlov himself had worked as a lawyer during his time at the Soviet Supreme Appeals Court. Long before 1951, however, Eastman had had second thoughts about the dictatorship of the proletariat, and especially about the dictator himself. He was now an established right-wing intellectual and a violent anti-Stalinist. Eastman thus appreciated, from first hand, both the background to Orlov's story and the importance, in Cold War terms, of the revelations he was about to make.

Despite these impeccable credentials, Orlov moved cautiously with this man he had never before met face to face. He introduced himself, not under his real name, but as "the author's representative." Whether Eastman believed that or not, he was under no doubts about the book. The manuscript, he declared, was "magnificent." General Orlov would, of course, need a translator for it and he, Eastman, would be happy to offer his services, in return for one-third share of the royalties. Even to someone quite unversed in the ways of the American publishing world, this seemed rather a greedy proposition. The Orlovs turned it over for a day of two and then turned it down. They borrowed a few hundred dollars from their New York relatives and then returned to their breakfast cereal regimen in Cleveland, to translate the book into English themselves. It took another year's hard slog but by the middle of 1952 everything was ready at last. Their hard work and patience were to be spectacularly rewarded. In March of 1953, a few weeks after arrangements had been made for the first extracts from the book to be published, the archvillain of the whole story, Joseph Stalin, died in the Kremlin. By waiting so long, Orlov had enabled the dictator to provide him with the sort of topical "peg" of which every writer dreams. Even so, he must have been rather disappointed that the dictator did not live long enough to see himself unmasked.

The hardback version of the book was brought out later that same year in New York by Random House, and was subsequently translated into German, Spanish, Japanese, and Chinese. Entitled *The Secret History of Stalin's Crimes*, it was the first authoritative and detailed exposure ever made of the truth behind the notorious Moscow show trials. Orlov was able to reveal, in Stalin's machinations between 1934 and 1938, depths of treachery, megalomania, vengefulness, and cruelty that not even his fiercest critics in the West would have credited.

Orlov's *Secret History* stands on its own and should be read on its own. All that are needed here are one or two examples of these indictments that he had been nursing for so long. There was, for instance, the inside story of the liquidation of Kamenev and Zinoviev, the two Bolshevik leaders who, in the early days of the regime, had formed, together with Stalin, the ruling trio of the Politburo. Ten years later, the morbidly suspicious dictator had determined to rid himself of his veteran colleagues, in case they should form a political nucleus around which opposition might gather. Their downfall began in the most unlikely way, with the murder, on December 1, 1934, of another member of the old guard, Sergei Kirov, who was shot dead in his Leningrad office by a young ex-Communist named Leonid Nikolayev.

This Kirov assassination was, from the outset, a most puzzling affair. No one had ever heard of the assassin. No one could imagine his motive, for Kirov was an immensely popular figure. No one could explain how the deed had been done for, popular or not, Kirov, as a Politburo member and head of the Leningrad Region, was closely guarded day and night. Puzzlement turned to utter bewilderment when official attempts were made to explain the crime. The first version was that the murderers were White Guard terrorists who slipped across the border from Finland. One hundred and four White Guard "culprits" were accordingly executed. However, it turned out that they had died in vain in more senses than one for, two weeks later, the Soviet press produced, out of the blue, an entirely new version of the crime. The White Guards were wiped from the scene as though those one hundred and four victims had never faced a firing squad. Instead, the murder was now blamed on the "Trotskyite opposition," headed by Kamenev and Zinoviev.

Orlov, who was abroad at the time, knew in his bones that both stories were ludicrous. The Soviet-Finnish border was far too closely watched for White Guard assassins to sneak across in pairs, let alone in scores. As for two old guard Bolsheviks assassinating a third, such an act would have cut across the most fundamental of party ethics which this breed of veteran Communist still adhered to, as well as being, in their case, a politically pointless exercise. On his next visit home, Orlov ferreted out the truth by discreetly questioning a number of highly placed friends in the hierarchy, all of whom he named in his book.

Stalin, it transpired, had himself planned the murder of Kirov down to the last detail, and the intention from the start had been to pin the blame on Kamenov and Zinoviev. The dictator had thus aimed to rid himself at one blow both of this outspoken Leningrad leader, who had drawn more applause at the 1934 Party Congress than he had himself, and also of two less dangerous Politburo members who, nonetheless, knew far too much for comfort about the dictator's climb to absolute power. With all this in mind, Stalin had replaced the Leningrad security chief, a man devoted to Kirov, with one of his own plastic figures. He had even arranged for Nikolayev, a man with a burning grievance caused by his own expulsion from the party, to be systematically incited to the murder as a protest against "bureaucratic injustice."

He did not turn out to be a very good assassin. The first attempt failed when the pistol he had been provided with was discovered, during a routine security check, in the briefcase where he was carelessly carrying it around. Clearly, Nikolayev needed a helping hand, and Stalin's minions saw that he got it. Not only was he mysteriously handed back his pistol and issued with another pass to the Headquarters building, but Kirov's guards were conveniently removed from the corridor when the assassin made his second approach. This time, he succeeded with one shot, and then fainted clean away at his victim's side.

The deed done at last, Stalin hurried in person to Leningrad to conduct the "investigation." But nothing went quite right for him. Nikolayev, who appears to have cottoned on to the fact that he had been duped, grew so incensed that, according to Orlov's account, he even shouted defiance at the dreaded dictator himself. There was no alternative, after that, but to try and sentence him in secret. The same expedients had to be used against his supposed employers, Kamenev and Zinoviev, who refused to confess to the crime and whom the state prosecutor could not succeed in framing in an even remotely credible manner. Finally, after weeks of threats and bargaining, masterminded once more by Stalin, the two veterans were persuaded, for the sake of "party unity," to take upon themselves the "political and moral responsibility" for Kirov's death, while denying any hand in the deed itself. For this, on January 15, 1935, a military tribunal, sitting *in camera*, sentenced Zinoviev and Kamenev to ten and five years' imprisonment repectively.

In fact, they never served out either sentence. Eighteen months later, in August of 1936, they reappeared in a Moscow courtroom at the head of a batch of sixteen old guard Bolsheviks accused of a variety of "counterrevolutionary" crimes. This time, the hearing was in public, and this time, beguiled by personal assurances from Stalin that their lives would be spared, the two men glumly confessed to all their "Trotskyite deviations." They had played their desperately loyal party role; Stalin promptly broke his solemn party pledge. On August 25, only twenty-four hours after sentence had been passed, the Moscow papers announced the execution of Kamenev and Zinoviev, along with all fourteen other defendants. It had been a long and muddled business, but the dictator had disposed of them at last.

Stalin's betrayal of these two survivors from the Bolshevik "Triumvirate" was perhaps the classic exposure in Orlov's catalog of the dicator's perfidy. But there were many other examples: the background to the 1936 purge of the Chekists for the crime of knowing too much, a purge that had culminated with the elimination of Yagoda himself; the inside story of how, in June of 1937, Red Army generals had followed the party leaders and the secret police chiefs into the courtrooms and the execution cells; and the almost incredible (even by Stalin's standards) tale of the attempt to frame three leading Soviet physicians for "causing the death" of, among others, the famous Russian author Maxim Gorky, whom Stalin had tried so hard to convert from a literary into a party legend. After all these revelations, written in a calm, authoritative tone, and without any ranting or special pleading, nobody could look at either the Soviet dictator or the system he had created in anything but a murky light again.

Chapter Thirteen

TOO MUCH, TOO LATE

The sensation made by Orlov's book was entirely public. However, preceding this there had been a domestic American turmoil about which nothing has ever been said. *Life* magazine had started, in February of 1953, to prepare extracts from Orlov's material, and on April 6, hard on the news of Stalin's death, the magazine printed the first of a major four-part series. It was only on that day, and only after opening that magazine, that the FBI learned that the greatest available expert on Soviet subversion and espionage had been living quietly in their midst for the past fifteen years.

An American official who was working in Washington at the time has described the reaction in government circles to this bombshell as a mixture of incredulity, horror, and wrath. Nineteen fifty-three was, after all, a far cry from 1938. Orlov had disappeared into an America wrapped in somnolent peace, a sleeping giant totally unaware of the battles that lay just ahead of it, and even more oblivious to the role of world leadership that would suddenly be thrust upon it after those battles had been won. Such security preoccupations as existed at the time—both domestic and international—concerned, in the main, Nazi Germany. The Soviet Union had barely reached the edge of Washington's chessboard.

By 1953, Hitler, and even Hitler's war, seemed like remote history by comparison with the global East-West conflict which had followed. In diplomatic terms, and particularly in Intelligence terms, the challenge of the Soviet bloc now overshadowed practically every square on the board. At home, the nation, in a convulsive overreaction against earlier ignorance and apathy, had both weakened and cheapened itself in the anti-Communist witch-hunts of the McCarthy era. The international horizon was equally dominated by Soviet threats and conundrums—not only on the ground, at danger points like Berlin or the Balkans, but also in space, through the contest for nuclear supremacy. Whereas the Washington of 1938 could barely boast of one professional expert in Soviet subversion and Intelligence, the Washington of 1953 fairly swarmed with them, and their combined knowledge and advice, however scrappy and distorted in parts, had become a key factor in the formulation of White House policy. This was the community which first discovered, through a magazine article, that a vital key to many of those Communist riddles which had puzzled them ever since the Cold War began had been available, all those years, in their midst.

Sheer disbelief seems to have been the strongest initial element in their reaction. That is scarcely surprising. Even the Time-Life Corporation, confronted with this KGB apparition from the White Memorial Library, had felt obliged to find someone, somewhere, in the United States who could confirm that Mr. Alexander Berg of Cleveland, Ohio, really was General Alexander Orlov of Bobruisk and Moscow.[1] But the FBI were after more than one private witness. They simply could not credit the whole story Orlov now told them of his

---

[1] The witness who came forward to put their minds at rest was the American writer Louis Fischer, who had known Orlov both in Russia and in Spain.

long underground existence, and they set out to reconstruct and verify its every detail, beginning in August of 1938.

Fortunately, both the former attorney general, Francis Biddle, and his immigration commissioner, Mr. Houghteling, were still alive; and these two retired senior citizens confirmed, not without a certain embarrassment, that Orlov had indeed been admitted to America in precisely the casual fashion he had described. The investigators, still nonplussed, next turned to the money. With great thoroughness, they had cost-of-living tables drawn up for a family of three (reduced after eighteen months to two), for the entire 1938–53 period, in order to establish whether it was possible for the Orlovs to have existed, as they claimed, on a modest budget of $1,500 a year. The sums just added up. Indeed, the conclusion was that they would have had (bearing in mind interest on savings) about $100 left in the kitty at the end.

Finally, the FBI sent their investigators to every town and every house which Orlov had named as a domicile, and to every library which he had consulted. Not only did it all check out; additional details emerged which were all to Orlov's credit, though he had not mentioned them himself. The agent investigating their long stay in Cleveland, for example, reported interviewing a War Bond salesman in the city who had once knocked on the Orlov's door during his rounds. The salesman distinctly recalled his surprise when the quiet-spoken "Mr. Berg" had promptly subscribed for a $50 bond, a sum which had seemed remarkably patriotic in view of the bleak appearance of the little apartment. Patriotic was, of course, just what the former Soviet agent wanted to appear. But whatever the motive, he could hardly be faulted for the gesture.

Whether out of a sense of frustration and resentment, or whether out of plain insensitive stupidity, the FBI now proceeded to handle Orlov in a very boorish way. For weeks after the appearance of the first *Life* article, they beleagured the New York apartment where he had moved, producing mountains of files and literally thousands of questions. To a top-level professional like the man they were interrogating, it was the least subtle "debriefing" he could imagine. It was also the least effective, especially when his interrogators, egged on by

their superiors and by the memory of those fifteen years of lost op-
portunities, tried to turn him into something little better than a common informer for their service. This was not the level at which a
former secret police general was prepared to operate.

His refusal led on to an even uglier phase in the relationship. The
bureau probably realized that at the best of times (i.e., the worst of
times for the refugee) Alexander Orlov would have been a difficult
man to bribe. But in 1953, as a successful author, money was the last
thing that he needed. His income from his writings during that year
was later estimated at $44,500, nearly twice the sum on which he
and his family had kept going for a decade and a half. What he *did*
need—and desperately—was an orderly and legalized existence in
America now that he had surfaced again under his true colors. This
was the lever that the security authorities, with totally misguided
doggedness, eventually tried to use against him, in order to force him
into compliance.

The official records reveal that on June 13, 1955 warrants of arrest
were actually issued against both Orlov and his wife, on unspecified
charges of "failing to comply with the conditions of the non-immi-
grant status on which they were admitted."[2] In addition, Orlov himself was indicted for "being an alien, who, after entry, was a member
of the Communist party of a foreign state." This piece of muddled
McCarthyism was as technically unsound as it was intrinsically ludicrous. The name of Comrade Feldbin, alias Orlov and the rest, would
have been struck off the rolls of the Soviet Communist party long
before the defector had crossed from Canada into the United States.

Fortunately, these rather sordid proceedings never got off the
ground. After the publication of his book, Orlov had become something of a literary sensation, and one whose political bona fides
emerged clearly enough, not only from his public disclosures about
the Soviet Union but from all the unpublished facts about his way of
life as a refugee in America. The friends he had made among the
professional classes—notably the doctors who had treated him and
his family over the years, and the lawyers and prominent journalists

[2] This particular detail is contained in a special congressional report on the Orlov
case, drawn up on May 31, 1956 (84th Congress, second session, Calendar no. 2098,
Report no. 2075).

who had handled his case—joined forces with his relatives and his publishers to put him beyond range of molestation and blackmail once and for all. Politicians were lobbied on his behalf, and the ultimate outcome was a special bill, passed by Congress in May of 1956, "to grant the status of permanent residence in the United States to Alexander Orlov and his wife Maria." It had been a long trek from Barcelona, Paris, Cherbourg, and Montreal. When that bill was finally passed, the beneficiaries were aged sixty and fifty-two respectively.[3]

Eight months before, on September 28, 1955, Alexander Orlov, accompanied by Maria, had given his first testimony before the Senate Subcommittee on Internal Security in Washington. Nine months after the bill, on February 15, 1957, the couple appeared before the same subcommittee again. Not until sixteen years later, and after both were dead, was an edited version of these hearings made available. Entitled *The Legacy of Alexander Orlov*, it was issued as a special tribute "to the memory of a remarkable man" and as a warning that what he had revealed about Communism in general and Stalinism in particular should not be forgotten.

When placed in its chronological sequence in the entire debriefing process, this testimony probably contains a few details which were additional to those Orlov had already given to the Intelligence authorities during the initial "bull-at-a-gate" phase of his interrogation. However, it certainly contains much less information than he was to produce, nugget by nugget, long afterward, when he was being treated with both human sympathy and professional expertise by his subsequent "controllers." Nonetheless, enough was said at those two congressional hearings to enlighten, and occasionally startle, the chairman, Senator James O. Eastland, and the chief interrogating counsel, J. G. Sourwine.

He told them, for example, the full story of Mark Zborovsky, one of the most dangerous of all the special agents sent out by Stalin to shadow and, if possible, neutralize his banished rival, Leon Trotsky. When Orlov had first arrived in America, he already knew that this agent (whom, at that time, he could only identify as "Mark") had insinuated himself into the intimate circle surrounding Trotsky's son,

---

[3] A similar private bill, introduced on their behalf on January 20, 1954, had failed to get through.

who lived and wrote in Paris under the name of Leon Sedov. Orlov produced the text of a long anonymous letter dated December 27, 1938, which he had sent from America to Trotsky. In this, he had warned the exiled Bolshevik leader not only that the son was at the mercy of a Soviet *agent provocateur*, posing as an ally, but that, through him, Stalin was planning the assassination of the father.

On Christmas Day in 1953, thirteen years after Leon Trotsky had indeed been butchered on Stalin's orders at his Mexican home in Coyoacan, Orlov learned that the sinister Mark Zborovsky had managed to enter the United States the year after the killing. Moreover, he was by now established as an apparently respectable immigrant who had been given American citizenship and who enjoyed a wide range of social and official contacts. As soon as that Christmas holiday of 1953 was over, Orlov had exposed Stalin's former henchman. Significantly, he had gone in the first place, not to the hostile FBI, but to the New York office of an assistant United States attorney, Mr. Atterbury. As a result, Mark Zborovsky had been effectively neutralized. Orlov was relieved in more senses than one. As he admitted to the Eastland committee, he had had an uneasy feeling, during that first Christmas after his spectacular reemergence, that the next assassination Zborovsky might well be planning was his own.

Another tangled story which Orlov now helped to unravel was the Soviet campaign, launched over the six-year period 1928–34, to flood the United States with counterfeit dollar bills. Some accounts of this had appeared at the time in the American press,[4] while Walter Krivitsky, in his own memoirs, published in 1939, had described how he had been given the tricky job of winding the entire operation up, once it became clear in Moscow that it had developed into an embarrassing fiasco.[5] But what even Krivitsky had, apparently, not known was the intended scale of the venture, and the degree of Stalin's personal involvement in it. These, and many other fresh details, were now revealed by Orlov.

The whole affair had been planned, he told the committee, in a bid to secure badly needed hard currency (through exchanging the counterfeit notes) and so help finance the industrialization of the

---

[4]   See, for example, *New York Times*, February 24, 1933 and May 6, 1934.
[5]   See Krivitsky, *I Was Stalin's Agent*, pp. 146–58.

Soviet Union. A secondary dividend was the anticipated dislocation of the American economy. Stalin had been the driving force behind the scheme from the start, and Orlov linked this with the fact that, as a political prisoner of the tsars, the future dictator had shared a cell, in 1908, with two notorious forgers of 500-ruble notes.

The American counterfeits, which were in $100 bills, were judged by United States Treasury officials to be "the most deceptive examples of the issue" they had ever seen. This was no wonder for, as Orlov told the Eastland committee, they had been prepared, on Stalin's orders, by the Russian State Engraving and Printing Office in Moscow. Some of the experts put on the job were survivors from the prerevolution days and, as Orlov commented, there had been no more complicated notes in the world than the old tsarist currency. Stalin had devoted the same care to the distribution problem; indeed, for this purpose he had specially purchased, through Canadian Communist intermediaries, the Berlin finance house of Saas-Martin.

Despite these elaborate preparations, the operation had flopped. Some of the bogus bills were passed in Texas in 1928 (their first appearance) and various small amounts, known in the trade as "floaters," were brought in over the years, either by innocent tourists or by far-from-innocent special couriers. But when, in January 1933, a more ambitious bid was made in Chicago to launch $100,000 worth of the counterfeit money all at once, three-quarters of the notes were seized before they had even been put into circulation. Some of the "bootleggers" were arrested and later convicted. The fact that their ringleader, a young Russian-born New York physician, Dr. Grigory Burtan, was also a prominent American Communist, pointed the finger straightaway at Moscow. The talk at the time had been of a potential "two-million-dollar ring." Orlov now revealed that Stalin had, in fact, hoped to plant $10 million worth of these forged bills in the United States. Even that target was only intended as a first installment.

This testimony sounded, to an American congressional committee, much more relevant than his earlier tale of how Trotsky's assassination in Mexico had been planned. But even closer to home was the discussion which developed, toward the end of Orlov's hearing, about the espionage network which the Soviet Union had managed to establish, already before the war, in the United States. By the year of his defection, he said, America had been placed on the same footing in Intelligence terms as Britain and France.[6] That meant that, from his own NKVD service alone (i.e., not including the Soviet military espionage organization) and counting only "legal" operations (i.e., those run by Soviet officials working out of diplomatic and trade missions), they were running at least eighteen spy rings. At the head of this chain in 1938 had been a certain Comrade Gusev, who had once served as one of Orlov's own subordinates. Gusev had under him six Soviet assistants in various parts of the country and they, in turn, each had three American assistants, normally members of the American Communist party. What the position was at the time of this hearing, in February 1957, Orlov could not say, as he had been out of touch for so long. But, as he remarked, in all the intervening years, only two of these spy rings were known to have been exposed. There was the notorious one connected with Whittaker Chambers, and a second, revealed by Elisabeth Bentley, who had come forward of her own accord to the authorities and revealed herself as a Soviet agent. Orlov grimly noted that this still left sixteen of the prewar rings unaccounted for, to say nothing of any larger, additional networks constructed during the years of the anti-Hitler alliance.

Coming in 1957, all this information about Soviet penetration in the thirties was merely a sobering catalog for the historical record. But had it been revealed in 1938—and properly evaluated and acted upon at the time—it might have gone some way toward saving the West from President Roosevelt's fateful illusion that the Soviet Union, with its spunky, commonsense leader, Uncle Joe, was the only proper country for America to do business with in sorting out the postwar world.

Orlov's next venture as an American author was a curious one. In 1963, the University of Michigan Press published his *Handbook of Intelligence and Guerrilla Warfare*, which he himself described as a simplified, reconstructed version of a guidance manual he had originally compiled in 1935–36 for use in a secret Soviet training school for "illegal" agents. The title is somewhat misleading, as less than 20 pages out of the 187 in the book concern guerrilla warfare, a subject

---

[6] That is, on a roughly equal priority below Nazi Germany which, by 1938, had become Moscow's chief target.

in which Orlov had had his own baptism of fire more than forty years before in Poland. However, this one short chapter, setting out the basic principles of guerrilla strategy, illustrated with practical examples from Orlov's operations in Spain, became, over the next decade, required reading for the leaders of so-called national liberation movements throughout the world. As many of these movements (notably in Southeast Asia and Latin America) were sponsored by Moscow or Peking against American-backed regimes, this single aspect of Orlov's work turned out to be ironically double-edged.

The rest of the *Handbook,* however, fitted in well with Orlov's long-term program of exposing to the general public the immense scale and the deadly, self-perpetuating thrust of Soviet Intelligence and subversion. He described the basic doctrine of the Soviet system which relied, far more than its Western rivals, on secret information gathered in the field by agents, as opposed to the mass of data available for evaluation from published sources. He then set out, in plain, concise language which the layman would understand, the various targets of Soviet Intelligence in the West; how the "legal" and "illegal" networks were trained and planted; and how the agents, once established, would try to operate, including their methods of recruitment and their systems of communications with base. There was nothing in this slim volume which would have been new to the already vast American Intelligence apparatus of 1963. But its three editions brought home to the man in the street what the West in general, and the United States in particular, were up against.

After this, Orlov started on a study of Soviet law, his other professional speciality. It was a scholarly project, well suited to the leisurely, almost serene life into which he and Maria had now settled. Then, on November 14, 1969, something happened to show that, though Stalin himself had been dead these sixteen years or more, the Kremlin had still not forgotten Alexander Orlov.

During the afternoon, there was a quiet knock on the door of the Ann Arbor apartment in Michigan where they were now living. Orlov opened it cautiously, and by only an inch or two, alerted by the fact that the buzzer which opened the downstairs entrance to the building had not sounded. An unknown figure stood on the threshold, and, without asking who was peering at him through the crack, held up a letter which, he explained rapidly in English, was from one of General Orlov's former colleagues in Spain. Orlov took the letter and, without opening the door any wider, asked the caller for his name.

"I am Feoktistov," came the reply. Then the man added: "I would like a few words with Alexander Mikhailovitch."

Realizing that the stranger either had no idea what he looked like or had failed to recognize him, Orlov told the man to wait and said he would deliver the letter. But this was not good enough for Maria (whom American officials always regarded as "the real security officer of the Orlov family"). She had heard part of the conversation from her bedroom, and now swept forward into the hall to confront the visitor. First, she asked for proof of his identity. He repeated his name, described himself as a member of the Soviet delegation to the United Nations in New York, and produced documents to prove it. "Are you armed?" Maria demanded next, and he assured her he was not.

She then closed the hall door behind her, keeping her husband on the other side of it, and embarked on a battle of words and wills with the Comrade Feoktistov—who was so obviously just another NKVD man operating under diplomatic cover—which went on for the best part of two hours. Orlov, realizing that his wife was trying to protect him by drawing their visitor out, listened to the whole exchange without showing his face again. It was a rather circular conversation, revolving mainly around Maria's sisters, who were still in the Soviet Union. Didn't she want news of them? Would she like to deliver a message to them? Didn't she care for them any more? But whereas Feoktistov, acting on instructions, tried doggedly to stick to family matters, Mrs. Orlov brought him back, time and time again, to politics, and to the Soviet police techniques she knew so well. After it was clear that he was not going to talk to the husband and could get nowhere with the wife, the visitor finally left. They both knew that matters would not be allowed to rest there.

Surely enough, another approach soon followed, on the telephone. This time, when Orlov revealed himself, the tactics switched to flattery. Everyone in the Soviet Union, said Feoktistov, now respected, and even admired, the author of *The Secret History of Stalin's Crimes*.

He was no longer, in this changed post-Stalin era, considered as an enemy of the people. Would the general be so kind as to present him, Comrade Feoktistov, with a personal copy of the famous book? The technique was even more transparent, as well as more nauseating, than the appeal to family ties. But the fact that the NKVD man was so easy to see through made him no easier to endure.

Protected by an American security apparatus that had now grown both grateful and more understanding toward them, they moved back to Cleveland. Here, for more than eighteen months, they remained undetected and unmolested, though Maria's health, which had been frail for some years, seemed to be growing worse under the daily threat of some renewed harassment. It was she who, once again, took the brunt of the final NKVD approach. This was signaled, on the morning of August 10, 1971, by another of those gentle taps on their door.

She did not, at first, recognize the man outside as that unwelcome visitor in Michigan. So Feoktistov handed over his diplomatic passport and meekly allowed himself to be shut in the corridor while it was examined. His timid manner, as well as his persistence, caused the thought to flash across her mind; perhaps he, too, has had enough, and has come to us to help him defect. She called her husband and they let the bogus diplomat in, hoping they were welcoming a new friend.

"When did you break with the regime?" Maria demanded eagerly.

"No, I am with them. I work for them," came the disappointing reply.

There then followed an exhausting repetition, with some variations, of the conversation at the Ann Arbor apartment. It appeared that Comrade Orlov had advanced much further in the esteem of the Soviet government and people. He was now actually loved by them, and could be made a Hero of the Soviet Union just for the asking. Indeed, the chief purpose of this renewed approach was to get the general's permission for Soviet publications to extol him and his anti-Stalinist work for the fatherland. Why did he not return, with his wife, to the honors that were their due? Would he like to give a list of his friends still in the Soviet Union, so that greetings could be passed on to them? Would he like to step outside, just for a moment, and greet Mrs. Feoktistov and their daughter, who were sitting in the car?

It was all unbelievably clumsy stuff. Orlov knew full well that what was awaiting him in Moscow was a bullet, not a medal; just as he knew that the people sitting in that car downstairs were not an innocent mother and child but a murder or kidnap squad. Yet, as he afterward told his friends, the NKVD man had let slip—purposely or accidentally, one fascinating detail. While they were discussing Orlov's break with Moscow, Feoktistov suddenly said:

"You know, I have seen that letter you sent in 1938 to Stalin and also what Stalin wrote about it."

And he repeated the gist of what the dictator had scribbled, more than thirty years before, on the file. The words were violent and obscene, almost too obscene for Orlov to pass on further. Yet they made him realize, with a surge of satisfaction, how sharp that old blackmail weapon of his had been, and how deeply it had been driven home.

Eventually, Feoktistov was pushed through the door and told never to show his face there again. He never did. But though all his efforts had failed in their main purpose, they did have one tragic effect. Maria Orlov literally worried herself into the grave during the weeks that followed. On November 16, 1971, she died in Cleveland of a heart attack.

Her husband survived her for only sixteen months. In that last, brief phase he had flung himself into his writing again—working simultaneously on both his unpublished memoirs and on a Russian version of the *Secret History*—all in an attempt to keep his loneliness at arm's length. But when, on April 7, 1973, he died, aged seventy-seven, in the same St. Vincent's Charity Hospital of Cleveland, under the same doctor, their good friend Dr. Henry Zimmerman, and of the same heart disease, it was, in his case, grief which had killed him as much as anything else. Maria had been the only person to share his life in their two such contrasting worlds, and the only one who understood the hopes and the disillusionments he had experienced in both. Going on without her must have seemed like walking in darkness. Their ashes now lie together in the crypt at Cambridge, Massachusetts, next to the urn of their daughter, Vera.

General Alexander Orlov was the brightest of all the Soviet Intelligence trophies which Stalin's reign of terror presented to the West. The tragedy was that, because of the general's own guile and the initial blunders of his American hosts, the trophy was allowed to stay hidden in a cupboard for the best part of two decades, only to be badly handled at first when it did appear. Orlov never lost a sense of bitterness about the clumsy and insensitive way his debriefing had started in 1953. The American official who stood closest to him during the last years of his life commented: "Every time I mentioned that episode, or he thought of it, he almost frothed at the mouth." But the government, and indeed Congress, had, after all, made handsome amends from 1956 onward, and Orlov finished up with absolutely no regrets about his decision to defect, and under no illusions that the fundamentals of Soviet policy had not changed as a result of Stalin's death.

Yet, despite the fact that he became, at the end, almost indistinguishable from a placidly typical American senior citizen, well liked and respected in his local Cleveland community, this transformation had not penetrated right down to the core of his being. It was not only that, like so many millions of fellow immigrants, he never shook off all the habits of his native land—in his case, for example, an abiding love of wine and of Russian *blinis*. Above and beyond that, he never entirely ceased to be a KGB general.

In the words of that same American official:

> Orlov remained a professional to the end of his days. He only revealed what he wanted to reveal and, as a rule, produced facts of his own in response to facts of ours. There were some secrets that he took to the grave with him, notably, what he had really been up to in that 1933–36 period, when he seems to have had a roving commission throughout western Europe. Perhaps some sense of personal loyalty remained to former friends and colleagues whom he thought he could still put at risk in the seventies. Perhaps, after the example of what had happened to Krivitsky, he even feared for himself if he unlocked certain boxes of tricks. One never knew. On some subjects, the curtain would simply come down, and that was that.

However, even after Orlov had published his books, given his testimonies to the Senate, and been through the rough mill of his FBI interrogations, nuggets would still come out of him which showed what a gold mine of information had been lost, in its day, to the West.

Once, for example, toward the end of his life, while he was reminiscing about the Spanish Civil War, he became unusually expansive. He disclosed that his secret telegraphic name for that operation had been "Schwed" and he went on to talk about the frequent conferences he had held on Spanish affairs during the period with the deputy "resident" of the NKVD in Paris, Comrade Kislov, whose telegraphic name for this assignment was "Finn." One day, as the two men were discussing the agents that they had managed to plant with the enemy forces of General Franco, Kislov singled out for praise the "invaluable services" of one such agent he was running himself, whom he described as "our cooperative British journalist." The source sounded so well informed and so important that Orlov had asked his colleague whether, despite the obvious security risk, this English spy might not be used as a live radio link for emergency communications.

"That's not on," Kislov had replied. "He would betray himself straightaway. You see, he has a speech impediment."

The only British journalist with a stutter who was then accredited as a foreign correspondent to Franco's headquarters was Kim Philby. Had Orlov produced that vital clue back in 1938, or even as soon as he surfaced in 1953, the career of the Kremlin's most spectacular British agent, the man who was to rise, still unsuspected, to the key post of head of Counterintelligence in the Secret Service, could have been cut short long before it had time to inflict its full, grievous damage on the Western world. As it were, the information came merely as an echo of this disaster. Orlov was the one storm petrel who, though he arrived, like the others, before the storm, only showed himself when it was already raging.

Chapter Fourteen

BALANCE SHEET

What these life stories represent is the first round in that East-West conflict which we now call the Cold War. In the twenties and thirties, only the Russians were aware that they were fighting this great ideological battle. Indeed, it was their own creation. The Western democracies, and above all America, hit back, to begin with, like blindfolded giants, and only gradually came to see the dark outlines of the menace they were resisting. It is the stripping off of those blindfolds which is the main contribution these early Soviet defectors made to the history of our times.

Even on a crudely physical marking-up of points, this first round comes out slightly in the West's favor. Of the key defectors dealt with, two (Agabekov and Reiss) were certainly murdered in exile by Stalin's vengeance squads; a third (Krivitsky) probably met his end in the same way. But Orlov lived on to be seventy-seven and then died of natural causes in a Cleveland hospital. Bessedovsky, if still among the living, is even older, and appears to have enjoyed a trouble-free old age as far as the KGB is concerned. As for Boris Bajanov, he is not only un- questionably alive today, but, as we shall see in a moment, exceed- ingly active. If we include some of the lesser figures in the score, the survival rate is even higher. Barmine, for example, has spent most of his long exile as an American citizen and only retired a few years ago as an official of the United States government. No single attempt on his life had ever been recorded. The same applies to Hedda Massing, who first came to New York as a Soviet agent more than forty years ago, and who still lives, tranquilly and honorably, in that same city today.

Nor, it seems clear, did those who avoided trouble have to wrestle with torments of remorse in their countries of adoption. The most striking common factor among these survivors is that not one of them ever regretted taking that decisive step of defection. If anything, their disillusionment with the tarnished ideals of Communism has tended to increase rather than diminish as the years in exiled freedom have rolled on. Mrs. Massing has supplied an instructive personal anecdote in this connection.

A few years ago, she received, at her New York apartment, an en- velope posted in Moscow. Inside was a copy of the special com- memorative stamp which had just been issued there in memory of one of the greatest of all Soviet spies, Richard Sorge, who had been honored, long after his death on active service, with the title, "Hero of the Soviet Union."[1] Accompanying the stamp was an unsigned typewritten message: "See what you have missed! Don't you now regret doing what you did?" Hedda Massing recalls that merely looking at the stamp and reading the anonymous jibe of that totally uncomprehending writer had made her, if possible, more thankful than ever that she had turned her back on this world of the police state, while the best part of her life was still before her.[2]

The tally of those alive or dead, and even the contentment of the survivors, is, of course, only a minor item in the balance sheet. Of those who died, from whatever cause, all but one had time to pass

---

[1] Sorge, who ended his career in Japan, was arrested and executed there in 1944.
[2] Conversation with the author, November 16, 1976.

on at least a good part of his knowledge beforehand. (The exception, in this, as in other respects, was Ignaz Reiss.) Furthermore, because of the closed structure of any Communist society, even a handful of insiders like these early defectors were, among them, in possession of a mass of secret information which was out of all proportion to their numbers. This emerges from their testimonies as one of the built-in weaknesses of all police states, then and now. Whenever any senior official from such a regime crosses the line, he brings out a cross section of the entire system with him.

There were individual cases, like that of Orlov, where much of the information came too late to be of use in its own contemporary setting. Some, like Krivitsky, spoke out just in the nick of time. But in no case was disclosure an instantaneous affair. The physical act of defection, so totally decisive in its outcome for the individual, was over and done with in a matter of a few hours, minutes, or even seconds: a car drive from Barcelona into France; a stealthy tiptoeing past snoring border guards on the Persian frontier; or even, in Bessedovsky's case, just one swift leap over an Embassy wall. But the psychological defection, which then had to follow to complete the process, usually stretched out over years. Indeed, it is problematical whether it was ever entirely accomplished, or ever could be, in any lifetime. Even the normal, nonpolitical immigrant usually maintains a mental toehold in his native land, however firmly and happily his feet are planted in his fatherland of adoption. But the man who decides to abandon, not just a country but an ideology—both of which he started out by enthusiastically serving—has far greater problems of equilibrium and identity to overcome. When Western governments threw away their chances with these men, it was usually because they tried to force such delicate transplants, and get out of them a rapid growth where no quick results were possible.

Nonetheless, whether or not the information came out early or late, and whether or not it was ever complete, by the outbreak of the Second World War these first defectors had, among them, drawn a solid enough picture of the threat which faced the West. And, even in the brief ten-year span covered by these escapes and debriefings, certain consistencies in Soviet aims and methods had already emerged. There was, for example, the Kremlin's penetration of foreign countries by the deadly sham of "popular front" democracy—a device tried out experimentally in Mongolia at the beginning of the decade and in full application, by the end of it, against much more critical targets like the French republic.

The same device, of fudging Communism with Socialism, and liberation with subversion, was also revealed as being hard at work throughout the period in the activities of the Comintern. Defector after defector had exposed this organization, and other international bodies like it, as instruments designed to undermine the Western democracies from within, as a cheaper and safer alternative to attacking them frontally on the ground. By the close of the decade, there was no longer any excuse to shrug off this threat. The gullible fellow traveler, like the "red dean" of Canterbury, had emerged as a familiar figure on the Western scene. Defectors such as Krivitsky were also helping to ram home the unpalatable fact that this ideological fickleness could easily spill over into political treason, and that the espionage recruits thus produced for the Kremlin were being drawn from the ranks of the privileged, as well as the underprivileged, in Western society. Unfortunately, Britain, which had most need to apply this lesson, was also the most reluctant to learn it at the time.

Even the one apparent paradox in Soviet behavior—the contrast between government and party attitudes—had begun to resolve itself by the end of the period, though this was to take much longer for the Western world as a whole to grasp. All these first defectors had brought with them the same warning in different forms. Communist Russia could neither be approached nor warded off in the same way as one might deal with normal states. These pursued only economic or political interests in their relations with each other and such relationships were always shifting to follow the shifting curves of the priorities themselves. The Soviet Union had this pragmatic political face as well. But its case was unique in that, for Moscow, this face was only a mask. Underneath lay the unchangingly hostile glare of ideology, the Marxist's eternal battle of faiths.

America itself was to experience a classic demonstration of this in the thirties. In 1934, President Roosevelt inaugurated his new and fateful policy of Soviet-American amity by establishing diplomatic relations between the two countries. America's token of good faith was the dispatch to Moscow of William Bullitt, an ambassador whose pro-Soviet leanings were almost dangerously pronounced. But Russia's response was to smuggle in, under cover of her official mission, the most ambitious Soviet network for espionage, propaganda, and subversion ever constructed in the United States. So far from the improvement in intergovernmental relations leading to a lessening of the ideological battle, it had merely provided the Kremlin with a long-awaited opening to intensify that battle.

This was never, of course, realized in Washington at the time—part of a general lack of comprehension which New Deal America displayed over the nature of Soviet Communism. In intelligence terms, this America, so far from being the land of unlimited opportunity, was the land of lost chances. The immediate expression of this was the complete neglect or inept handling of such crucial sources as Orlov and Krivitsky. But there were longer-term effects as well, and these went far beyond the professional game of spy and counterspy.

When America did launch its belated onslaught against Communist subversion, it attacked, not the actual menace, formidable enough though this was, but its own caricature of that menace. The McCarthyite hysteria of the early fifties was, in part, the bewildered reflex of a nation waking up, from an unnaturally long slumber, in a dark and unfamiliar room. There was no time to get the measure of the surroundings and, moreover, nothing at hand by which to measure them. Even if McCarthy could have stampeded a more educated public opinion (which is unlikely), he could hardly have manipulated a large and influential Counterintelligence organization, complete with its infrastructure of archives, field operators and trained analysts. Yet such an organization simply did not exist for Soviet affairs, when, at the end of World War II, America suddenly found herself at the head of what rapidly became the anti-Soviet camp. It was small wonder that distorted shadows on the wall could be passed off as solid objects. There was hardly anyone around who could tell the difference. As a result, the Kremlin became better served by this breed of antagonist than by any of its defenders. To this day, the cry of McCarthyism is an emotive smear which can be used to counter many a well-justified attack on Communist penetration tactics.

In Europe generally, and in Britain in particular, the position was very different, as the Krivitsky interrogations showed. Where mistakes and omissions were made in London, these occurred despite a background of knowledge and not because of a background of near-ignorance. Such transatlanic contrasts endured throughout the war and after it. It was not just differences of personality and political persuasion which made President Roosevelt so ready to woo Stalin and Winston Churchill so unwilling to trust the Russian bear any further than he could throw it. Britain's long professional experience of both tsarist Russian and Soviet Russian aims and methods also played a role. There was, above all, the conviction in London that nothing about those aims or methods had been changed by the historical accident of the anti-Hitler alliance. And it was the cumulative influence of the first Soviet defectors which, in turn, had helped to form that conviction.

It is fitting to end where we began, with the saga of Stalin's runaway secretary; for if there is one defector's story which symbolizes both the continuity of the Soviet threat and the slow awakening to it in the West, it is that of Boris Bajanov. We left him in Paris in the thirties, working as a journalist for the right-wing Russian émigré press, and as a "consultant" for Mr. Dunderdale of British Intelligence. He had already survived several OGPU attempts on his life and was beginning to sleep a little more soundly in his bed as some of the agents detailed to kill him were themselves, like Blumkin, wiped out in the Moscow purges, while others, such as Maximov, his erstwhile companion in the flight across Persia, had committed suicide. Yet, by now, another dictator even more formidable than Stalin was rising up in Europe—Adolf Hitler. This introduced problems into Bajanov's private world also.

Like so many anti-Communist émigrés, he was in something of a dilemma over Nazism. He was too much the instinctive enemy of Yagoda's OGPU, and all it stood for, not to find Himmler's Gestapo equally odious; and he soon recognized in the Nazi leadership those same symptoms of amorality and power lust which had repelled him, as a young man, in the Kremlin. But émigrés, like beggars, cannot be choosers. He would have been less than human had he not hoped that this savage new weapon of Hitlerism might, in some way, be turned toward the liberation of his homeland.

Britain, no less than Nazi Germany, was measured by this yardstick. So much so that when the British government, at the beginning of 1939, tried to seek a general understanding with the Soviet Union, Bajanov promptly severed all his ties with London. Soon after the ill-fated British mission had set out for Moscow, Bajanov was approached once more in Paris by his British Intelligence contact with another request for advice and information. He declared indignantly that it was now all over; he was no longer prepared to give any assistance to a country that was seeking to ally itself with his enemy, Soviet Communism.

"Remember, we have long arms," the British agent warned him.

"Stalin's are longer," replied Bajanov, "and so far I have kept out of them."

Six months after that exchange, war broke out. Like millions of others, Bajanov was sucked up in the vortex though, characteristically, even now he managed to be master of his own destiny. His first move, in the winter of 1939–40, was to Helsinki, where, with the blessing of Finland's soldier-president, Field Marshal Mannerheim, he started raising a battalion of anti-Communist troops from the Red Army prisoners-of-war captured by the Finns. He had collected more than one hundred fifty volunteers when Stalin thankfully agreed to a ceasefire with his tiny but unbelievably tough opponent. The short Russo-Finnish War ended; Bajanov's embryonic unit was disbanded accordingly; and he himself returned to Paris.

In the summer of that same year, 1940, the fighting came a lot closer than the lakes of Finland. The Nazi Wehrmacht punched through the Western defenses, driving everything before it. British forces withdrew to their own islands, and the capital of the French republic, like so many other capitals, became a German-occupied city. In view of what Hitler already had in mind for Russia, it was not to be wondered at that Bajanov, whose anti-Soviet sympathies were notorious, should have been left unmolested by the Gestapo.[3] (Had his

---

[3] He told the author that throughout the war, he only had contact with the Gestapo on one occasion, when a written summons to appear for questioning arrived through

activities as a collaborator of British intelligence been on their files, it would, of course, have been quite a different story.) But Bajanov was nonetheless surprised to receive, in May 1941, a polite request to go to Berlin and present himself to Hitler's minister-designate for the eastern territories, Dr. Rosenberg. The purpose of the summons was even more astounding.

Bajanov found himself being asked, as the leading expert on Soviet Russia, how the civilian population there would behave under military occupation. That would depend, he replied, on the purpose of that occupation. Was it to enable the Russian people to regain their liberty? Of course not, came the cold response, its aim would be to strengthen the Third Reich. "In that case," Bajanov said, calmly calling a spade a spade, "you will lose the war." And he declined to give any further help or advice, despite threats which his interlocutors were well able to put into practice.

How he managed, after that, to get away from Berlin at all, let alone without half the bones in his body broken, was a mystery that Bajanov himself could never really explain in later years. Quite apart from the defiance he had shown, there was the security aspect. He was now one of a handful of men who knew the secret of "Operation Barbarossa." But get away he did, returning again to Paris as though nothing had happened. Hitler's attack on Russia, which duly followed a few weeks later, did, however, transform his life. The Western democracies, on whom he had been pinning his hopes for an anti-Bolshevik crusade, promptly allied themselves with Moscow in the common front against Germany.

Suddenly Bajanov—always so active and positive—felt nonplussed and defeated. There seemed no way in which he could carry on his struggle. Hitler, the only man still left fighting the Soviet Union, was not only an unsavory prospect, but a forlorn one as well. As Bajanov had declared in Berlin, with their policy of outright conquest, the

---

the post. As it was delivered in this innocuous way (as opposed to an arrest without warning at 3:00 a.m.), Bajanov calmly decided that he was in no danger, and turned up. His *sang-froid* was justified. The Gestapo had somehow got hold of the wrong end of the stick about his activities in Finland, and profusely apologized when he put the record straight.

Germans were marching eastward into disaster. So, for the first time in his life, he opted right out of politics, laying aside even the journalist's pen which had supported him ever since his arrival in Paris from India in 1928. He raised enough capital on which to eke out the war years by selling, for a handsome price to the Japanese military authorities, his voluminous card index of Soviet personalities.[4] When the war was over, he started out on a new career entirely, the construction of precision equipment for French technical laboratories. This slumber of the political bystander, contented if not happy, lasted for some twenty years. Then, in the spring of 1975, a later and more famous Russian émigré, Alexander Solzhenitsyn, came to Paris and shook him out of it.

The two distinguished exiles, separated by more than a generation, spent the best part of a week closeted together. Despite a difference in philosophy (Solzhenitsyn is a devout believer and sees the salvation of Russia in the arms of the Orthodox Church, whereas Bajanov is an atheist who holds any religious solution to be anyway outdated), the two men got on well. Both, after all, shared a whiff of greatness as well as total, uncompromising sincerity in their hatred of Communism. Yet the results were not as planned.

Solzhenitsyn, who at first had wanted to write a biography of Bajanov, finally left it to his new friend to write his own memoirs. Bajanov, who had hoped to persuade Solzhenitsyn to become the prophet of a new anti-Communist resurgence, found the great author determined not to be deflected from his writing. So, in the end, Bajanov got landed, not only with his own biography but also with his own movement. It is an ambitious concept. At the core of his thinking is a cry to the Western world to revitalize itself through the leadership of its elite, a rejuvenation process which he sees as necessary to save the Communist world, as well as the free one.

He has set out his ideas in these words:

> You know, as I do, that our civilization stands on the edge of an abyss. . . . Those who seek to destroy it put forward an ideal. This ideal has been proven false by the experience of the last sixty years;

---

[4] Compiled mainly, as he later confessed, from official announcements made over the years in the Soviet press.

but the masses, taken in by tireless propaganda, believe, to some degree, that it is genuine, and their belief is a great source of strength. . . .

The defenders of our civilization, on the other hand, are severely handicapped. Of course, common sense, reason, and a free economy based on private enterprise and property constitute, among them, an incomparable engine for human progress in mankind's history. But you cannot inspire the masses with reason.

Moreover, the defenders have allowed themselves to be portrayed as monstrous lackeys of capitalism, exploiters without altruism or ideals; whereas, in truth, it is the Communists and their revolutionary allies who are the real gangsters, having, for decades, organized what can only be called a global holdup for their profit. . . .

As a result, those who fight to defend our way of life are pilloried, and even take on a somewhat shame-faced air themselves. Only in your England, a country of ancient culture and tradition, does the party which defends civilization dare to call itself "conservative." In any other Western country, that label would be a guarantee of electoral defeat. Even in England, it can be damaging.

But the problem of bringing back freedom to Russia is not insoluble. Indeed, the force of many circumstances makes it far more feasible today than forty, or even twenty years ago. The Russian leadership are cautious, petty, and exhausted people—second- or third-raters almost by definition, otherwise they would hardly have survived Stalin's purges. Most important, the youth of Russia no longer believes in the system, despite the fact that they have known nothing else. If the West, above all the Anglo-Saxon West, the Americans, British, Germans, and so on, develop their confidence and their unity, they can win the battle for our civilization and set humanity on the true path to progress, not the twisted path of Marxism.[5]

It would be hard to find a better message than that to sum up, not only the life of Bajanov himself, but also the lives, and deaths, of all the other Soviet storm petrels.

---

[5] Letter to the author, September 3, 1976; translated from the original French.

INDEX